I Get
Paid for This

D1608872

I Get Paid for This

Kicking Ass and Taking Names in Vegas

Rick Lax

Photos by Bryan Adams

HUNTINGTON PRESS
LAS VEGAS, NEVADA

I Get Paid for This
Kicking Ass and Taking Names in Vegas

Published by
  Huntington Press
  3665 Procyon Street
  Las Vegas, NV 89103
  Phone (702) 252-0655
  email: books@huntingtonpress.com

Copyright ©2011, Rick Lax

ISBN: 978-1-935396-50-5
$15.95us

Cover photo: Bryan Adams

Inside photos: Bryan Adams: 7, 12, 45, 59, 73, 86, 116, 131, 133, 135, 138, 139, 140, 149, 150, 159, 167, 169, 174, 206, 210, 216, 217, 226, 229, 233; Rick Lax: 17, 19, 25, 26, 33, 46, 60, 66, 78, 81, 92, 134, 153, 154, 156, 157, 179, 180, 181, 185, 186, 194, 198, 199, 200, 202; Slyvie Kindle: 19, 125, 126, 136; Al Powers: 50, 146, 147; Courtesy of subjects: 83, 114, 173, 205; Bob Burchess: 111; Magentic Public Relations: 130, 137; ©imacon/iStock Image: 134; ©Holly vector/Dreamstime: 138; ©Lawrence Wee/Dreamstime: 142, 143; Gabe Fajuri: 177; James Baldwin ©MD Archives, 1982: 191

Production & design: Laurie Cabot

All rights reserved. No part of this publication may be translated, reproduced, or transmitted in any form or by any means, electronic or mechanical, including photocopying and recording, or by any information storage and retrieval system, without the express written permission of the copyright owner.

Sylvia:

Happy you were here for some of this.
Wish you could have been here for more.

Ally:

Thanks for a fun 3 years. Guess it's time for me to move out.
Break it to Monkeybunny gently.

contents

Seven-Day Workweek

Stunt Journalist

I've got the best job in the world.
What do I do?
Whatever I want.
Then I write about it.
I work as a "stunt journalist" for *Las Vegas Weekly*.

Stunt journalism isn't about objectivity or fairness or anything fancy like that. It's about telling a good story. The formula is simple: *Do something crazy and then say what you did.* Bonus points if you undergo a life change or make a fool of yourself along the way. Triple-bonus points if you look within, scrutinize your psyche, and then extrapolate.

I didn't set out to become a stunt journalist. It just happened. When I attended the University of Michigan, I lived next to *The Michigan Daily* building. One day, bored, I wandered in and met one of the editors. The next morning I awoke to a phone call:

"Can you write a story for me?" the editor asked.

"I've got Italian in an hour," I told him.

"No you don't. The Modern Language Building just flooded and classes are canceled. That's your story."

The Michigan Daily made my piece the front-page lead. Seeing my name in print felt good, so I decided to write another story. But just as I began working on it, the Black Student Union and the American-Arab Anti-Discrimination Committee and

30 other student groups banded together to boycott the paper.[1]

It was a tricky situation for everyone involved. Tricky for the boycotters because, well, how do you boycott a free newspaper? And tricky for *The Michigan Daily* writing staff because they had to 1) cover the boycott with fake objectivity, or 2) pretend the boycott wasn't happening, even though it was the most newsworthy story on campus.

I picked option 3: I left the *Daily* to write a piece for the *Ann Arbor Paper*. It was about my friend's band.

"Write it up on your own," my friend told me, "and then I'll give it to the rest of the band to check through. I think that's what they did in *Almost Famous*."

"Sounds good to me," I replied.

To review, I let the subject of my story determine my method of fact-checking based on what he claimed to have seen in a movie starring the daughter of the blond woman from "Three's Company."

This would be a good time to mention I never formally studied journalism.

Anyway, the story came out, nobody read it, and I felt like crap. I'd put a lot of work into it. Maybe not into the fact checking, but into the prose.

There's got to be an easier way to see my name in print, I thought.

And then I discovered memoir.

Unlike journalists, memoirists don't have to do any research or interviews. And unlike novelists, memoirists don't have to create compelling plots or think up memorable characters with relatable personalities and fitting names.[2]

---

[1] Here's an excerpt from the anonymous email that started the boycott:

> *The Michigan Daily* has become a publication that manifests the institutional racism and ignorance that plague communities of color, and threatens the progress of the campus community at large. Most recently, these manifestations have become more blatant and demeaning. They include:
> - The use of the term "Buckwheat" in a racist manner in the Arts section.
> - The misidentification of faculty, administrators, and guest speakers of color in picture captions.
> - The frequent misspelling of minority-student names.
> - The application of stereotypes to manipulate the perception of minorities.

[2] Sometimes, for legal purposes, memoirists have to change names. But even this can be phoned in. Case in point: Most the names of the minor characters in my first book, *Lawyer Boy*, were taken from the TV show "Saved by the Bell." Let's look at a paragraph from *Lawyer Boy*:

> Violet, my friend Samuel's ex-girlfriend, wanted to know whether she could throw her deadbeat subleasee's stuff out the window (she couldn't); Robin the ex-girlfriend wanted to know whether she could get out of a six-month lease with her fiancé's stickler father (maybe); Borders barista Molly wanted to know what she could do to help her boyfriend, who was on trial for racketeering (*way* out of my league).

Violet, **Molly**, and **Robin** are the names of **Samuel** "Screech" Powers's short-term love interests in

Memoirs practically write themselves.

To keep would-be memoirists out of the market, professional memoirists say things like, "If I had a nickel for every schmuck who told me he wanted to write a memoir, I'd have a billion dollars. It's harder than it looks." Professional memoirists say this every chance they get, even if nobody has ever told them that they want to write a memoir. And if nobody *has* ever told them that, it's only because they've heard so many professional memoirists discussing how many hypothetical nickels they've accumulated from wannabe memoirists.

But really, it's *so* easy.

And while there are many good reasons to write a memoir (attention, sympathy, empathy[3]), money is not one of them. See, even incredibly talented/incredibly modest memoirists like me can only make so much from them. To survive, we have to get

---

"Saved by the Bell." **Violet** was Screech's geeky girlfriend, played by Tori Spelling. **Robin** was a gold digger who liked Screech only after his grandmother's spaghetti sauce took off. And **Molly** was the girl who kissed Screech after his command performance in the JROTC obstacle course relay race.

[3] Abigail Thomas, author of *Thinking About Memoir*, has a different perspective. She says there are many good reasons *not* to write a memoir:

> Memoir is not a place to get revenge, or to appear angelic, or to cast oneself as victim. If that's on your mind, write fiction. Memoir should not be self-serving, even accidentally. If you come out as anything but profoundly human, you've probably get the wrong motives for doing this, or you haven't stood far enough back, or come close enough … But poor little me is not a good motive for memoir. Neither is good little me. If that's the point you're setting off to prove, or (even worse) illustrate, you aren't going to get very far.

She is wrong.

Memoir is *the* place to get revenge. Yes, you have to change your enemy's name and identifying characteristics, but *he'll know who he is.* (Worried about a defamation lawsuit? Then just follow memoirist Ann Lamott's advice: "Give him a teenie little penis so he will be less likely to come forth.")

Memoir is *the* place to appear angelic. In my first book, I'm constantly fighting crime, doing favors for people, and resisting the temptation to cheat. True, I didn't present myself as an *arch*angel, but that's only because I didn't want to lose credibility. Per my editor's suggestion, I put some in some 'bad' stuff, like the time I broke plans with my then-girlfriend to study for my Constitutional Law final exam.

I'm such a monster, right?

Thomas says that if you want to get revenge or come off as angelic, you should write fiction, but to me, that seems like a roundabout way of doing it. I mean, if you put your mind to it, I'm sure you could write something sappy like *Where the Red Fern Grows*—something that people would read and think, *Whoever wrote this has warmth in his heart.* But it's so much easier to tell people that you chased a guy down the streets of downtown Chicago to retrieve a stranger's cell phone. At least, that's what I did.* Took me five minutes to write the scene.

Thomas says Bad Little Me/Good Little Me is a bad motive to write a memoir, but the way I see it, the only alternative is Average Little Me. And nine times out of ten, tales of "mediocrity" are actually tales of Good Little Me or Bad Little Me in disguise. So go ahead and brag. Tell the world your story, you hero.**
*I really did do this, by the way.
**Nota Bene*: Take this footnote with a grain of salt; Stephen King called Abigail Thomas's last memoir "The best memoir I have ever read"; my mom called my last memoir "pretty fun."

regular, non-memoir writing gigs.

I found my gig at *Las Vegas Weekly*. I combined what little journalism knowledge I had with my memoir-writing skills. I wrote stunt stories. They're halfway between traditional news stories and memoirs. I wrote about stealing a urine mat from the Wynn casino and about giving the half-time peptalk at a Harlem Globetrotters game.

After a year, my editors began asking me to write stories about *other* people. Normal stories about normal Las Vegans. Bartenders, cab drivers, dealers—people like that. My editors said that if I wanted to "really understand Las Vegas" (i.e., if I wanted to keep my job), I'd have to go outside myself and talk to the people who make the city tick.

Problem #1: Las Vegas workers are their own breed. Especially the men and women who work on the Strip. They don't feel comfortable opening up to guys who, say, steal urine mats for a living. They're guarded. They're trained to be that way. First rule of the Vegas tourism industry: *Smile and keep your mouth shut, unless you're apologizing or recommending a Cirque show.*

I realized that if I were ever going to get these workers to talk to me, I'd have to relate to them. I couldn't just ask sympathetic questions; I'd have to walk a mile in their shoes.

Problem #2: A mile is a really far. Back in grade school, when we had to run the mile in gym class, I'd consistently finish third-to-last. Just ahead of this boy who had asthma and this girl who was morbidly obese. Year after year.

Surprisingly, though, I excelled at the 50-yard dash. I walked away from my first-, second-, and third-grade Field Days with 50-yard-dash blue ribbons. I only failed to take blue ribbons home in the fourth and fifth grades because in 1993, Lone Pine Elementary School transitioned out of the 1st place=blue/2nd place=red/3rd place=white ribbon system and into the socialist everybody-goes-home-with-a-green-participation-ribbon system.

The point is, I'm good with short bursts.

So what if, instead of working a typical Vegas job for a really long time, I worked a lot of Vegas jobs for a really short time? Wouldn't I then be able to relate to the people who make the city tick?

Of course not.

The people who make the city tick aren't idiots. They recognize a stunt for what it is. Working, say, seven jobs in seven days would earn me the same amount of street cred that K-Fed got for doing *Celebrity Fit Club*.

But maybe I don't need street cred. Maybe I don't need to relate to the people who make the city tick to "really understand" how Las Vegas works. Maybe, if I held seven jobs in seven days, I could figure out how the city works on my own. I could pull off the stunt journalist's triple-pointer: I could become part of the city's workforce, look within myself, examine my psyche, and then extrapolate.

And that, dear readers, is what stunt journalists call a "premise."

DAY 2

Street Performer

If you walk by Paris Las Vegas at the right time, you'll see Elvis, Darth Vader, Wonder Woman, a silver boxer, a green toy soldier, and a guy wearing a pink bra and white go-go boots. He's got the words "MANWHORE FOR TIPS" painted on his stomach in black capital letters, and, for a dollar, he'll take a picture with you.

"My wife's supportive," he says.

The casinos used to kick street performers like these off the Strip, but after several rounds of litigation, the performers figured out that the casinos didn't have the right.

Civil rights attorney Maggie McLetchie tells me, "For over thirteen years, the ACLU has been litigating the question of how the First Amendment applies on Fremont Street and on the Strip. And the courts have repeatedly held that each area is a public forum."

"So I can perform there, for tips?" I ask.

"You can't obstruct foot traffic and you can't beg aggressively, but aside from that, yes, performing for tips is legal."

With the law on my side, I take to the Strip alongside professional busker/personal friend Jungle Josh. He brought with him a sound system, a folding table, and a six-foot long Colombian Red Tail Boa Constrictor.

Her name is Isabelle.

I don't like snakes. I don't have an irrational fear of them; I'm not afraid they're going to slither into my apartment at night and pin me to my bed. I have a *rational* fear of them. They're dangerous. But Josh assures me that Isabelle is different—"Very nice, very friendly."

At 7 p.m., we arrive at his spot, 15 or 20 feet from the Mon Ami Gabi restaurant. It's 100 degrees out and I'm wearing a collared shirt, a tie, and a vest. I'm sweating. As we unpack our tricks, some guy asks me, "Where's the nearest Half Price Ticket booth?"

"I have no idea," I say.

He rolls his eyes and mutters, "Asshole."

Josh removes Isabelle from her red bag and sets her on the folding table.

"I'm going to go grab some water," Josh tells me, and before I can object, he's gone. So there I am, standing on Las Vegas Boulevard with a snake I've only just met.

Almost instantly, I learn the most important thing about snake ownership: *If you've got a snake with you, you don't matter.* Rather, you matter only in that you're the guy who can answer three questions.

Here are the questions, and here are the answers I gave:

QUESTION #1: "What kind of snake is that?"
ANSWER #1: "What kind of what is what?" (*I look down.*) "Ahhh! Where the fuck did that thing come from?!"

QUESTION #2: "Is it real?"
ANSWER #2: "It's actually a robot. I've got the remote control in my shoe. Looks realistic, doesn't it?"

QUESTION #3: "Does he bite?"[4]
ANSWER #3: "*All the time.* He's bitten three people tonight, and they weren't even messing with him. If I were you, I wouldn't stand where you're standing— you're in his striking zone."

I must be a terrible actor; whenever I get done telling a child how dangerous the snake is, she inevitably runs up to pet it.

Josh returns with a bottle of water and asks me if I'm ready to get started.

"Ready."

He moves Isabelle behind us.

"Do you want to go first?" Josh asks. "Or do you want me to go first?"

"I was hoping we could do shows together," I suggest.

I'm eager to start performing, but not ready to do a whole show on my own.

"We could alternate tricks," I offer.

"I don't think that's a good idea. That would kill the momentum."

"Can we just try?"

"We can," Josh says, "but I don't think you'll be happy with the results."

Josh flips on the mic and gathers a crowd.

"Street magic! Street magic in ten seconds! If you want to lead a normal and boring life, keep on walking."

A crowd forms and Josh encourages them to stand in line.

"Just like you're at Starbucks," he says.

Twenty or thirty people oblige.

---

[4] Everybody assumes the snake is a "he," so another good way to respond to this question would be, "No, *SHE* doesn't bite," as if you were all offended.

Josh pulls a half dollar through the fibers of a blanket. Then he introduces me. I change a red ball into a green ball and then into a yellow ball. Then I reintroduce Josh. He cuts a rope in two and then restores it. Then he reintroduces me. I borrow a cell phone and put it inside of an inflated balloon.

We make zero dollars. Josh was right about momentum. We'd lost people between each trick. In fact, *nobody* stayed for the whole show.

Some guy asks Josh if he can pose with the snake for a photo.

"That's what she's here for," Josh says, placing Isabelle on the guy's shoulders.

Josh walks back over to me and says, "How about *I* do a full show, and then *you* do—"

The guy holding the snake interrupts with a string of profanity: "Where the fuck did you go?! You leave me with this fuckin' snake on my shoulders?!"

Josh takes back Isabelle, apologizes, and prepares himself to show me how it's done.

"Next magic show begins when the plumbing demonstration is over!" Josh bellows.

He's referring to the Bellagio fountains, which are going off behind us. When they stop, Josh begins. He does the coin and blanket trick, then the rope trick, and then a trick in which a chosen card appears in a sealed Ziploc bag.

He gets three dollars in tips.

Not great, but moving in the right direction.

I'm up next.

I have trouble attracting a crowd, so Josh attracts one for me: "Ladies and gentlemen," he shouts into the mic, "in just seconds, Las Vegas' own Rick Lax will be performing the most amazing magic you've ever seen."

Is he building me up too much?

"Folks, you're just seconds away witnessing a miracle."

I think he is.

A single girl steps forward to see a trick. She's about 10, and her parents aren't thrilled. They stand six feet behind, frowning.

"I'm Ricky," I say, and I extend my hand forward. The girl shakes it and says, "I'm Sadie."

And with that, I begin my show with a card trick. Once the parents see that Sadie isn't going anywhere any time soon, they join us. And then more and more people come to see what Sadie's family is looking at.

I direct the whole show to Sadie. After the first trick is done, I say, "Now, Sadie, if you start applauding, I bet everybody else will too."

She does; they do.

I do another card trick, then the ball trick, and then the balloon trick, and then I deliver my "hat line"—the line that lets people know I'm working for tips:

"At this point in the show, you're probably wondering, *If I put a couple bucks in Ricky's hat, will he be offended? Is he too proud for that?* And the answer to those questions is no. I won't be offended. I'm not too proud for that. Now, Josh over there"—I point—"goes nuts when you tip him. Makes him furious. He's a purist. But me? I don't mind. So feel free."

And then I do my last trick, in which an invisible pack of cards materializes in my pocket.

It's more impressive than it sounds.

Anyway, the show is worth four bucks. Again, not great ... but moving in the right direction.

Josh has me do another show. That one is worth $8.21. Right direction.

"You're getting better and better," Josh tells me, "but you could change up your hat line. Try something like this: 'Now, with most shows on the Strip, they tell you the price beforehand. But I let you decide the price *after* the show. So if you think the show is worth a five, a ten, or a twenty, you can leave a five, a ten, or a twenty. The casino doesn't pay me to be out here. I live on your tips. I need them to feed my rabbits.'"

Humor, sympathy, guilt, myth busting—that's the *Encyclopedia Britannica* of hat lines.

"You want people to think that you're above ones," Josh says. "You want those fives and tens. That's why I take ones out of the hat as soon as they go in. Ones breed. Now go ahead and do one more show. I'm thinking of giving the snake to the girls, so we can focus on the magic."

"The girls" are other street performers. They dress up as angels. The blond one wears a black bra, black shorts, black wings, and pink leg warmers. The brunette wears a white bra, a white skirt—well, technically it's a skirt—white wings, and white leg warmers. Like the MANWHORE FOR TIPS, they take pictures with tourists for tips.

As the girls come to our spot, a twentysomething guy who, I'm guessing, hasn't seen a shower for over a week, walks by carrying a pair of heels. He wants to know if anybody is interested in buying them.

"What size are they?" asks one of the angels.

"They're nines," he says.

"No thanks."

The girls decide against Isabelle, too, so Josh uses her to draw in his next crowd.

"Can my snake have a bite of your ice cream?" he asks a boy.[5] The kid walks over and holds his cup before Isabella's head.

Josh pulls a huge crowd this time. Sixty or seventy people. Accordingly, he puts on a huge show. Mixes in lunges and jumping jacks. He's blocking a good deal of the sidewalk, so some pedestrians are walking behind us, right by Isabelle's stand. They usually don't notice her until they're inches away. And then they freak out.

Josh finishes his show and delivers the hat line. He's rewarded with a ten, a five, and a handful of ones. About twenty bucks total. He's in the groove.

I'm up again, but right after I begin, the Bellagio fountains start up. And then two Elvii show up. And then some drunk asshole decides he wants to take over my act. He won't let me get five words out without yelling about how hungry he is, about how, if I were a real magician, I'd make a cheeseburger appear. Then, some other asshole throws a handful of escort advertisement cards at my face (which, sadly, is the best part of my set in that it wins me some sympathy from the otherwise nonplussed crowd). Then the "HOT BABES DIRECT TO YOU" truck pulls up behind me. It's got a massive photo of three topless women on it, and I watch my spectators' eyes move from my playing cards to the truck.

Two bucks.

"You think I could do this professionally?" I ask Josh.

"Oh, you've definitely got the chops," he says. "The question is, could you do your five minute show a million times in a row, night after night after night?"

The answer is no.

I got through one night, but my tenth show wasn't as energetic as my first. If I had gone on longer, my energy would have only declined further. If I had to do the same show, day after day, week after week, year after year, my enthusiasm would bottom out. And then I'd get no tips.

Of course, when I watch unenthusiastic performers, I'm the first to complain. I'm the first to say that they're "just going through the motions." When I visit the Strip, I expect my waiters and my dealers to be perky and eager 24/7. And when they're not, I bitch about it.

Maybe I could cut them some slack.

---

[5] Far cleaner than the line he'd been using earlier: "Hey, Lady, want to hold my snake?"

DAY 3

Strip Club Restroom Attendant

Here's how a Mafia protection racket works: A Mafioso shows up at your door and says, "If you pay us a thousand bucks a month, we'll keep you safe."

"Safe from what?" you ask.

"All kinds of things," you're told. "We can keep your business from burning down and we can keep your family from getting hurt."

"That's never been a problem before," you say. "I think I'll pass."

"Well," the Mafioso say, "I'll stop by tomorrow, just in case you change your mind."

That night, somebody shatters your front window with a stone and thwacks your son with a bat. And then you realize, *you need protection from the Mafia because the Mafia's in town.*

Same thing with restroom attendants.

You go to the bathroom, you wash your hands, and then you look around the counter for a paper towel. You find nothing. And then, from across the room, you see a man walking towards you with a paper towel and a smile. At first, you're grateful. But then you realize, *you couldn't find a towel in the first place because the guy walking towards you confiscated them.* He created the problem he's ostensibly solving, and he did it so you'd give him money.

What I'm trying to say is, I had some moral qualms about job #3. But as I drove to the Crazy Horse III strip club, I wasn't worried about ethics; I was worried about being demeaned. Restroom attendantry isn't exactly the most glamorous profession.

Then, I started worrying about my worries.

When did I become such a classist?

You can find the Crazy Horse III strip club a mile west of Mandalay Bay. You can find the Crazy Horse III's men's restroom between the bar and the wheelchair lift. Just walk past the servers in the black-and-red corsets, past the tattooed brunettes with the thongs pulled halfway down their butts, past the six-foot blonds with the two-inch nails, and underneath the mesh lampshades.

As I made that walk, a short dancer with skinny legs and a goofy smile approached and started doing the Running Man—you know, the 1980s dance move. Easily the cutest, most original approach I've ever seen at a strip club.

"I'm here to work," I told her.

She frowned and walked on.

Inside the men's room, I met my coworker for the night, Brian. He's almost 60 and he used to work as a salesman. He's friendly, he's articulate, and he relates with everyone. Black, white, old, young, fancy, drab—everybody loves Brian.

"This job is about service," Brian tells me. "I try to provide it the best I can."

He takes me to his filing cabinet and shows me his business license.

"I'm an independent contractor. I pay my taxes. I actually spend a lot on this job, and I've got to keep track of that, too. At any given time, I've got about $3,000 in supplies in here, and I pay for them myself."

That's the second function of bathroom attendants—the one that morally distinguishes them from Mafia protection rackets. Restroom attendants provide patrons with breath mints, cologne, and candy—things the patrons wouldn't otherwise have but for the attendant's presence.

Brian has the best-stocked restroom in Vegas. He doesn't just have Peppermint Starlight Mints, Wintergreen Starlight Mints, and Jolly Ranchers; he's got Hershey Nuggets, Tootsie Pops, Peanut Butter Snickers, Marlboros, Parliaments, Camels, several dozen colognes (including four different types of Axe Body Spray), lint rollers, and ChapStick.

Most popular snack: Wint-O-Green Lifesavers.

Most popular cologne: Acqua Di Gio.

Okay, that's the clean stuff. Now let's talk about the dirty:

"What kinds of bad things go down in here?" I ask. "What should I be expecting tonight?"

"The worst things are people passing out in the stalls, multiple men in stalls, drug usage, and fights. That's why we have security."

I brace myself for the worst, but keep my focus on the bread and butter: "Let's go over the towels," I say.

Brian has a simple technique. He folds a stack of two towels in half, diagonally, and hands them out with a friendly, "How's it going?" He's got specialized greetings for the regulars. The most common one is, "What the fuck?", delivered in a low gravelly voice. It's his catchphrase.

He demonstrates: "Whaaaaat the faaaaaak?"

I mimic: "Whaaaaaat the faaaaaak?"

"Maybe you can develop your own catch phrase," he suggests.

And with that, I'm ready to begin.

First guy: Very tall, washes his hands, takes the towels, drops a buck in the tip jar.

Second guy: Also tall, also washes his hands, also drops a buck in the jar.

Could it be this easy?

I try a change-up for the third guy: I give his towels an extra fold. Bad idea. He looks at them funny, unfolds them, and then leaves no tip.

No tip from the fourth guy, a preppy-type wearing a fancy shirt and a knit tie.

Fifth guy: Red t-shirt, says he's from Iowa, leaves a tip *before* he washes his hands.

Sixth guy: Looks pissed off, doesn't use soap, leaves a ten-dollar tip.

Brian folds the ten in half and slips it in his breast pocket. Brian, apparently, has the opposite strategy of Jungle Josh. Brian displays the ones and hides the higher denominations.

But why?

We'll get into that in a minute. First, here are some statistics. They're based entirely on my personal observations of a handful of men, and they're grossly rounded. But putting that aside, I'm pretty sure they're 100 percent accurate.

- 50 percent of men wash their hands after they pee.
- 50 percent of hand-washers leave a tip.
- 15 percent of hand-washers/non-tippers do this thing where they reach into their front pockets as if they're going to bring out tips, but then their hands never come out. Or they come out empty. Sometimes this move is accompanied by a shrug. Presumably, this is meant to make the restroom attendant think, *This guy wanted to tip me but he didn't have any cash on him.*[6] *He's okay in my book!*

As the hours pass, I meet a kid who's desperately trying to look like Al Pacino's *Scarface* character. I meet a guy who, effortlessly, looks just like "Family Guy's" Peter Griffin. And I meet a man with the biggest smile I've ever seen.

"Good night?" I ask the grinner.

"*Great* night," he replies. "Great weekend. Same as the last two."

"Why's that?"

He extends his right middle finger and pokes it in and out of the hole created by his left thumb and index finger.

"I've taken girls home with me the last two weekends," he says, continuing the obscene gesture. "And here's why: I'm the whitest black person I know."

"Okay … " I say.

"Here's how it is: There are black people and there are niggas."

And then the guy enumerates the differences. Brian laughs heartily, and I point

---

[6] At a strip club. Right.

out that he's stealing Chris Rock's old material. The guy furrows his brow and walks away. Brian is not happy with me. He doesn't say it, but I sense that I've overstepped my bounds.

A couple minutes later, a man stumbles into the bathroom with a beer bottle in one hand and a tune in his head. The tune has lyrics, and the lyrics go like this:

Pussy, pussy, I'm going to get me some pussy tonight.
Pussy, pussy, pussy, pussy, I'm going to get me some pussy tonight.

I'm pretty sure it's an original.

The man pees, fumbles with the soap dispenser, sloshes some water around, takes two towels from me, throws them on the ground—unintentionally, I believe—and then puts his hand up for a high five.

I give it. Not my finest moment. I wasn't thinking. It was instinctual. Somebody asks for a high five and I just go for it. I'm sure there's some evolutionary basis for this.

Brian lets me use some of his hand sanitizer.

The interesting thing is, it's the only time I use the hand sanitizer all night. The whole experience is far cleaner than I expected. No stray poop, no vomit, no nothing.

"You came on a good night," Brian says, "in terms of there being no mess and no drama. But especially in terms of tips. You came on a really good night."

But did I ... or is that what Brian just wants me (and everybody else) to think?

I know this sounds crazy, but I think that Brian wants people to believe bathroom attendantry is—pardon me in advance—a crappy job. Why else would he hide the tens and twenties? I think he's going for pity tips.

I assumed restroom attendantry was a job of last resort. But the truth is, Brian is doing just fine. I don't want to get into monetary specifics—that's the *one* thing Brian doesn't like discussing, how fabulously wealthy he is—but I will say that the guy makes more than, oh, the average stunt journalist.[7]

People felt good when they tipped Brian and me. I could see it in their faces. They felt like they were helping out the little guy. Guys don't feel that way when they tip dancers or waiters or bellman, because it's expected of them. But when guys tip us, they feel like they're doing a mitzvah.

And maybe that feeling is worth more than a buck.

---

[7] Again, based on personal observations and casual math.

Beauty Shop Clerk

DAY 4

Studio Lites is more than a clothing shop. Studio Lites is, well, I'll let Chris the owner describe it to you: "We're a head-to-toe store. Everything from wigs to shoes. We've got clubwear, lingerie, bathing suits, corsets, jeans, wigs, costumes, and toys."

The shoes are for go-go dancers, but, according to Chris, housewives and students buy them, too. I'd say that the dresses are for strippers, only my roommate (who isn't a stripper) once bought a dress at Studio Lites and wore it to her best friend's wedding.

If you walk into Chris' store, he's going to make sure you walk out looking great. He's not just trying to make a sale. And here's how I know: Two years back, I was working on a story that involved my B-cup roommate walking around with giant silicone breasts.[8] They're like implants, only they don't go under your skin. We stopped by Studio Lites to pick up a specialty bra that would hold the external implants. Trouble was, Chris's bras held triangular external implants, and ours were rounded.

"Well, we'll still take the bra," I said, "I guess we'll just make the best of it."

"It's not going to look good," Chris told us. "You'd be better off buying a regular bra from Walmart."

Because he knew it would look bad, Chris wouldn't let us buy the bra from him. I've been recommending Studio Lites to my stripper friends ever since.

And now I've come back to work there.

Chris greets me at the front counter and turns me over to one of his sales clerks for a walk-

---

[8] Textbook stunt journalism.

around tour of the shop. She's about 20, she's quiet, she's friendly, and I forgot her name.

"We've got wigs for fashion and medical. Over here, we've got the inexpensive wigs—pink, red, blue, if you're going to be a Smurf—and then, over here, for daily fashion, for cancer patients, we've got the more expensive line with real hair and realistic lace fronts."

We walk to the far side of the shop.

"Over here we've got our costumes"—(crowns, fangs)—"and we've got our masks here"—(Carnival-style, Zorro-style, George Bush-style) —"and panty hose here, and jewelry here, and makeup here. We carry Ben Nye brand—good pigment for stage. And here's our liquid latex, and here's our swimsuits, and the corsets and waist cinchers are over there. We sell those to Renaissance, Rockabilly, and Steampunk people. And this is our section for cross-dressers—butt pads, hip pads, breast forms."

I recognize the silicone insert holder bra that Chris wouldn't sell me two years ago.

Chris rejoins us and explains, "About ten to twenty percent of our business is transformation. That's the cross-dressers and drag queens. But it's not like I have to carry special clothing for them. Large for a woman is a medium for a guy. And speaking of … "

A man walks through the front door. He looks like a typical grandpa. Maybe a bit shorter than average. He's wearing a blue baseball cap and a nylon windbreaker.

"He just flew in from rural New York," Chris tells me. "Tonight, I'm going to transform him."

"Into a woman."

"Right. And then we're going to take him out for a night on the town."

"How often does this happen?"

"For him? It's been two years. He hasn't been able to break away from the wife and kids. Now, Rick, I tell you what: If you'd be willing to put a wig on, right now, I'd be able to sell this guy anything … "

"I don't follow … "

"Young, good-looking guy like you—if he sees you dressed up, then he'll be thinking, *What would it take for* me *to look like that?* And then he's going to start buying."

"Maybe there's some other way I could help today … "

Chris calls back the clerk and asks us to lower a set of wig shelves. They're too high and they're uneven. So we take the wig heads off the shelves, set them on the glass counter, move each of the shelves down a notch, and then put the wigs back.

Next, the clerk asks me to remove all the babushkas and do-rags from the glass case, wipe down the inside with Windex, and then replace everything in an aesthetical-

ly pleasing display. After that, Chris has me re-shelf a hundred or so wigs. The most efficient way to do this, it turns out, is to grab two mannequin heads at a time in pre-choke-slam holds.

All the mannequin heads were the exact same. Same size, same features, same makeup. But the wigs made them look different. One mannequin head was sexy, one was flirty, one was wild, one was dramatic, one was old, one was conservative. I'd never before realized how dramatically a woman's hair affects her appearance.

Next I'm given a tagging gun and asked to shoot price tags onto a rack of new dresses. The gun has a needle for a barrel, and I only poked my finger once.

Not to brag.

Another man enters the store. Another average Joe. Let's call him Joe. Joe greets Chris with a huge hello, and Chris responds with an underwhelming hi. This is out of character for Chris, who's usually all about customer service. The man wanders into the wig section and Chris calls me over.

"How much do you know about the fetish community?" Chris asks.

"Not too much," I say.

"Well, Joe over there wants me to do his makeup, but the last time I did, he was really obnoxious about it. So now, I have to punish him. So I'll have my girls deal with him. That guy is a submissive, and he wants me to be a dominant, and so I have to play this part. I can't just do his makeup and give him what he wants, because that's not *really* what he wants. He wants me to ignore him."

"Will you *ever* do his makeup?"

"Oh, maybe one day down the road. Maybe I'll surprise him. But not any time he *wants* me to do it."

Joe tries on a long blond wig. After he agrees to purchase it (for $195), Chris goes over and cuts the wig's bangs. I walk by to ask Chris if he needs help with anything else. From far away, Joe looked calm and relaxed. But up close, I can see that he's breathing heavy and that he's got a subversive smile.

"I think we can let you go for the day," Chris says. "Very good work."

When we shop, we don't just form relationships with the people who sell us clothing; we form relationships with the clothing itself. Before we buy a shirt, we don't just imagine what we'll look like wearing it; we imagine how we'll feel wearing it. And then we try it on, to preview this feeling. This emotional connection is probably even stronger with fetish items like corsets, latex, and wigs.

Chris understands this. He understands that most women (and cross-dressing guys) are never going to look as sexy the women on the billboards and the print ads, or the strippers at Crazy Horse III, or the girls who dress up as sexy angels and take photos with tourists for tips. But, with a little help, Chris can make them *feel* that way. And when you think about it, that's almost more important.

DAY 5

Poker Player

I play poker once a week. I don't play to make money; I play because it's fun. Usually I break even. But every now and then, I'll have three or four winning sessions in a row, and after I do, this thought will invariably cross my mind: *Do I have what it takes to be a pro?*

Playing poker for a living is a whole different ballgame. When you play for recreation and you lose, you go home bummed out. When you play for a living and you lose, you go back to your parents' home and you stay there.

My game is Limit Hold 'em. That's different from the Texas Hold 'em you see on TV, where players "go all-in" and lose all their money in a single hand. In limit poker, you can only bet, raise, win, and lose a tiny amount each hand. It's less exciting, but also less dangerous.

Who else plays limit poker?

Old people.

Canes, motorized scooters, and oxygen tanks are the norm. On TV, poker is flashy and sexy. In reality, poker is liver spots and open-mouthed chewing.

I don't feel bad about taking old folks' money because 1) Feeling that way would be patronizing, and 2) They don't feel bad when they take mine. And they often do. A lot of septuagenarians and octogenarians are fantastic, ruthless players.

I've heard people compare professional poker players to leeches. "All they do is take money from other people."

My reply is, "So does everybody else."[9]

---

[9] Think about it like this: Professional poker players sell brainy entertainment to tourists.

Now, if you want to talk about leeching, listen to this: I have some female friends who supplement their income by, as they put it, "hustling." They get dressed up, they go to a fancy casino, they wait for rich guys to pick them up, and then they lead the conversation to this:

Rich Guy: "Do you want to play blackjack?"

Sexy Girl: "I don't know how."

Rich Guy: "Let me teach you."

And then they go to the table, they drink, they play dumb, and they gamble with the rich guy's money. If they lose, oh well. If they win, they take a percentage of the winnings. Usually half. Some girls take money off the table after every winning *hand*. (Some do this openly, some do this covertly.)

Oh, and how about this one: My roommate has friends who work as Champagne Drinkers. Here's how that gig works: They get dressed up, go to a club—I won't say which one, but it's on the Top Five list—they walk around, and they wait to get hit on. Eventually a group of guys will approach and invite them to their table for some booze.

"Do you have any Champagne?" the girls will ask.

"We've got vodka," the guys might reply. "Come have some of that."

And then, as instructed, the girls will respond, "We've been drinking champagne tonight and we

Unlike towel confiscation, I don't have any moral reservations about poker playing. It's not morality that's kept me from trying my hand at professional poker; it's discipline. Sometimes I play marginal starting hands (hands that should be folded), and sometimes I stay in pots too long, hoping for a miracle card that will 'make' my hand.

Professionals don't do this. They fold. They cut their losses.

And that's what I've got to do, starting now.

As Annie Duke would say, I've got to decide to play great poker.

At 2 p.m. I arrive at The Venetian Poker room. It's got 39 tables, and about half of them are full. I sit down and pull $135 out of my wallet. Everything I had on me. I get my chips, I get two cards, and I look down at them.

They're both kings.

I'm rich.

Two kings is a fantastic starting hand. It's the second best, actually. Right behind two aces. So before I can even get comfy in my chair, I raise the pot. A bunch of people call.

That's fantastic, too. Poker players hope for "loose" tables where nobody folds and everybody pays off the good hands.

The dealer reveals the first three "community cards"—the cards that everyone at the table shares. One of them is an ace. That's not good. It means that if somebody has just one ace in his hand, he's got my kings beat.

But nobody bets. Then another card comes down, and nobody bets. And then the last card comes down, and it gives me a straight to the ace. Suddenly my hand is really good again. I bet, and the woman to my right—possibly Native American, certainly obese—raises me. Turns out she's got a straight to the ace, too.

Maybe I jumped the gun with my enthusiasm.

I'm dealt a string of bad hands, and I fold them all. With no hands to play, I spend the time assessing my opponents. I'm the youngest at the table by a decade. I think most of the players are in their 50s. But not the guy at the far end. He's eighty-something. His arms are yellow and red and bruised. There's a giant sore on his elbow. He moves slowly. It takes him forever to look at his cards and forever to put in a bet. I'd call him a sad sight, only he had *so* many chips in front of him. Far more than anyone

---

don't want to mix. Order some champagne."

Champagne, you see, is the most expensive drink on the club's menu. And you can drink a bottle of champagne a lot faster than you can drink a bottle of vodka.

So the guys order the champagne, the girls chug it down, and then they move on to the next table. The club makes a thousand bucks, the girls make $200/hour, and the guys leave pissed off. And then, without fail, the guys return to Vegas the following year to fall for whichever club scam is in vogue.

else at the table. About 350, probably.

I'm dealt the king of clubs and the nine of clubs. It's a good hand, but it's not great. It's the type of hand I usually play, but probably shouldn't.

You're a professional now, Rick.

I fold. Then the dealer reveals the three community cards. They're all clubs. I would have had a flush, and I probably would have made a lot of money with it.

I'm upset, but I try not to be upset for too long. After all, I made the right decision, given the knowledge I had at the time. That said, I'd rather be rich than right.

As the hands go by, the old guy at the far end racks up more and more chips. As he does, I notice something about him that I'd somehow failed to notice before. He has three teeth that periodically emerge from the front of his mouth and slip back in, like gophers.

Now, when I tell you that these teeth "emerge," I don't mean they stick out a little. I don't mean that he flashes them. I mean that they come an inch and a half out of his mouth, seemingly connected to nothing.

Does he have some sort of novelty teeth that rest on the tip of the tongue? Does he have the loosest/smallest set of dentures in the history of orthodontics?

No explanation sufficed. I'm telling you, these teeth were *flying* out.

Before long I'm down $50, which is more than I made after hours of street performing.

I fold a couple more good-but-not-great hands, and then I'm dealt a pair of nines. I catch a third nine at the very last second, and I win my first big pot. Of course, if that third nine hadn't come up, I would have lost. I got lucky.

But I'm supposed to winning because of skill, not luck.

Before long, I win another huge pot. I've got the ace-nine of diamonds, and three more diamonds come up on board, giving me a flush.

Then I'm dealt an even better hand: a full house. The trouble is, Old Man Teeth has four-of-a-kind. So he takes a $100 pot from me. He's now got about $450 in chips in front of him.

I count my chips. I've got about $300. I'm up $170.

It wasn't that hard to get there. Between hands I'd been firing off emails and surfing the Internet on my iPad.

Maybe poker playing is the right job for me.

Or maybe not. Over the next two hours, my luck changes. I start losing. Nothing dramatic, no big pots. But the other nine players chip away at my stack, little by little. Before long, I find myself playing king-nines, suited six-eights, and all those other marginal hands I'm not supposed to be playing. I can't help it. I see my hand moving towards the felt and there's nothing I can do to stop it.

A guy from Jersey sits down next to me. He says he imported Christmas crafts into the U.S. until he made some foolish deals in 2007. So he went out of business and sold his warehouses.

"Best thing that ever happened to me. Everybody else who stayed in the business, everybody who kept his warehouse, just *disintegrated* when the bubble burst. Now they're all treading water and I'm having a comfortable retirement."

We chat about Vegas shows, Vegas restaurants, and Vegas nightclubs. Before long, I realize that I'm more interested in our conversation than I am in the game.

I look back down at my chip stack. I've got $131 in front of me. I've blown through my $170 winnings and lost $4 on top of it.

That's when I realize: *I will never be a professional poker player.*

I cash out.

In some ways, I'm very disciplined. I can write books and work out six days a week. But when I sit down at a poker table, I can't help but play marginal hands, and I can't help but chase cards. I guess I just like to gamble.

DAY 6

Oyster Shucker

When I was three, my mom walked me around Caesars Palace and taught me the Roman gods. Jupiter was the king, Juno was the queen, Neptune was the water guy, Pluto was the death guy, Mars was war, Venus was love, Mercury was the messenger, and Bacchus was wine. A decade later, Caesars

opened up the Forum Shops, a mall that featured an auto-animatronic fountain show, like Disney's Hall of Presidents, only starring Roman gods.[10]

---

[10] Only unlike the Presidents from Disney's Hall, the talking statues at the Forum Shops are virtually incomprehensible. These dinosaurs have been stammering on since 1992, and honestly, they should have hung up their togas years ago.

For years I assumed the pudgy, seated figure in the center of the action was Caesar. After all, he's sitting on a throne; he's wearing an olive-leaf crown; he resembles the Little Caesars Pizza mascot. Turns out he's actually Bacchus, the Roman god of wine. It took me multiple viewings to realize this; the fact that Bacchus begins the show by declaring "I am Bacchus! God of wine!" in a booming voice was apparently not a dead giveaway. Bacchus' boom overtakes his diction to the point of unintelligibility. He sounds like Santa Claus after nine too many cups of eggnog.

In Bacchus' defense, the guy is made of marble, which probably makes speaking difficult. (Remember how the Tin Man sounded before Dorothy put oil to his mouth?) Plus, Bacchus is the god of wine, so he's probably wasted. And he's probably pissed that he used to be a respected demigod but is now reduced to performing the same five-minute skit, 14 times a day, seven days a week, year after year, before confused Midwestern tourists.

I guess what I'm trying to say is, if I were in Bacchus' position, I'd be an alcoholic too.

A few minutes into the wine god's incoherent monologue, he cries, "Let the festivities begin!" That's when things get really confusing. The fountain rotates, and the other three statues (Venus, Apollo and Pluto) join the conversation. Unlike that of Bacchus, these gods' voices can't compete with the overpowering Copland-esque soundtrack. Fortunately, they've got visual tricks: Apollo plays the lyre, Venus creates a meteor shower. Then a couple of laser-powered horses gallop across the sky.

I recently re-watched the Festival Fountain show, and when it was through, I asked a group of four

I made my first serious magic purchase at the Caesars Forum Shops. The magic store, Magic Masters, was located right next to the talking fountains. I spent about 80 of my (parents') hard-earned dollars on a set of four trick decks of cards: A Svengali Deck, a Stripper Deck, a Rising Cards Deck, and an Invisible Pack.[11]

After the sale, the magician behind the counter pulled a book from the bookshelf and a secret passage appeared. We walked through it, into the back room, and he taught me the inner-workings of each effect.

The magic shop has long since closed, but the mall is doing well. A couple years back, Caesars added another 175,000 square feet to it.[12] It's within that new space that you can find P. J. Clarke's Restaurant & Bar.

The original P. J. Clarke's opened on New York's 55th street in 1884. Throughout the decades, regular patrons have included Jackie Kennedy (Sunday brunches with John Jr. and Caroline) and Frank Sinatra (sat at Table 20). The P.J.'s at Caesars opened in early 2011. Like the original, the Caesars restaurant features black-and-white photos, red-and-white checkered tablecloths, thick drinking glasses, thick cuts of bacon, and most of all, oysters.

I arrive at 2 p.m. and one of the cooks leads me to the uniform room. I pick out a white apron, I put it on—"Loop, swoop and pull"—and I head to the back room for a brief lecture on oysters from one of the chefs.

Here are the highlights:

Texan women what they thought it was about. Two of them admitted they didn't know ("I couldn't really understand what they were saying"; "I stopped paying attention and just kind of zoned out"), but the other two had their own hypotheses: "Caesar was having some kind of party? Like a birthday party, maybe? And the other statutes were entertaining him?"; "No, it was Zeus, and he was punishing the other gods for something. Right?"

As best I can tell, the Festival Fountain show has no plot. It took me years to realize this, because the show's music suggests a dramatic narrative. (Its mood moves from anticipatory to revelatory to dangerous to triumphant.) But in terms of story, the Festival Fountain is less like the (relatively) new Fall of Atlantis show at the back of the Forum Shops (in which King Atlas' children fight over who should get to control Atlantis, and then the gods step in, stop the fighting, and sink the city), and more like Disney's Hall of Presidents (in which the American presidents introduce themselves and say what they're famous for [i.e., "Hi there! I'm Benjamin Harrison! I passed the McKinley Tariff and the Sherman Antitrust Act!"]).

I say Caesars should keep the fountain, but cut off the show. Remember what stand-up comedian Mitch Hedberg said about a broken escalator: "An escalator can never break; it can only become stairs. You would never see an 'Escalator temporarily out of order' sign, just 'Escalator temporarily stairs. Sorry for the convenience.'" Well, a non-talking statue fountain is still a statue fountain, and that's nothing for which to apologize.

[11] Remember that trick I mentioned in the street performer section? The one in which an invisible deck of cards appears in my pocket? The one that's more impressive than it sounds? *That*'s the Invisible Pack.

[12] Bringing the total to 636,000.

The original P. J. Clarke's opened on New York's 55th street in 1884. … Like the original, the Caesars restaurant features black-and-white photos, red-and-white checkered tablecloths, thick drinking glasses, thick cuts of bacon, and most of all, oysters.

There are west coast oysters and east coast oysters. Some people who love west-coast oysters won't touch east coast oysters, and vice versa. At any given time, P. J. Clarke's in Vegas shucks at least three west coast oysters and one east coast. In New York, that's reversed.

Each oyster has its own flavor profile. Some are salty, some are sweet, some are from murky water, and some are tumbled deep. Today, most oysters are Gigas. Gigas replaced Olympias. There are hundreds of types of Gigas, but the popular ones that P. J.'s serves up are Gold Creek and Penn Cove.

Today, I'll be shucking those and Kumamotos, which come from Japan.

The lecturing chef turns me over to the executive chef, who tells me about the importance of serving food quickly: "From the sea to the plate—the faster it gets from place A to place B, the fresher it tastes. We treat it like a nine-one-one emergency."

I notice an anchor tattoo on the head chef's arm, so I ask him about it.

"It's because back in the kitchen, I run a tight ship."

There's more to it: The head chef used to live on a boat, scraping barnacles, and one day, he hopes to have a boat and restaurant of his own.

The head chef turns me over to the oyster shucker, Daniel. In the turnover process, there's a brief discussion as to whether they should send me to another Forum restaurant to bring back a chive stuffer.

"I can do that," I say. "No problem."

"No," Daniel says, "we're not going to make you do that. There's no such thing as a chive stuffer. It's just an initiation ritual thing we do with the new guys. But you're only here for a day, so we'll spare you."

"We won't make you find the pizza-dough repair kit either," the head chef says.

Well that's a load off.

Daniel the shucker was born in Vegas. He grew up on pizza, burgers, and strawberry shakes. He learned about oysters in Denver.

He walks me back through the kitchen, through the walk-in refrigerators (which smell fantastic), and to the live oyster bar. The seats are all empty, but Oyster Happy Hour starts in a couple of minutes, so they'll fill up shortly.

"Oysters are bivalves," Daniel explains. "Same as clams or mussels. There's the cup,"—he points—"there's the cap, there's the beak, and there's the hinge. First you've got to crack them open. To do that, you rest the oyster against a rolled up dishcloth, like this,"—he demonstrates—"and you steady it with your palm. Then you take the blade and you try to find a good place to start the crack. Then you push, hard."

His oyster pops.

"After that, you glide your blade along the top, to separate the muscle from the shell. And once you do that, you can pop the top off. Now, when you do that, some oysters are going to look thin and transparent—about five percent of them. We throw those out. We're looking for opaque oysters with thick liquor. Like this."

He presents a healthy oyster.

Two middle-aged ladies sit down. They say they're from Minnesota, that they love oysters, and that they're starving. Because it's happy hour, oysters are going for a buck each, and they order 18.

Off we go.

I've got three shucking knives from which to pick. Long, short, or short and bent. I pick the short and bent. I roll up the hand towel and pick out what I think will be an easily shuckable oyster. I rest it on the towel, press it down with my palm, and push the tip of the blade into the sweet spot.

Nothing.

I push harder.

Nothing.

I put the blade tip in a different location and try again.

Nothing.

Disheartening; I'd imagined myself a natural. After decades of sleight-of-hand practice, I'd come to think of myself as good with my hands. I'm pretty strong, too. But my dexterity and strength just don't translate. I can't get the oyster open for the life of me.

I should say: I'm not going at the oyster with full force. I don't want the blade to slip and jam into my hand. Nobody likes a bloody oyster.

After three minutes of nothing, I realize that if I want to crack this thing, I'm going to have to use all my might. So I do, and at the four-minute mark, the oyster cracks.

I can only imagine what the two ladies at the oyster bar are thinking. Daniel has been shucking nonstop, and he's been engaging them in pleasant conversation, too. Hopefully he distracted them from my incompetence.

Next I've got to separate the meat from the shell. This doesn't come naturally, either. But eventually the muscle snaps, and I remove the top. Then I cut the oyster from the bottom—it's connected on both sides—and then I turn the oyster over to make sure it's fully separated.

Done.

Daniel, of course, has already finished the other 17 oysters. I'm sure he could have done the eighteenth, too, only he didn't want to make me feel bad.

I scoop up a heaping mound of ice from the sink, I set it on the tray, and then I plate the oysters. They're slippery, so if I stick the shell into the ice at the wrong angle, the oysters will slide out, down the side of the tray, and onto the table. I manage to keep all 18 on the plate, with spare real estate for the dipping sauces and lemon wedge.

The women chew, swallow, and smile.

A group of three twentysomethings sit down next to the Minnesotans. The girl in the middle is wearing an "It's My BIRTHDAY" tiara. They're from Slovakia, and they want 24 oysters.

If you want to work in the Vegas F&B industry, you've got to be an actor. You don't have to be trained, but you've got to play a part—that of the knowledgeable, grateful server.

I shuck the next oyster in about three minutes and the one after that in two. Daniel and I split the order into two plates and we put 12 on each. After we serve the group, Daniel encourages me to taste what we've been shucking. First I try an east coast oyster, then the west coast. My palate sucks, but I can tell the difference.

I first tried oysters when I was about ten, and I hated them. Now I'm kicking myself for two decades of missing out. The west coasts taste great.

A group sitting across the restaurant orders a dozen oysters, and this time, three or four of mine make the final cut. As we're shucking, Daniel is still talking to the Minnesotans about restaurants in their hometown area, and he's talking to the Slovakians about oysters. One of the Minnesotans makes some dumb joke—something about the weather back home—and Daniel laughs deeply. The lady who made the joke smiles. Mentally, I award him an Oscar, or whatever the food and beverage industry's equivalent is.

If you want to work in the Vegas F&B industry, you've got to be an actor. You don't have to be trained, but you've got to play a part—that of the knowledgeable, grateful server. Especially if you want to serve cocktails. Casino clubs and pools no longer have "job openings" for "cocktail servers"; they have "roles" for "cocktail servers/ models." You don't go in for an "interview"; you go in for an "audition."

At first I thought casinos used those terms to make Vegas-via-L.A. servers feel better about themselves (i.e., *Well, they didn't pick me for that pilot, but I guess I can put my acting skills to work here*). But after spending the afternoon behind the oyster bar, I see that I was wrong. It really is a performance.

DAY 7

Casino Executive

Everything I know about casino management comes from "Las Vegas," the James Caan TV show. And I've only seen a few episodes. In other words, I don't know much about casino management.

The same can't be said of Felix Rappaport. Before he became the president of the Mirage, he'd worked at seven other Vegas properties. He'd actually worked at the Mirage before, too, back in '91. Only this time around, he's in charge of 4,200 people and he's got a corner office. *The* corner office, I should say. It used to be Steve Wynn's. The walls are made of glass, and they overlook a private putting green and garden. Every bird in sight is chirping and none of them are pooping.

"Coming back to the Mirage felt like a real homecoming," Felix tells me. "I see a lot of the same faces I saw twenty years ago. But a lot of new ones, too."

"Like mine," I say.

"Yes. And on that note, it's time to get started. Everyone's waiting for us."

Felix and I walk from his office to the main conference room for the Management Committee meeting. This is where the Mirage's vice presidents update Felix as to the goings on throughout the property. That's the small goal, at least. The big goal is to think up new ways to capitalize on emerging trends while staying true to the Mirage legacy brand.

Everything I know about casino management comes from "Las Vegas," the James Caan TV show. And I've only seen a few episodes. In other words, I don't know much about casino management.

The Special Events director speaks first. She's got a formal presentation. She begins by handing out a thick packet of stapled paper, which includes a drawing of a polar bear on a unicycle juggling five pieces of pie with one hand.[13] Also, the requisite Dilbert carton.

---

[13] The image is accompanied by this quote: "It is a continuous rotating pie of multi-tasking and prioritizing. It takes a focused, organized, passionate individual to juggle the variety and number of events with efficient success and knowledge."

The packet explains what the Special Events director does. For example, every year she plans a New Year's Eve Party, a Super Bowl party, and a Chinese New Year party. And then, she plans more experimental events. Like the pickle-eating contest.

"Our next event is Slotlander," she says.

"Is that a *Zoolander*-themed slot tournament?" Felix asks.

"No, *Highlander*," she replies.

"You realize there hasn't been a *Highlander* movie in the past twenty years," Felix points out.

Next up is the CFO.

"I don't want to alarm everybody and get back to cutting expenses," she says, "but we do have to pay attention to ancillary, discretionary costs. Cell phones, for instance. Those expenses are creeping up again. People who have company paid-for devices— think about whether these employees really need these phones *today* versus whether they needed them when we gave them out."

The CFO also brings up the new Kardashian Boutique. It's a strong brand and the Kardashians could bring a lot of publicity to the Mirage, but the store needs to be placed within the framework of the traditional exotic/oasis/relaxing Mirage brand. That's the tricky part.

The VP of Hotel Operations talks about how Mirage is expanding the M Life Player Reward card program into the non-gaming universe. Traditionally, you could only rack up reward points (which translate into casino comps) by gambling. Mirage is now planning on expanding the program to diners and shoppers. The first step is getting those cards in the guests' hands.

"You know," I say, "you can't get the cards in the poker room."

This gets everyone's attention.

"When I sit down to play blackjack, the pit boss always asks me if he can make me a card. But at the poker room, when I sit down, the dealer always asks me if I have a card, and when I say no, he says, 'Well, you should get one—we give you a buck for every hour of play.' But then he says that to get the card, I have to *leave* the poker room, *walk* across the casino, find some desk, and ask for it there. So I never go. I've actually *never* seen a poker player get up and get one."

"It's not actually *across* the casino," someone at the other end of the conference table points out. "It's close to the poker room."

Felix jumps in to defend me: "The point is, Rick *feels* like it's a burden. And these cards help us. We shouldn't ask our guests to go out of their way to get them. We want to make them as easy to get as possible."

"And," I say, "even if the place where you go to get the cards is right next to the poker room, the last thing a poker player wants to do when he finally gets a seat at a table, finally gets comfortable, is leave the seat, leave the game, and go try to track down some desk."

A couple people jot down notes.

"Now, Rick, did you have some other thoughts about the property?" Felix asks.

"Well, as long as we're on rewards," I continue, "I should tell you about my dad. He stayed here at the start of the summer. He got some offer in the mail—two comped nights, I think—and he stayed here for a total of three. He said that he played more than ten hours of blackjack, over three days, at a fifty-dollar minimum bet table. And then he asked you to comp the third night and you said no. So then, when he came back later this summer, he stayed at Mandalay Bay."

The Table Games VP explains, "A lot of players feel that way. They feel like, if we've agreed to comp two nights up front, all of their play should go to a comp for their third night. But the truth is, when we comp those first two nights up front, we're expecting that our guests will play during those nights, and the up-front comps are meant to cover that play. In other words, it's not like all ten hours of play went to that third night."

"Well, my dad thought they did. I'm not saying he was right; I'm just telling you about your guest's perception. And if it's a misperception—and it sounds like it is—he's probably not be the only one who holds it. The other thing that upset him was, he felt he was getting the same deal as slot players. He made some comment about how he knew that slot players were getting the same two-night comp deal, and he wanted more. Now, whether or not he deserves more than a slot player is a separate issue, and maybe he doesn't, but the point is, right or wrong, he felt like he didn't get what he deserved."

The meeting ends at noon, then lunch time.

Felix and I walk through the lobby, though the atrium, and through the casino. Along the way, he bends down to pick up a gum wrapper from the floor. He doesn't pause or make a big show of it; he just dives down, on instinct, scoops it up, and tosses it in the nearest trash can.

We arrive at Onda Ristorante, the Mirage's Italian place, and we meet up with Onda's head chef and the Mirage's executive chef. This is no ordinary lunch; this is an audition. The Mirage is trying to fill Onda's assistant-chef spot.

We take a table against the restaurant's back wall and the auditioning chef comes out to welcome us. He looks nervous. Of course, he's not being judged on his demeanor; he's being judged on his food. He'll be cooking up his own recipes, not recipes from the Onda menu.

He walks back to the kitchen and Felix asks the remaining chefs and me our favorite vacation destinations. Before we can answer, the auditioning chef returns with the first dish: heirloom tomato carpaccio with lemon thyme vinaigrette, sea salt, and extra virgin olive oil.

It's a small dish, and I finish it in a minute. When I look up, I see that everybody else's plate is 90 percent full.

"Did you guys not like it?" I ask.

"It's not that," says the executive chef. "We just want to make sure we have room to taste everything."

Ah.

Next up is the penne with sweet sausage and roasted peppers, and then comes the seafood risotto with Maine lobster and fresh spot prawns, which really impresses the executive chef, who describes himself as a "risotto snob."

"How likely is it that he'll get the job?" I ask.

"He'll probably get hired," the executive chef replies. "Derek"—that's the Onda head chef—"has worked with him before, and likes what he does."

Out comes the Chilean sea bass with rapini and fennel saffron sauce (my favorite dish so far—tastes like butter without being too buttery, if that's even possible), and then the truffle-crusted New York strip steak with black pepper and chianti reduction (least favorite; too dry).

I don't know much about food, but I know what I like, and I'm pleased with the meal. So are Felix, the executive chef, and the head Onda chef. The guy is going to get the job. Only he doesn't know that yet.

The chefs call the candidate from the kitchen.

"How do you think you did?" asks the executive chef.

"Okay," the candidate replies. "I'm not happy with the steak."

"It was a bit tough."

"Yes," the candidate agrees, even more nervous now.

"But we all enjoyed the rest of the meal. The penne in particular. And the risotto." The candidate exhales.

The chefs move into culinary specifics, and I excuse myself for the slot meeting.

The slot offices are located between the sports book and the California Pizza Kitchen. This is where Mirage executives determine the week-to-week movement of the machines. On any given day, the slot crew might be bringing in four *Hangover* games, shifting two *Sex and the City* machine banks from the high roller area to the main floor, or phasing out a row of video poker machines. Stuff like that.

Currently, the slot execs are trying to break up some of the larger machine banks, to create more walking paths. Of course, the best way to break up machine banks is to get rid of machines. And fewer machines means poorer machine selection. And poorer selection could mean less revenue.

"But not necessarily," I say. And then I tell the slot execs about a study I read in Malcolm Gladwell's *Blink*. It was conducted by Sheena Iyengar, who went to a grocery store in California and set up a table with six different jams. Among the shoppers who stopped to taste them, 30 percent ended up buying. After that, Iyengar put 24 jams on the table. What was the result? Only 3 percent bought jam. The customers weren't happy with the big selection; they were overwhelmed.

"Maybe you'd see the same positive effect if you cut back on the machines," I say.

I thought I'd dazzled the small group with this info, but they'd heard it all before. They knew about the potential benefits of having fewer machines.

Of course they know this. They're professionals.

I stay quiet for the rest of the meeting. *One skill of a great leader*, I tell myself, *is knowing when to keep your mouth shut.*

Last up is the employee meeting. This one takes place in one of Mirage's ballrooms. The big hall is occupied with convention-goers, so we take the small one. The room is filled with about 20 tables, set up in a giant rectangle. About 30 people are sitting around these tables, waiting for Felix to arrive. There's one guy in a security guard uniform and two women in maid uniforms (actually, "Guest Room Attendant" is the proper term). There's a maintenance guy, there's a dealer, there's a chef, there's a zookeeper, and there are a couple suits. Felix paces around the room, and facilitates the introductions.

"Let's go around and say our names, our job titles, and how long we've been working here at the Mirage."

There's José, who works at the pastry shop, there's Dan from sales, there's the guy who invented the chaise lounge rental system (like cabana rentals, but without the cabana), and there's Willy Wheaton, who shops for the villa guest VIPs (and, in his free time, is a pastor and a mortician), and there's Heather from the concierge desk, and there's a lady who's in charge of Title 31 compliance (something to do with money laundering), and there's the guy who counts revenue in the cages (as he's been doing for 21 years), and there's the repair guy (20 years), and there's Rose from the uniform department, Eric from the Receiving Dock, Tara from the aquarium (Felix: "Do you name the fish?" Tara: "Some of them. The big puffer fish—we call him 'Big Guy'"), and there's Cheryl the blackjack dealer from Philly, and there's Eddy the Tower Villas supervisor, and there's Joe the valet attendant, and there's me.

"Rick here is working as a casino executive for one day," Felix says. "Basically, he wanted a day where he did absolutely nothing."

Big laughter.

"The purpose of this meeting," says Felix, 'is for you to ask questions or raise complaints. Now, if you have a problem with your boss, you have to go through human resources. But other than that, I'm here to hear you out."

"The espresso machine in the employee dining room," one employee says, "has been broken for two or three months."

I didn't catch who said it, but as soon as it's said, murmurs of agreement spread around the rectangle. Several more comments about the employee dining room follow. The most important lesson of casino management: Make sure your employee dining room is really good.

One of the guest room attendants—she's from Haiti and she's wearing a blue hairclip—says, "I can't find anything to eat in there. Something healthy. They just put out white wine and chicken and that little popcorn shrimp."

Felix lets the chef respond to this.

"The salad bar has seventeen items. And we've always got rotisserie chicken, burgers, and cheeseburgers; there's always a fish option with no sauce, steamed veggies with no sauce, and a whole deli section, and soups."

The woman has another complaint: "People are leaving their room service trays in the hallway, and I always have trouble packing up my cart and getting around them. I have to pick them up, and that's not my job."

"If a guest calls room service," Felix says, "we pick the tray up right away. Of course, ninety-five percent of people don't call, so we have them laying around. And you're right, it is a problem. It's been a problem everywhere I worked. But we've got to have the right attitude about it. I walk around and I pick up trash, all the time."

The maid looks skeptical, and I want to tell her that Felix is telling the truth about the trash, but I keep my mouth closed.

The most important lesson of casino management: Make sure your employee dining room is really good.

"We should all be doing that sort of thing," Felix continues. "This is our home. But it's a competitive environment, too. When we opened in eighty-nine, it didn't matter what we did. We'd make money. Caesars was our competition, but they were in decline. Now there are twenty-five great properties on the Strip. Fortunately, MGM Resorts International has most of them, but it's a competitive world. That's why we've got to be focused on guest services. We can't be the newest casino on the strip—we're not Aria or Cosmo—but we can be the friendliest."

The gift shop worker has an issue, too: "The handling of the salad bar tongs in the employee dining area."

"What do you recommend?" asks Felix.

"I have three ideas: Have your own tongs, have a sink, or have a hand sanitizer."

"We've been fortunate so far," says Felix. "Some other hotels have had foodborne issues …"

He's referring to Aria, where a small group of guests contracted Legionnaire's disease at the property, and then came together to sue MGM Resorts International and Dubai World for negligence.

"We'll get it fixed," Felix says.

When the employees are out of complaints, the meeting ends and they return to their regular jobs. My workday as a casino executive is over, but my work as a stunt journalist is only just beginning.

It's time for me to tie together everything I've learned the past seven days. It's time to look within, scrutinize my psyche, and extrapolate.

What do I feel?

I feel something, but it's not profound. It's nothing clever, either.

I feel an affinity for my coworkers.

I feel an affinity for Felix, for Daniel at P.J. Clarke's, for Chris at Studio Lites, for Brian at Crazy Horse III, for Josh the busker, and even for Isabelle the snake.[14] At least, at the end of the night, Isabelle didn't terrify me as much as she did at the start of it.

Maybe I simply never got past the honeymoon phase with any of these Strip workers. Or maybe it's something more …

Before moving to Vegas, I lived in Chicago for three years. In Chicago, friendship groups revolved around school and nationality. (Unfortunate but true: Chicago is one of the most segregated cities in the country.) But here in Vegas, everyone is friends with their coworkers. The bartenders hang out with the bartenders, the cocktail servers hang out with the cocktail servers, the dancers hang out with the dancers, and the street performers not only hang out with each other, they live together.

I don't believe Vegas friendship bonds are stronger than those in Chicago, but I do think they form faster. For two reasons:

1) Las Vegas is a transient city. People move here and leave here all the time. So if you want to make friends with anybody, you've got to do it quickly.

2) Las Vegans are united by a single goal: *Get as much money from tourists as we can.* I don't think this is bad; I think it's beautiful. And I'm not alone. Many Las Vegans recognize the beauty and importance of this singularity of purpose. Mayor Oscar Goodman had an 86 percent approval rating[15] because he transformed the city into a corporation. He, more than anyone else, understood that we're all in it together; that we don't need to fight with each other, that we need to keep our focus on the big picture: Getting people to Vegas and emptying their wallets once they get here. That the economy sucks and that our numbers are down only increase the importance of these objectives.

---

[14] I feel an affinity for nobody at the Venetian poker table, but that's probably because I walked away a loser. If I'd won, I'm sure I would have felt a deep and meaningful connection to everyone.

[15] When asked about this, he said he was looking for the other 14 percent so he could "have them whacked."

Sure, on a small scale, our dance clubs compete against our strip clubs, and our bars compete against our frozen-daiquiri stands, and our street performers compete against the Bellagio fountains, and our casinos compete against each other. But still, we're all united by that common goal: *Get people here and get them spending.*

And how do we do this? By doing our jobs well. By playing our parts. The Mirage creates a comfortable locale through tropical ambiance and friendly customer service; Daniel the shucker charms Midwestern soccer moms with nonstop passion and polite laughter; Brian the restroom attendant creates instant rapport with bathroom goers with personalized greetings.

In L.A.'s entertainment industry, they fight all the time. The writers fight against the producers, the studios fight against the other studios, the actors fight against the other actors. And all the fights are very public. Pick up any given *Variety* magazine and see for yourself.

Las Vegas is very different from, say, Los Angeles, another city in which a lot of people work in the same industry. In the entertainment industry, they fight all the time. The writers fight against the producers, the studios fight against the other studios, the actors fight against the other actors. And all the fights are very public. Pick up any given *Variety* magazine and see for yourself.

When Las Vegans fight, we keep it behind closed doors, so as to not scare the tourists. And the truth is, we don't fight that often because we're all in the same boat. We all realize that the casino across the Strip isn't the real enemy; the real enemy is the casino in Macau. More and more "Vegas-style" casinos are popping up around the world, and they're killing our bottom line. So while the fine men and women who make Las Vegas tick might not like the direction our city is going in, they do like each other.

I like them, too. And I walk away from them with a better understanding of how the city works.

And perhaps more importantly, I walk away with a couple of backup plans, in case the whole stunt journalism thing doesn't pan out for me.

The Stunt Pieces

If you don't like this chapter, there's no point in going on. It's the best one in the book. Here's how I know: Nobody ever walks up to me and says, "You're the guy who wrote that opinion piece about Senator Ensign's bill, which, if passed, would deny federal funds to state and local governments if they took advantage of the *Kelo v. City of New London* ruling!" But people often walk up to me and say, "You're the guy who lived in the bathroom!"

"Yes," I proudly reply, "I *am* the bathroom guy."

Readers like my stunt pieces the best.

Media critics, by comparison, don't like stunt journalists. They think we're glorified emotional tourists. They think the premise of every stunt piece is, by its nature, flawed. They argue that the purpose of a stunt piece is never what the author claims within the piece (e.g., "Would ditching caffeine for a whole month improve my dating life? I had to find out!"), and always to tell a good story/get a paycheck.

My response?

You're a media critic. We only watch you on cable news shows because you're prettier and handsomer than the politicians. Now go away and let us tell some good stories.[16]

Here are the good stories:

---

[16] Notice how I didn't really address the media critics' argument? Yeah, that's because it's solid.

Mr. Olympia and the Fake Muscle Suit

Some guy was on my leg-extension machine. Sure, the gym had two others, but this guy was on the one I wanted to use.

Typically, in that situation, I follow standard gym protocol: I wait until the guy is done with his set, and then I ask, "Mind if I work in with you?" But this situation was different. The guy was huge. Bengal tiger huge. So I was too intimidated to even approach him. I was afraid he'd say, "You think I'm going to alter my workout for you?" Or worse: He'd ignore me, as if somebody of such small stature didn't even blip his radar.

I'd just moved to Vegas, just joined Las Vegas Athletic Club, and I didn't want any trouble. So I got on the calf machine, thinking, *Man, the guys in Vegas are built. What do they put in the water here?*

Fast-forward three years.

I now know that guy was Jay Cutler (a.k.a Mr. Olympia). I know he's actually a nice guy, and that he and I aren't so different, after all: We both want to get bigger. The difference is, Cutler sees himself as moving towards perfection; I see myself as moving away from deficiency.

Most people think of "body image" as a women's issue, particularly here in Las Vegas, where sexy female physiques are used to advertise every casino and nightclub on the Strip. But guys are under pressure, too, by local billboards and ads (Chippendales, Thunder from Down Under, American Storm), by Old Spice commercials, by *Men's Health* cover models and by the Mark Wahlberg, Matthew McConaughey, and Jake Gyllenhaal movies we're dragged to. The subtext of all of it is, *if you want hot girls to like you, you need big arms, ripped abs, and toned legs.*

Guys feel insecure about their bodies, too. We just don't talk about it.

Well guess what?

I'm talking.

Y Y Y

I was never obese, but I was once overweight. I liked sugar cereal and I liked big portions. Cinnamon Toast Crunch, Pops, Cocoa Puffs—the usual suspects. At the time, I didn't realize how unhealthy those overflowing cereal bowls were; I only realized that I didn't look like Hulk Hogan, Ultimate Warrior, Macho Man Randy Savage, or the other guys I'd watch on TV as I chowed down.

At 14, I passed out in the middle of my first marching band practice. I woke up on the grass, surrounded by my new classmates. But that wasn't my most embarrassing marching band-related memory.

This one time, at band camp, one of the drummers asked me, "Ricky, do you have boobs?"

"Huh?" I replied, as if I didn't hear or understand the question.

"He said, 'Do you like boobs?'" offered one of the girls, trying to cover for him.

That I needed a girl's help to get me out of it only made the situation even more humiliating and emasculating.

I lost weight at 16, and was thinner by college. Freshman year, I went to Michigan State and lived in Case Hall, with all the football players. One day, in the elevator, four or five of them got on and squished me against the back wall.

"Sorry, man. Didn't see you there," one of them said.

After that, I got more serious about lifting. Over the past decade, I've gained some muscle mass, but I still look nothing like Macho Man. And recently, I finally accepted that I'll never look like him.

It's a good thing, I told myself. A lot of women don't like bulging veins and stretch marks. A Wahlberg body is one thing. A Schwarzenegger body is another.

But then I stumbled on a shortcut. Trouble was, the shortcut would take a couple weeks to arrive by mail. So in the meantime, I set out to meet someone who'd already achieved the physique he was after. Along the way, he had gotten some help from a different type of shortcut …

Y Y Y

Joe Rossi is a personal trainer. He's 44, and he's lived in Las Vegas most of his life. When I met him at the Las Vegas Athletic Club on Sahara near Decatur, he was wearing a black-and-white Under Armor shirt and matching shorts and shoes.

"One of my clients got me this whole getup," Rossi explained. "She knows I spend all my money on food."

Rossi's in fantastic shape—especially for a 44-year-old—but as a kid, he had asthma and pneumonia, and he was overweight.

"When I got out of the pool," Rossi says, "the other kids would call me 'whale' because my skin was so shiny."

Rossi started bodybuilding in his late teens, and after he started lifting, he started doping.

"I started taking testosterone cypionate and Dianabol. I got them from a sports doctor. I felt that to compete at the level I wanted to compete at, I had to."

About seven weeks before Rossi's first event, his parents caught him using.

"They threw all my drugs in the garbage," Rossi remembers. "I was devastated, but I understand. Those drugs can be dangerous. A couple weeks ago, this trainer at Gold's—he was a serious bodybuilder in the late seventies and early eighties—he died of heart failure. Right in the gym. They tried the AED machine, but it didn't do anything."

And that's not Rossi's only death-at-the-gym story:

"When I was eighteen, there was this guy performing cable crossovers, a lower-chest exercise, and his heart exploded. At least, that's what they said; I think what happened was a chamber blew out. Either way, the guy dropped dead."

Rossi's been off the drugs for a long time. He maintains his physique with diet, exercise, and discipline. But he still remembers when he first went off the banned substances: "There's a physical and psychological addiction. It wasn't easy."

Ultimately, that might be the best reason not to do steroids: Eventually, you have to stop. And when you do, it's not pretty. Your body will shrink and your brain will resent you. Luckily, the shortcut I'd discovered had no potential for addiction …

Y Y Y

Flex Design Costumes manufactures realistic muscle suits. They take flesh-colored bodysuits and glue on 60 hand-cut pieces of foam. Then, they press on another layer of fabric, airbrush and sew. The muscle suits take three weeks to make and cost $850.

Mine showed up on the porch in a large, thin box. I removed the suit and was pleased to see that its color matched my skin tone well. I slipped the suit on and zipped it up. Then I put on a pair of running shorts and checked myself out in the mirror.

My usually small forearms had ballooned to the size of softballs. My calves were like grapefruits. And I finally had that sought-after V-taper. The extra-broad shoulders and padded butt even made my waist look smaller. I felt a powerful, surprising, instant ownership over my new physique. *This*, I thought, *is the body I deserve.*

Everything was lovely … until I realized I'd have to take the suit off.

And when I did, I looked pudgy. But I didn't feel down about it; I felt inspired. I felt motivated to turn my real body into something resembling the one I got on flexdesigncostumes.com. And I hadn't even worn the suit out in public yet. Even though I was excited to see people's reactions, I was nervous, too.

Y Y Y

Jay Cutler is the #1 bodybuilder in the world. He's the most endorsed (MuscleTech, Muscular Development, SmartShake—the list goes on), and he's the current Mr. Olympia, winning the title four times over the last five years. He's 5-foot-9, 300 pounds. His arms are 22.5 inches around and his thighs are bigger than your waist.

The youngest of seven, Cutler grew up on a farm in Massachusetts. He bailed hay, chopped wood, and raised cows, chickens, geese, horses, and pigs. He was always a big kid, and Cutler discovered bodybuilding young.

"My sister's boyfriend was into lifting, and one day he brought this magazine to the house. There was a picture of Chris Dickerson on the cover—he won Mr. Olympia in nineteen-eighty-two. I wasn't sure what bodybuilding was, but I was sure that I liked the way it looked. As a kid, I watched superhero cartoons—Superman, Batman—and when I saw the bodybuilders in that magazine they looked like the superheroes from the cartoons. So I equated bodybuilding with power."

Cutler saved up his money, and when he hit 18, he spent $300 on a yearlong gym membership. He was disciplined from working on the farm, and he used that drive at the gym, waking up early, putting in the hours.

Did his new body attract lots of women?

"I started dating a girl when I was sixteen, and I'm still with her. We've been married twenty-two years," Cutler says. "Nobody goes into bodybuilding to get chicks. It's way too hard. And I don't know about you, but the women I know aren't interested in cooking up chicken breasts ten times a day."

Cutler is constantly eating. He attributes 85 percent of his physique to his nutrition; 15 percent to his training.

"How many times during this interview, so far, have you thought to yourself, *I hope this wraps up soon so I can eat*?" I ask.

"Honestly, a couple."

Cutler has more discipline than anyone I know, but I wouldn't call him obsessed. He's just a professional who knows what it takes to succeed. I'd characterize his drive as healthy, though a lot of his peers don't have such sound psyches.

Cutler says about half of bodybuilders have muscle dysmorphia, a disorder in which guys think they're not muscular enough.

"They think they're not big. If you see a bodybuilder in the gym wearing a long-sleeved shirt in the summer, it's because he thinks his arms look small."

"And do you think you're big enough?" I ask.

"I see photos of myself at my absolute best. So I have this picture in my head. And when I train, I'm always trying to get to that point," Cutler says. "I've never been insecure about my looks, but right now—this is the worst I look all year. Right now, it's my

off-season, and I'm in my bulking phase, so obviously I don't look great."

When somebody compliments Cutler during the off-season, he doesn't feel pride; he just thinks, *You should see me at competition time.*

When the interview ended and Cutler walked outside, everybody stared. That's his whole life: stares, points, and cell phone-camera pictures. Some people know who he is. Some are just impressed. And some think he's a freak. But one way or another, everyone looks.

Y Y Y

I slipped the muscle suit back on.

Over that, I put on red track pants and a tight, white, long-sleeved Nike turtleneck weight-lifting shirt, to hide the suit's telltale neck and wrist lines. My fake abs popped through the fabric, as did the veins in my fake biceps. If you didn't know me, you'd never suspect something was up.

I drove to the grocery store. Everybody in the parking lot looked so unfit. I felt bad for them, and I felt bad about parading my newly cut body before them.

Or maybe they all saw me and thought, *look at the juicehead moron.*

As I freed a shopping cart from the rack, an older lady with short blond hair paused to watch, her mouth agape. In her defense, my incredibly tight shirt wasn't usual grocery store attire. The only guy who would wear that shirt to go shopping is the type who wants to be gawked at.

I'm typically a healthy shopper, but wearing the muscle suit, I was exceptionally so: lettuce, pomegranate juice, fat-free salad dressing, Gardenburgers, eggs. I'd wanted to get some ice cream, but didn't want to piss off the other shoppers (i.e., *He eats that crap and looks that good? How is that fair?*).

In the cereal aisle, I passed by a group of four. Two guys, two girls. The guys were built and the girls were cute, but they barely looked up at me. Which gave me a depressing thought: *If I can't catch these girls' eyes looking like this, what chance would the real Rick have?*

Looks weren't a problem when I wore the suit to the Las Vegas Athletic Club on West Flamingo the following night.

Good abs on a guy are the equivalent of big breasts on a girl. Guys looked at my ripped abs, then up to my eyes, then away. A second later, without fail, they'd look right back to my abs. They must have assumed that after they broke eye contact with me, I'd break eye contact with them, and they could score a free glance at my stomach candy. It was a pitiful display ... *and,* I realized, *it's precisely how I check out women.*

Oops.

When I stopped strutting around and started working out, I found myself lifting way more than usual. How was that possible? It's not like my new muscles were real. I've got two hypotheses:

1) Imagining yourself bigger is a common weight-lifter visualization technique, and the suit made that infinitely easier. I didn't even have to try; I just looked in the mirror and saw myself huge, which might have tricked my brain into thinking that I could lift more than I actually could.

2) I didn't want to embarrass myself or arouse suspicion. If I were to curl 25s, looking the way I looked, people would wonder. So I curled 40s instead. Normally I can't do that.

I was well off to what might have been the best workout of my life … until I had to pee. So my workout came to an abrupt end, followed by a really fast drive home.

The unplanned, inconvenient, bladder-trying drive forced me to contemplate the lengths to which I'd gone to feel big. Should I feel embarrassed? Was I crazy? Was I alone?

Susan Bordo is a professor of gender studies at the University of Kentucky, and she literally wrote the book on this topic: *The Male Body: A Look at Men in Public and in Private*. I told her my story and asked whether men's bodily insecurities were as bad as those of women.

"In one way," Bordo replied, "it's worse, because not only are men dissatisfied with their bodies, but many feel ashamed that they have those insecurities. They see it as unmanly to care about how you look. So it's a double-whammy."

And, as it should be obvious by now, working out more is the wrong way to make these insecurities go away.

"Few people who suffer from body image dissatisfaction are truly content with a healthy body. The anorexic strives for a body that is never thin enough, the surgical junkie's face gets tighter and eyes more cat-like every year, and men and boys with muscle dysmorphia can never be big enough."

Bordo's message was crystal clear: *Chill out, Rick.*

Y Y Y

I'll never have a perfect body. I'll never look like I do in the fake muscle suit. And even if I did look that way, I'd probably still feel dissatisfied. For all I know, the guys on the Chippendales billboards and in *Men's Health* feel that way, too. Maybe even Mark Wahlberg does.

I'll probably retire the muscle suit, and I'll probably keep lifting. But I'm not going to beat myself up because I don't look like Macho Man. That said, if my workouts go well these next six months, come Halloween, you just might see a former band geek wearing a leopard print tank top and a leopard print cowboy hat, and carrying around a box of Slim Jims. If you do, toss a compliment his way. You might even get a Slim Jim out of it.

Medium Unwell

On Friday afternoon I met with a medium and contacted my "dead" mom. Notice how I put "dead" in quotation marks? *Yeah, my mom's not dead.* She lives in Michigan, where she designs websites, does half-hour sessions on the elliptical machine at Life-time Fitness, and eats Gardenburgers with my dad at J. Alexander's. Of course, I didn't share any of that with the medium; I told the medium my mom was dead, and I let her take it from there.

I don't want to reveal the medium's name, but I will reveal that it's close enough to "charlatan" that she might want to consider changing it. So for now, let's call her Charla.

Charla is an older lady—about 70—with hair extensions and incredibly white teeth. When I met her—I don't want to reveal her place of business—she was wearing a pink tank top that showed off her wrinkly cleavage.

"You must be Rick," she said. "You look nervous."

"I am," I replied, "I've never done anything like this before."

I meant that I'd never before attempted to expose a medium, and if Charla was truly clairvoyant (as she claimed to be), she might have known that.

She escorted me to the séance area, and I pulled back a bead curtain and walked inside. The tiny room was adorned with scented candles, psychedelic posters, and a massage chair. We sat across from each other at a three-foot-by-three-foot table draped with a red tablecloth and topped off with a green placemat.

"You want to contact your mother," Charla told me.

Don't get all excited; I told Charla's assistant beforehand that I wanted to schedule an appointment to contact my mom.

"When did she pass?" Charla asked, taking my hands into hers.

"About a year ago."

"And how did she die?"

I looked down, took a deep breath, looked back up at Charla, and said, "Dog bite."

And then there was a long pause. During this pause, I began to worry. I began to worry that Charla could see through my lies, that I'd gone too far with the "dog bite" line, that I should have saved the crazy stuff for the end of our 30-minute session. And when I couldn't take the silence any more, I started talking:

"I mean, not just a dog bite. That's why she went to the hospital in the first place, but once she was there, she got this infection, and then they moved her, and she got this other thing, and one thing led to another ... "

"Have you thought about filing a medical malpractice suit?"

That was the last thing I expected to hear from Charla—legal advice.

Mediums, of course, can't talk to the dead. Or rather, they can talk to the dead, but the dead can't talk back.

"My father and I talked about it," I said.

"You might want to consider it. If your father has the means, of course … Does your father have the means?"

"I guess … " I replied.

Charla nodded solemnly, and I tried to get her back on track.

"So … we can get in touch with my mom, here, today?"

"You don't feel it?" Charla asked. "You're already in touch with your mother. I can sense her presence all around you. Right now. I can see tiny shapes all around you. Little geometric shapes."

"And the shapes … are my mom?"

"Did you mother do something with math or science?"

"Not really … "

"What did she like to do?"

"Figure skating. She loved figure skating."

"That's what it is!" Charla exclaimed.

"That's what what is?" I asked.

"The shapes—they're cold and white … like ice!"

I took the cue and feigned enthusiasm.

"Do you ever figure skate?" Charla asked me.

"No."

"Here's why I'm asking: Your mother is telling me that she'd like for you to go figure skating. She wants you … to go out on the ice … and see the world from her eyes."

"Ever since she passed over," I said, "I can't even watch figure skating on TV. I try to, but I just close my eyes and change the channel."

"Well she wants you to do something creative—that's what she's telling me right now."

"Anything else?"

"She's telling me … that she wants … she wants you to do something to clear your mind … to go hiking at Red Rock or go to Mount Charleston, by the canyon, where there's a waterfall … to reconnect with her."

My mom knows I hate hiking. So even if she were dead (which she's not), and even if dead people could talk (which they can't), she'd never send me to Red Rock. Maybe to the Red Rock casino, but that's it.

"Did your mother leave anything for you?" Charla asked.

"After she passed, I found this chest," I improvised, "and I unlocked it, and inside—"

Just then my phone rang. It was my mom. I'd told her to call me at that time. I'd planned to put her on the phone with Charla, and have her tell Charla that she was alive and well. But I chickened out. Charla was so warm, so comforting, and so clueless, I just didn't have the heart to do it.

"I'm so sorry," I said to Charla, as if my phone's ringer had disturbed the energy aura she'd build up over the past half-hour.

"Don't worry about it. We're coming to an end, anyway. Was there anything else you wanted to know?"

"There is one thing: Sometimes … I get the feeling … that my mom is trying to contact me. Is that weird?"

"You mother is trying to contact you," Charla assured. "She's calling out to you. She wants you to know that she loves you and that she's okay."

Charla and I hugged, and I considered fake crying. Then I reached into my wallet to pay her, at which point Charla said the funniest, least believable thing I'd heard all day: "That's right; I almost forgot about the payment!"

The fee was unreasonable in that Charla was totally wrong, but reasonable in that Charla charges much less than, say, a psychologist.

Of course, you get what you pay for.

And if you did pay for a psychologist, he might remind you that death is scary, and he might tell you that a belief in spiritualism is a denial of death. But mediums, of course, can't talk to the dead. Or rather, they can talk to the dead, but the dead can't talk back.

That's what I think, at least. And my mom agrees. She told me so yesterday.

Hustle and Flow

I hadn't given much thought to urine splash before I peed at Encore Las Vegas. The urinal I used had a blue, Velcro-like mat against its back wall and another atop its drain cover. These mats are called "Splash Guards" and they're meant to reduce urine splash. There's just one problem: They don't. But don't take my word for it; ask the khaki pants I was wearing.

A couple Mojitos later, I gave the Splash Guards a second chance. Same result. If anything, the mat made the problem worse. So either my stream is somehow fundamentally different from that of most men or Steve Wynn got ripped off.

The day after what I've come to refer to as "Urinegate," I emailed Becky Nathan, guest relations manager at Encore Las Vegas. I told her about the Splash Guards, about my khaki pants, and, in an unprecedented display of maturity, I refrained from using the term "pissed off." I asked Nathan whether the Splash Guards had ever been tested by Encore, by Steve Wynn, by their manufacturer, or by anyone.

Nathan wrote me back promptly: "I want to personally thank you for taking the time to share your comments regarding Encore. You have certainly demonstrated loyalty to our resort and the feedback you provide is invaluable. I have forwarded your concerns regarding the splash guards in our men's rooms to our management team for review."

While waiting to hear back from Encore's management team, I whizzed by some other casinos to see what, if anything, they did to combat urine splash. What I saw shocked me.

O'Sheas Casino turned urination into a game: "PISS OFF! The Ultimate Pissing Contest." For 25 cents, O'Sheas restroom patrons can answer the age-old question: "Can you piss more than Uncle Billy Bob?" The wall-mounted coin-operated machine portrays Uncle Billy Bob as a single-toothed redhead farmer wearing overalls and a trucker hat. He's holding a beer bottle, and if you can produce 20 ounces of pee, well, urine luck: His bottle lights up.

The Las Vegas Hilton takes a similarly cavalier attitude towards matters urinary. Above the urinals at Hilton you'll find life-size photographs of women reacting to men's genitalia. Above one urinal, a woman in an asymmetric black dress holds out a tape measure, her mouth agape. Above a second, a blond woman wearing midriff-baring red top smiles like a kid at a candy store and snaps a photo. Above a third, a disappointed looking brunette in pink holds her thumb an inch away from her first finger.

Nobody was peeing at the third urinal.

I visited nearly every bathroom on the Strip, but the only Splash Guards I came

---

**O'Sheas Casino turned urination into a game:
"PISS OFF! The Ultimate Pissing Contest." For 25 cents,
O'Sheas restroom patrons can answer the age-old
question: "Can you piss more than Uncle Billy Bob?"**

---

across were the ones at Encore and Wynn.[17] Maybe Mr. Wynn is the one guy in Vegas cognizant of the urine splash crisis, or maybe, when it comes to urinals, the guy's a spendthrift.

A dozen Splash Guards cost $70. Anti-Splash International, the company that manufactures the mats, recommends changing them every one to two weeks. If Encore and Wynn have 100 urinals between them (a conservative estimate), and if they change the mats as recommended, it would cost the two hotels over $20,000 a year—and that figure doesn't even include the cost of paying restroom attendants to change the mats.

I found that pricing information on the Anti-Splash International website, Anti Splash.com. The site's PRODUCT OVERVIEW section says that Splash Guards "control the spread of public health organisms" and "prevent splash back of urine onto clothing," but offers no proof of either claim. I emailed Anti-Splash International and asked, "What kind of testing have you done on your splash guards?"

"If you could be more specific," an Anti-Splash administrator responded, "we would be happy to answer any questions."

The question seemed straightforward to me, but I expanded it nonetheless: "How, exactly, do you know that the Splash Guards reduce urine splash? For instance, have you ever set up a test in which you streamed liquid into a urinal with a Splash Guard, one without a Splash Guard, and then measured how much liquid rebounded from each?"

No response. Fast forward a couple of days. I still hadn't heard back from the Anti-Splash administrator (nor from Becky Nathan at Encore), so I took matters into my own hands. I stuffed a couple of trash bags in my briefcase, bought a pair of rubber dishwashing gloves from Vons, and drove to Encore to swipe a Splash Guard so I could perform my own testing.

The bathroom was empty when I walked in, but still, I had to act fast. Somebody

---

[17] Authors note: Since this story's original publication, other casinos have brought in Splash Guards.

could enter at any second, and that somebody could be an attendant or a security guard. I dashed into the far stall, opened my briefcase and slipped on the gloves. I approached the nearest urinal, reached inside, and pulled out the dripping, urine-soaked Splash Guard. I dashed back into the stall and dunked the Guard into the toilet bowl 10 or 20 times to clean it. I wrung out the mat, wrapped it inside the trash bags, and stuffed the bundle back into my briefcase. I washed my hands (like a dozen times), and walked back to my car feeling just like Danny Ocean at the end of *Ocean's 11*, only dirtier.

When I got home, I discovered this terribly-timed email from the Anti-Splash administrator: "Rick, if you give me your location, I can direct you to one of our customers that is near you and you can try our product out yourself."

I replied that I'd already "obtained" a Splash Guard myself, but that I would still like to see specific information of product testing.

Then I moved into Phase Two.

I removed the lid of my bedroom toilet, carried it outside and rested it against a tree. I poked a straw through a piece of paper towel, took a swig of Black Cherry Kool-Aid and spat the liquid through the straw, against the porcelain. Four or five droplets splashed off the porcelain and onto the paper towel. Next I taped the Splash Guard against the toilet lid and repeated the blow test. Once again, four or five droplets splashed back.

Based on my informal test, the Splash Guards did not reduce backsplash. It definitely reduced perpendicular splash, but I think most men actually enjoy watching their urine dissipate against a smooth porcelain backdrop. I should also note that the

Splash Guard did not increase urine splash, as I'd originally suspected. Perhaps I just perceived an increase in urine splash because yellow liquid shows up better against a blue background than against a white one.

Sure, my test falls a little short of *Consumer Reports* standards, but to the best of my knowledge, it's the most scientific test performed on the Splash Guards to date; consider this email from the Anti-Splash administrator:

"As far as quantifying the precise amount, I don't have that information at hand, but I can probably get it if you really need it. I personally have run an informal and unscientific test for my own curiosity, though. I just taped a piece of construction paper near a board, which I hung one of our backguards on, and then had at the pad with my kid's supersoaker. I then counted the drops on the paper. I tried it again without the backguard and was disgusted by how much splash back there was … Just as a rough estimate, I would say conservatively that at least nintey percent of the mist (yeah you're breathing that stuff!) that comes off an unprotected surface is eliminated, and almost all of the larger droplets were contained."

I responded and said that I really did want to see information quantifying the precise amount. I never heard back, and until I do, I've got to believe that no such information exists. I admit that my test was no more scientific than that of the Anti-Splash administrator. But consider the tester; objectivity is on my side.

I never heard back from Becky Nathan at Encore, either. The Splash Guards are still in the Wynn and Encore urinals—including the one I swiped (I returned it one Saturday afternoon). Wynn and Encore might be the most gorgeous hotels on the Strip, and I'm not going to stay away from them over such a trivial matter. But until they take out the Splash Guards, I'll be keeping my khaki ants at home in the closet.

Notice how there's no "p" in them? I'd like to keep it that way.

How You Play the Game

The Harlem Globetrotters are cocky bastards. They're not whimsical, they're not inspirational, and they're certainly not American heroes. They're sadistic bullies who'll do whatever it takes to win, no matter how cruel or degrading.

I could be biased. See, last week the Globetrotters played the Washington Generals at the Orleans Arena, and I had money riding on the Generals. Like Krusty the Clown, who lost his life savings betting on the Generals, I figured the team was due.

You'd think placing a bet on a basketball team that's three-and-a-half decades into a 10,000-game losing streak would be easy, but none of the sports books in town would take my bet. According to the manager of the Venetian sports book, "Las Vegas casinos only take bets on legitimate sporting competitions, not exhibition events. You can't bet on the all-star game, and you can't bet on *American Idol*."[18]

"But can't you make an exception for the Generals? They haven't won since nineteen-seventy-one."

"Call up an offshore sports book and place a bet with them," he suggested.

I called my dad instead. He's a lifelong Globetrotters fan, and was willing to take my bet. We agreed that I'd give him $1 if the Globetrotters won and he'd give me $1,000 if the Generals did.

Before the game, I told Generals team captain Ben Augustine (6'6", 210 lbs.) about my bet.

"I'll try my best out there," he assured me, "but I have to tell you, I've been playing with the Generals for four years and haven't won yet, so I can't make you any promises."

"But you'll try?"

"Of course I'll try. I always try. Everyone on the team does. Every time we take the court, we do our best to win."

"But you never have."

"Not yet, no. But to me, it's not about winning or losing; it's about how you play the game. Energy, efforts, hustle, winning loose balls, crashing the boards—that's what's most important."

I took my seat at the press table, and the announcer introduced the Washington Generals starting lineup. Children booed. The jeers provoked the Washington Generals coach into grabbing the microphone from the announcer and giving this speech:

"I hope you kids didn't come here today expecting to see the Globetrotters win,

---

[18] Authors note: Since this story's original publication, this law has changed.

because if you did, you're going to be sorely disappointed. Today the Washington Generals are going to make history, right here in Las Vegas—the armpit of America."

I know that sounds bad, but you have to remember where this guy is coming from. He's been coaching the Generals for years and has yet to win a game. He's frustrated with the league, and probably with himself. The Las Vegas swipe was textbook Freudian projection, and he shouldn't be blamed for it.

The announcer cued up "Sweet Georgia Brown" and introduced the Globetrotters, who ran onto the court and into their trademark circle formation. In a desperate, transparent plea for attention, the Trotters passed basketballs behind their backs, rolled them along their arms, and spun them on their heads.

In a desperate, transparent plea for attention, the Trotters passed basketballs behind their backs, rolled them along their arms, and spun them on their heads.

The Harlem Globetrotters took an early lead, and every time the Generals came close to closing the gap, the Globetrotters cheated. For example, when Washington General Christopher Spartz was about to make a layup, one of the Trotters ripped his jersey off. The shirtless, humiliated Spartz ran off-court to the sound of 1,000 sadistic children laughing. The referee called a foul and escorted Spartz to the foul line. When Spartz was about to take his first free throw, one of the Trotters pulled his pants down, and again, the kids went wild.

These children clearly have no appreciation of what a serious issue bullying is. According to the United States Department of Health and Human Services, 160,000 students stay home from school on any given day because they're afraid of getting bullied. And as for those doing the bullying, (i.e., the future Globetrotters of America), 60 percent of them will have at least one criminal conviction by the age of 24.

Considering their predisposition for humiliation, you must be wondering how the Globetrotters kept public opinion on their side throughout the game. Well, let me tell you: They did it through shameless pandering. For example, during the quarter break, one Globetrotter invited a cute little girl onto the court and spun a basketball on her finger. Then he gave her a T-shirt.

At halftime, I joined Spartz and team captain Augustine in the Generals locker room. The coach was all business:

"Listen up. Listen up. Not a bad half, but you've got to do a better job protecting the ball. On defense, call your man out; call out 'thirteen'; call out 'forty-nine.' You've got to set better screens, too. If you stay focused, your shots will start falling. We know we're a better team in the second half, so let's make history happen here tonight."

After the coach's speech, Augustine introduced me to the rest of the guys and told them about my bet. Some of them laughed—bad sign—but others asked if I had any pointers for them.

"Actually, I do. The Trotters pretty much run the same play every time, but you never seem to catch on. They weave the ball at the three-point line for ten seconds, then they pass to the tall guy at the free-throw line, and he feeds it to one of the shorter guys who comes in from the side and dunks. Same play again and again, but you look so surprised every time it happens."

"What else?"

"I'll tell you what else: We just elected a guy named Barack Hussein Obama to be our president. Some small-budget Indian movie called *Slumdog Millionaire* just won the Golden Globe for Best Picture, and it's probably going to win the Oscar, too. This is the year of the underdog. I know a lot of kids came here tonight to see the Globetrotters win. But don't think about them, think about the underdogs. Think about the boy who always gets picked last in gym class, and win this game for him."

The Generals rallied in the third quarter. I was clearly a major influence here, but the Generals coach deserves most of the credit. When the referee wasn't looking, the coach switched the official game ball with a remote-controlled basketball. When the ref figured out what was going on and switched the ball back, the coach put a clear disc over the Globetrotters' rim so none of their shots could fall in. And when the ref figured that one out, the coach walked over to the scoreboard control pad and upped the Generals' score by 16 points.

When the referee wasn't looking, the coach switched the official game ball with a remote-controlled basketball. When the ref figured out what was going on and switched the ball back, the coach put a clear disc over the Globetrotters' rim so none of their shots could fall in. And when the ref figured that one out, the coach walked over to the scoreboard control pad and upped the Generals' score by 16 points.

I know that sounds bad. But again, you have to remember where the Generals coach is coming from. His team has been stripped down, humiliated, dehumanized—not just for the past hour, but for the past three and a half decades.

I knew the Generals were in trouble when one of the Trotters stole the ball from team captain Augustine by crawling under his massive legs. Augustine looked completely befuddled, and throughout the final five minutes of the game, the rest of the Generals did too.

The Globetrotters won 81-68. Children cheered and rushed to the court to have their photo snapped with Sweet Pea Shine, Big Easy Lofton, Flight Time Lang, and the rest of the domineering braggarts.

An hour later, I got a phone call from my dad.

"Who won the big game?" he wanted to know.

"It's not about winning or losing," I told him. "It's about how you play the game."

Take Me Higher,
But Keep It On the D.L.

I'm 5'11". I'm about two inches taller than the average American male. And yet, I'm insecure about my height.

It's all my roommate's fault. She's 6'1", inconsiderately, and she likes to wear heels. Her friends are tall, too. They're all showgirls and former showgirls, and, like my roommate, they don't shy away from pumps, stilettos, and platforms. So when we go out as a group, I'm the short one.

There's nothing wrong with being the short one—just ask Beethoven (5'3"), Ghandi (5'3"), or Spike Lee (5'5"). But being tall sure has its perks. Particularly for men; tall guys are more likely to get responses to their personal ads; tall guys are more likely to get married; tall guys have more children on average.

According to author Arianne Cohen, (who is 6'3" and clearly biased), "Talls annually earn $789 more per inch than our average-height counterparts, racking up $1.5 million in extra assets over 40 years."

But why is that? Why does the taller candidate usually win the election? Why is the average Fortune 500 CEO six feet tall? Why are taller people so successful in life? Are they more intimidating? Or is it all about confidence?

I set out to investigate.

ITallerShoes.com sells elevator shoes. Not the monster-mash boots used by the guy who plays Frankenstein at Universal Studios, but shoes that secretly boost their wearer's height by two to four inches. The boost comes from a hidden, extra-thick sole.

Shoes like these are generally marketed to shorter guys, but there's no rule that says guys like me can't wear them, too. I was mildly embarrassed about placing an order, but ITallerShoes.com assured me, "The plain package has no words such as 'elevator shoes' or 'instant height-increasing shoes.'"

So I ordered two pairs. The first, a pair of brown dress shoes with tailored trim and perforated toecaps, made me 3.2" taller. The second, a pair of casual brown leather walking shoes with tri-colored racing stripes and elastic laces, boosted my height by 2.8". I was worried that the walking shoes would look odd and obvious, but they didn't. Actually, they looked more stylish than all my normal shoes.

On Friday, I slipped on the 3.2" dress shoes and met my roommate and her also-tall friends at the Griffin. They were drinking wine, wearing heels, and standing around the bar like they owned the place. As tall people tend to do.

I stood right next to them and ordered a merlot. Fifteen minutes passed, and none of them commented on my growth spurt.

Why hasn't anybody saying anything? Do they even notice a difference? Are they so used to hanging out with extra-tall guys (6'3" and up), that my height increase hasn't even registered with them? Or worse: maybe they know I'm wearing elevator shoes, but aren't saying anything because they're embarrassed on my behalf.

The second glass of merlot loosened me up. And for a while, I didn't think about height. After all, we were all standing at the same level, and height observations usually surface when there's a disparity. But when some average-sized people walked in the bar and stood right next to us, I began to appreciate how physically domineering we were.

I felt bad for the men in the other group. I felt like we were inadvertently emasculating them with our very presence. I wanted to say, "Don't fret; I'm not really this tall."

After a half hour, I came clean and removed the elevator shoes. I handed one of them to my roommate's friend Katy (who, like my roommate, stands at 6'1"), and she said, "Oh my God. I need to buy these for every guy I date!"

My roommate chimed in: "I dated a guy who did wear shoes like that, on our first date. Then, on our second date, he was much shorter, and I was like, what the hell happened? And later, one day at his apartment, I saw the shoes on the ground by his door, and I was like, ohhhh."

"Did you feel tricked?" Katy asked.

"Yeah," my roommate replied.

"But you kept on dating him," I pointed out.

"I guess I did."

I asked my roommate's other friend Claudia (who stands at a relatively paltry 5'10") whether she could ever date a shorter guy.

"Depends on how much shorter the guy is," Claudia replied. "I couldn't date 5'7"or under. I used to joke with my ex that if we got married, he'd have to wear the heels."

I'm guessing Claudia found that joke funnier than her ex did. If the girl I was dating said that to me, I'd cry my way to the plastic surgeon's office for distraction osteogenesis (i.e., leg lengthening).

I re-donned the elevator shoes, and we left the Griffin to wander around Fremont Street. The stares were nonstop, and so were the comments:

"There go the supermodels."

"Damn! Look at those tall blonds!"

"Holy shit."

Basically I was ignored. Understandable; a tall guy isn't as noteworthy as a tall girl. (In America, the average guy stands five inches taller than the average woman.) But being ignored gave me a chance to observe the guys who were checking out the girls. Guys, I found, check out tall girls differently. With shorter girls, the eyes move down gradually, from the head to the butt. But with tall girls, the eyes drop like an Acme anvil. There's a pressing need to see whether the girl is really that tall, or whether she's wearing 6" stripper shoes.

We approached one of the Fremont Street stages and watched the "Dream Team Divas" perform a dance show. I'll tell you this much: I sure didn't have any trouble seeing the stage.

After the performance, we went backstage and snapped a photo with one of the Divas, who's also a friend of my roommate. It looks like a picture of six average-sized people with one short girl up front … only the "short" girl isn't short at all; she's 5'5", a half-inch taller than the average American woman.

Standing next to the average-sized Dream Team Diva and the average-sized girls at the Griffin, I felt a boost of masculinity. But my confidence spike was like a cocaine high: artificial and temporary.

I realized that the shoes would eventually have to come off. And when the shoes did come off, back home, the ground looked shockingly close, and my roommate looked taller than ever.

The elevator shoes didn't offer me the confidence that (ostensibly) comes with being tall, but perhaps others perceived me as confident. But when it comes to winning elections, negotiating a salary, and getting the girl, isn't that what counts most?

Not Just a Bathroom, a Home

We don't have utopia, but we do have Town Square. And in a lot of ways, Town Square is better. The grass is greener (because it's Astroturf[19]), the music is clearer (because the speakers are hidden in the planters), and the bars stay open later (does Utopia even have bars?). But like Sir Thomas More's fictitious island society, Town Square is too good to be true. I found that out the hard way … by moving in.

Ɏ Ɏ Ɏ

On a recent Wednesday I hopped aboard Mike Wethington's golf cart for a grand tour of Town Square, the 1.5 million-square-foot "lifestyle center" located just south of Mandalay Bay. Mike, Town Square's general manager, drove me past the botanical garden, around the footbridge and stone waterfall and throughout Town Square's 22 buildings, whose architecture shows Parisian, San Franciscan, Bostonian, and Barcelonan influences.

"We've got over seventy different façade types," Mike told me. "Our intent was to make Town Square look like a city that developed over the years."

Quick examples: The Lucky Brand Jeans store has a mansard roof, the Express store has a mission-style roof, and the Tommy Bahama store has, appropriately, a Bahamian/colonial/plantation/antebellum-style roof. Only Sephora's roof, which displays a "2007" historical marker, betrays Town Square's through-the-years architectural motif. But aside from the girls who work at the sunglasses kiosk below, I doubt anybody's given much thought to the marker, let alone noticed it.

For lunch, Mike and I met up with Town Square Marketing Director Mary Kathryn at Anthony's Coal Fired Pizza. Anthony's, a Floridian import, serves "pizza well done"—and that's not just a slogan; Anthony's keeps its ovens at 800 degrees. Over chicken wings (also coal-oven roasted), eggplant Marino, and vegetable pizza, I asked Mike and Mary if they had read *Review-Journal* columnist Geoff Schumacher's recent piece on Town Square.

In case you missed it, Schumacher called Town Square "the new Downtown,"[20]

---

[19] The Town Square cleaning crew combs through the blades to remove debris and preserve springiness. The combs run just above the layer of fine black gravel (spread between the blades), which visually approximates sod and cushions pedestrians' steps.

[20] Wrote Schumacher:

> Town Square is achieving something that the real downtown can only dream about right now. As hard as the real downtown has tried in recent years to redevelop and attract legions of locals, its results pale in comparison with the numbers visiting Town Square …

and the comment sparked more controversy than a Mel Gibson movie. Apparently some Las Vegans think Downtown Las Vegas (the one with the low-res TV on the ceiling and the football-shaped souvenir glasses) is still Downtown Las Vegas. Go figure.

Mike and Mary said they were aware of Schumacher's article and pleased with it.

"Town Square was designed to be like a real downtown," Mike told me, "a place where people would come to meet. Schumacher's comment is a compliment to our intent and design."

"We had thirty-thousand people visit us on Halloween last year," Mary added, "and fifteen-thousand for Santa's arrival. We're not just putting on events; we're starting family traditions. And we want to draw families, year after year."

"With all those families coming through," I said, "security must be a big issue here."

"The biggest crime people commit at Town Square ... " Mary replied, " ... is shopping too much! A lot of wives get in a lot of trouble here."

The Lucky Brand Jeans store has a mansard roof, the Express store has a mission-style roof, and the Tommy Bahama store has, appropriately, a Bahamian/colonial/ plantation/antebellum-style roof. Only Sephora's roof, which displays a "2007" historical marker, betrays Town Square's through-the-years architectural motif.

I got the sense she'd gotten a lot of mileage out of that line.

"The most typical crimes are shoplifting and vandalism," Mike said, on a more serious note. "Maybe somebody goes at a mirror in the restroom, scrapes it. We've had some vehicle break-ins, but that's it. We haven't had any major incidences, and that's

---

Town Square is where the prime demographic of locals goes now to shop, eat, hang out with friends and meet new people. The restaurants are good, the nightlife is energetic and the shops have trendy things people want to buy. The movie theater is the valley's best. It has great freeway access and acres of parking. It's safe and clean ... By the way, this is not an advertisement for Town Square.*

*Mary: Take note: Schumacher's piece would make a perfect Town Square advertisement—especially the whole "this is not an advertisement" bit.

because we have a strong, around-the-clock security presence. We have to; our bars close at four, we get deliveries in at five and six, and we get office tenants arriving at seven and eight. Plus, we've always got families and children around."

Mike's comment brought us to the Town Square Children's Park (both literally and figuratively; we started walking there after our meal). Mike and Mary talk about the park the way most parents talk about their children. Let's just say I wouldn't have been surprised if they'd pulled out photos of the park from their wallets.

When we arrived, I saw what all the fuss was about. Town Square Children's Park has a 35-spritzer pop-jet fountain, a 40-foot-tall tree house, a hand-painted puppet theater, and a hedge maze adorned with an animatronic elephant, monkey, dolphin, and flamingo.

The hedge maze, I came to realize, isn't actually a "maze" (a tour puzzle in which some paths take you to the goal and others lead to dead ends); it's a single, jagged, looping path bisected by a connecting path. In other words, it has no dead ends. I suppose that just provides further evidence in support of Mike's spiel about Town Square being safe for children.

As I exited the "maze"—it wasn't hard—I felt a thought emerging. I felt it on the tip of my brain. Little by little, my mind started putting the pieces together: safe for children … no serious crime … bountiful employment opportunities … good nightlife … and then it hit me: *Town Square is the perfect place to live.*

I began imagining a new life for myself—a life filled with luxury, beauty, indulgence, and relaxation—a life free from crime, boredom, poverty, long drives, and real dirt. Then I enlisted Mike and Mary's help.

"Describe the perfect day in Town Square," I said.

Mary didn't hesitate for a second: "You could start your morning at The Coffee Bean. Get a latté, maybe a muffin, pick up a newspaper and read it outside. Then you could stroll down the street and do some window-shopping. Then lunch at Brio Tuscan Grille—maybe enjoy a glass of wine. In the afternoon, you could catch a movie at Rave or relax at the Eleven Spa."

Mary paused to think, and Mike continued right where she left off: "You could grab dinner at Texas de Brazil Churrascaria. Then listen to some live music at Blue Martini, maybe ride the mechanical bull at Cadillac Ranch, maybe sample the 160 different beers at Yard House, maybe catch the game at Bar Louie. And at that point, if you're still not tired, you could grab late-night breakfast at Johnny McGuire's."

That's when I decided: *I'm going to move into Town Square.*

Y Y Y

When we arrived, I saw what all the fuss was about. Town Square Children's Park has a 35-spritzer pop-jet fountain, a 40-foot-tall tree house, a hand-painted puppet theater, and a hedge maze adorned with an animatronic elephant, monkey, dolphin, and flamingo.

Here's the email I sent Susan Holland, Town Square's leasing manager: "Hi Susan, I'm in love with Town Square, and I'm thinking about renting some property there. Tell me, are all your renters as happy as they seem to be?"

Holland's reply: "Thank you for the compliments, and we strive for each customer to have an opinion like yours. In terms of leasing, are you interested in retail or office? Thank you."

My reply: "Of course; compliments are well deserved in this case! But if I'm going to become part of the Town Square family, I'd like to be considered more than a 'customer.' Seems a little formal—don't you think? I'd like to think of myself as a 'resident.' I'm interested in a one-bedroom apartment. How much would that run me?"

Holland's reply: "Our upper levels are all designated as office space. There are no current plans for any type of extended living."

No extended living?

Huh?

Surely Holland was mistaken. Surely Turnberry Associates didn't construct this modern-day Shangri-La only to forbid people from moving in. That'd be like grilling a flank steak in front of an emaciated puppy and then tossing it in the trash. Perhaps Holland was playing some kind of practical joke?

Nope; here's what senior leasing director George Radu had to say about Holland's email: "She is correct: We do not have any residential units at the Town Square Lifestyle Center."

Ah. Therein lies the discrepancy: "Lifestyle Center" is the noun phrase; "Town Square" is merely the (incredibly deceptive) proper noun. The thing that makes it so deceptive is that the center area of Town Square not only looks like a real town square—a publicly owned area used for public gathering—but it functions as one, too. Of course, real town squares (e.g., Trafalgar Square, Tiananmen Square, Times Square) are owned by governments; the Town Square center area (like Town Square Major) is owned by Turnberry Associates, a 50-year-old, $7 billion real-estate-development and property-management corporation.

And just as the Town Square center area isn't a real public town square, Town Square Major isn't a town. It's a shopping mall[21,22]—sorry, "lifestyle center." I got in touch with UNLV Professor of Sociology Michael Borer to discuss the phenomenon of private space functioning as public.[23] Here's what he had to say:

"Consumption sites—especially outdoor malls like Town Square—are neither totally private nor totally public. They perform the same functions of traditional public spaces, but they're ultimately controlled by property owners, who can regulate the spaces through laws and design elements. The amount of regulation—security and surveillance—and how that amount is perceived will determine the inclusivity or exclusivity of that space."

Town Square must have found the perfect amount of security and surveillance because the place seems safe and free, yet everybody there is well-to-do and quick-to-spend.

"A traditional public space," Borer went on, "is one where all are free to enter, interact, and leave at their will. Shopping malls, or 'lifestyle centers,' can never meet such lofty ideals. But if regulation is kept low, they can provide spaces for people to gather, to interact, and to share not only goods and products, but ideas and beliefs as well."

It's not all bad, is professor Borer's point, but the "lifestyle center" isn't all-new either: "Renaming 'shopping malls' 'lifestyle centers' supports the idea that our identities are dependent upon the things we buy. And when it comes to 'lifestyle centers,' nothing is new; everything is just rebranded to meet the 'needs' of a 'diverse' consumer base. Even 'the mall' itself has been rebranded, and identities become simply things that are bought rather than built."

The rebranding isn't accidental. Turnberry Associates designed Town Square to resemble a real town for one purpose and one purpose only: to increase sales.

Well, I thought, *if Town Square is going to act like a town, I'm going to treat it like one. Residential units or not, I'm moving in.*

---

[21] Nomenclatural irony: The "National Mall" in D.C. is a real town square.

[22] As best I can remember, in the two hours I spent with Mike and Mary, they never once used the term "shopping mall."

[23] The Supreme Court addressed this issue in the 1946 First Amendment case *Marsh v. Alabama*. In the majority opinion, Justice Hugo Black wrote, "Ownership does not always mean absolute dominion. The more an owner, for his advantage, opens up his property for use by the public in general, the more do his rights become circumscribed by the statutory and constitutional rights of those who use it."

Y Y Y

On Friday I vacated my cozy tri-level townhouse and moved into the handicapped-accessible bathroom in front of Town Square's south parking garage. I wanted to move into the bathroom by the north parking garage because it's twice as big, but some guy had apparently moved in before me, and after 15 minutes, I realized he wasn't planning on moving out any time soon. Damn squatter. So I schlepped my belongings to the south side.

When the coast was clear, I dragged my stuff into the bathroom and locked the door behind me. I arranged the fake plants I'd brought, made my bed and taped up a Robert Pattinson poster by the toilet. And then, when the feng shui was satisfactory, I began my new life as the first resident of Town Square. I climbed into bed, pulled out my MacBook Air and started to write.

The words poured out of me. I wasn't just settled in physically; I was settled in emotionally. I was no longer plagued by the day-to-day worries and social insecurities that block most writers' creative output. I'd moved on up and gotten a piece of the

pie—and unlike the Jeffersons, my perfect new life couldn't be abruptly canceled by CBS without a proper series finale.

That's when the knocking began.

Most of the time, when somebody knocks on your door and you don't answer it, the knocker goes away. Maybe she knocks a second time, or maybe she ties a pamphlet to your door handle, but that's as bad as it gets. However, when you live in a handicapped-accessible bathroom and somebody knocks on your door, they keep knocking until you do something about it. And the longer you wait, the louder the knocks get, and the louder the knocks get, the more difficult it becomes to get any work done.

Finally, finally, the knocking stopped. But I knew it was only a matter of time before a new knocker came to breach my covenant of quiet enjoyment. Fortunately, I had foreseen this would be a problem—that's why I brought with me a "PRIVATE PROPERTY/NO TRESPASSING" sign.

After the first knocker left, I duct-taped the sign to the door. In retrospect, this was a stupid thing to do. A Town Square janitor noticed me putting the sign up, and then he got on his walkie-talkie. Now, I can usually talk my way out of situations like these, but the cleaning guy didn't speak English, and, well, that made it hard.

A security guard came by a minute later, looked at my sign, and then at me.

"Well?" she said.

"Well," I replied, "some lady was knocking on the door, and she wouldn't stop."

"Yeah, that's how it works with bathrooms."

"Yes, but this isn't just a bathroom; it's my home."

At that point the security guard got on her walkie-talkie and started off a chain of numeric code-ridden walkie-talkie calls (e.g., "We got a six-twenty by the south parking garage. Call Ed and get the four-forty on this guy."). Eventually the guard got in touch with Mike Wethington.

"I know Mike!" I said.

"We'll see," she replied. "He's on his way."

Mike showed up five minutes later—he wasn't kidding about security's efficiency—and wanted to know what the hell I was doing in his bathroom. It was a totally reasonable question. I told him about my desire to move into Town Square, and judging by his response, he was more sympathetic than upset.

"You can't live in Town Square. We're not zoned for it. We're in the McCarran Airport FAA flight path. It's not the primary path—that's from the east—but when the wind shifts, they open this up to more traffic. So, yeah, zoning restrictions bar all residencies. Sorry, but you can't stay here."

After just 20 minutes of living in Town Square, I was being evicted.

Y Y Y

Here's the kicker: During the course of "moving into" Town Square and writing this story, I bought a T-shirt, a three-pack of underwear, a pair of shorts, a bracelet and a necklace (from H&M), a couple of frozen yogurts (from Yogurtland), a couple of iced diet green teas and a hardcover book (from Borders), and groceries (from Whole Foods). All in all, I spent over $250. The only other malls at which I drop that kind of cash are the Forum Shops at Caesars and Venetian's Grand Canal Shoppes. When I walk into a "normal" mall, I typically spend $50, get bored, and leave.

Why is that? That was the question I asked Golden Gate University Department of Psychology Chair Kit Yarrow (whose book, *Gen BuY*, came out September 8, 2010). Here was her answer:

"Malls like Town Square, the Forum Shops and the Grand Canal Shoppes are really squarely designed as entertainment complexes. People will come for the novelty, thrill, opulence, and entertainment, and feel as if they're on vacation. Vacations tend to spur spending as people give themselves permission to buy because it's a 'special event.' Also, stimulating environments rub off on products—purchase considerations actually seem better and more valuable."

"So that's why these 'lifestyle centers' have grown so popular?"

"It's more than that; the lifestyle centers offer the visual stimulation of a 'city' without the hassles. They're designed to accommodate the interests of all ages and both genders—in other words, there's something for everyone. So couples, kids, families, friends can share in an outing. Of course, the longer people linger, the more they spend."

Which is a good thing … or a bad thing, depending on how you look at it.

"My main concern," Yarrow continued, "is that the kids who use these lifestyle centers as their playgrounds become acculturated to all the things that are for sale there. That's one of the reasons why young people today have higher expectations than previous generations about what they 'should' be able to have or afford."

So maybe Town Square isn't better than Utopia after all. Sure, your kids won't get lost in Town Square's hedge maze (because it has no dead ends), but they also won't learn how they navigate their way through the real world. Unlike the Town Square hedge maze, the real world is full of dead ends, and unlike Town Square, the real world is full of crime, and poverty, hunger, and (gasp!) boredom. Town Square provides an escape from all that, but the escape is temporary. Trust me.

Still, while Town Square might be a crappy place to live, it's a beautiful place to spend … and to laugh and to play and to hang and to chill and to stroll and to sit and to dine and to drink.

Unconventionals

The opposite of a specialist is a generalist. A generalist knows a little bit about a lot of things. There are two ways to become a generalist: You can travel around the world, seeking out the brightest thinkers, newest ideas, and latest technologies, or you can become a writer, move to Las Vegas, and cover conventions.

I picked option two.

Las Vegas hosts about 18,000 conventions each year.[24] As a journalist, I easily get access to these events. Yet writing about conventions is still tough. I can only say, "A bunch of bald white guys walked around a beige room," so many times.

So I try my best to select unique conventions, and to write about them in unique ways. Here—let me show you:

---

[24] The biggest and most famous convention is the Consumer Electronics Show, which draws 140,000. Less famous Vegas conventions include the concrete convention, the accordion convention, and the Gerard Butler convention.

Dawkins, Randi, The Myth Buster, & The Moon Hoaxer

I'm standing in a lukewarm hot tub with 30 atheists. A big guy named Rick is teaching me the history of the modern Skeptic Movement. He's explaining how magician James Randi and biologist Richard Dawkins have debunked psychics, mind readers, remote viewers, astrologers, homoeopathists, acupuncturists, and God.

This, I imagine, is how the Sophists must have felt—philosophizing in crowded Greek bathhouses as their fingers and toes pruned. Then again, the pre-Socratic philosophers spent their time forming hippy-dippy theories ("All things come from water," "Everything is in flux"), and the modern Skeptics spend their time picking those theories apart.

This, I imagine, is how the Sophists must have felt— philosophizing in crowded Greek bathhouses as their fingers and toes pruned. Then again, the pre-Socratic philosophers spent their time forming hippy-dippy theories ("All things come from water," "Everything is in flux"), and the modern Skeptics spend their time picking those theories apart.

Over a thousand Skeptics gather annually in Las Vegas to disprove, discuss, debate, and inquire. The year I attended, they were joined by a man who swore the moon landing was faked, a man who claimed he could cure terminal diseases over the phone, and one million pissed-off ghosts.

So did this motley crew play nice? The answer might surprise you.

It's Thursday afternoon and I'm pulling into the South Point parking garage. I'm heading to The Amaz!ng Meeting (TAM!): A Celebration of Critical Thinking and Skepticism. It's the eighth annual meeting. I'm running late.

The Richard Dawkins press conference is supposed to start in 10 minutes, and I haven't even parked, let alone walked through the casino and to the convention hall, let alone checked in at the press registration table, let alone fired up my laptop up and typed up some clever questions. Oh, I've scraped by with dumb ones in the past, but Richard Dawkins topped Prospect magazine's list of *Top 100 British Intellectuals*, so clever queries were de rigueur.

I double-time through the casino, breeze through the registration process—nobody asks for ID—and locate the room in which the press conference is set to take place. I take a seat next to a young man holding a giant crystal ball in his lap. I deduce that he's not a 'genuine' fortune teller (i.e., one who genuinely claims to tell fortunes), but a Skeptic pretending to be one. Presumably, to show how silly fortune tellers are.

"Do you know what I'm going to ask Dawkins?" I say to the pseudo seer, secretly hoping he'll write my questions for me.

"You plan to ask Dawkins … "—the mock oracle stares into his ball and squints—"questions pertaining to skepticism."

Thanks, Nostradamus.

Dawkins, author of *The God Delusion*, enters the room wearing a light-brown blazer over an open-collared shirt. Within minutes, he's fielding questions about arresting the pope and why American political leaders have to end their speeches with "God bless America."

And then it's my turn to ask something. Here's what I come up with:

"When I checked in to the conference, they didn't ask for my press credentials or for my drivers' license or anything. They just gave me this press badge and let me in. Do you think they should have been more skeptical?"

Seemed appropriate.

"You think you should have been frisked for fear that you were armed?" Dawkins replies.

A couple people snicker, but Dawkins goes on: "I think it's a rather nice characteristic to be trusting. We live in a deeply mistrustful world. And when you go through airport security, as I do, you get the feeling that the world runs on mistrust. I get the feeling, when I remove my shoes, that bin Laden has won. I think I'd rather take my chances in being blown up. So maybe we in the Skeptic movement are very trustful. It's an interesting paradox that you possibly may have unearthed."

When I asked the question, I wasn't thinking about violence. What I'd meant was, *Do you think TAM! organizers should be more concerned about freeloaders skipping the $425 registration fee?* But it's not surprising that Dawkins interpreted the question the way he did. He's not only one of the smartest guys in the world; he's also one of the most controversial. Crudely put: There are people who would like to see him dead.

Having casually unearthed a mind-shattering paradox—this according to Britain's top intellectual!—I exit the press conference and walk through the convention hallway. I see skeptical conventioneers wearing T-shirts from previous TAM! gatherings, from the Center For Inquiry, and from SkeptiCamp.

Everybody is talking about the Million Ghost March. Apparently, to protest this year's TAM!, mediums from across the globe have called upon one million dead souls to haunt South Point. Word is, the mediums specifically called upon the ghosts of Michael Jackson, Liberace, and Hunter S. Thompson.

A young conventioneer tells me the Million Ghost March is a joke, originally posted on a Skeptic-friendly, Onion-like website (and then reposted on woo-woo websites that didn't get the joke), but before I can investigate further, I'm told that James Randi, the man responsible for the whole convention, is ready for our interview.

James "The Amazing" Randi has spent 70 years performing magic and investigat-

James Randi

ing paranormal claims. As a lifelong magician myself, I was honored to spend some one-on-one time with the prolific Kris Kringle dead-ringer.

"Does being a magician make you more skeptical, or are Skeptics attracted to magic?" I ask.

"The first one," Randi replies. "It makes you more skeptical. Magicians see how easily people are fooled and how quickly people make assumptions. Let me give you an example … "

Randi crumples up his cocktail napkin with his right hand. He takes it with his left. He readjusts. Then he opens his left fist.

The napkin is gone.

"We all make assumptions," Randi continues, "and often our assumptions are wrong. You assumed that I transferred the napkin from my right hand to my left—in part because I was looking at my left hand—but I actually kept it in my right hand the whole time."

Well, Randi may have assumed that I assumed that he put the crumpled up napkin in his left hand, but in actuality, I knew that he didn't. See, I've been performing false transfers myself, for 22 years, so I know one when I see one.

Of course, Randi's assumption about my assumption only proves his initial point: We all make faulty assumptions. Happens to the best of us.

Randi and I weren't the only magicians at TAM! The current president of the James Randi Educational Foundation (JREF) is a magician (DJ Grothe), the TAM! press manager is a magician (Austin Luton), and three of the TAM! lecturers/performers are magicians (Michael Weber, Johnny Thompson, Jamy Ian Swiss).

Penn & Teller couldn't make this year's TAM!, but even the most skeptical Skeptic wouldn't question their skeptic street cred. Five nights a week, Penn & Teller perform a "mind reading" illusion in which they satirize the tactics commonly used by psychics, mediums, and so-called body language readers. During the trick, Penn delivers the line, "All psychics, mind readers, and mediums are, without exception, bullshit. Their tricks are evil and immoral." And when he does, the audience bursts into applause.

So you have to wonder: Do Penn & Teller have a self-selecting audience (i.e., do only Skeptics see their show?), or do average Americans *like* Skeptics now? Are the tides turning against Sylvia Browne, John Edward, and Uri Geller, and toward James Randi and Richard Dawkins?

Perhaps. But still, not everybody is on the same page.

Adam Savage, co-host of Discovery Channel's "MythBusters," just finished his lecture. The Skeptics are pouring out of Ballrooms A & B, but they're not talking about Savage; they're taking about "the moon-hoax guy."

"What was that moon kid's problem?" one Skeptic asks.

"Do you think the moon hoax guy flew all the way from Australia just to do that?" asks another.

I don't need a mind reader to tell me who the "moon-hoax guy" is; he's the one everyone is pointing at. He looks just over 20 and he's got a moustache and he's wearing a black suit.

Everybody's talking about him, but nobody is talking to him. So I walk up and introduce myself.

His name is Jarrah White. He describes himself as "The Grandson of Apollo Hoax Theory." He believes the Apollo moon-landing video was faked. He believes we've never been to the moon. He believes we can't go to the moon because the radiation would kill us along the way.

In other words, White is a skeptic.

But he's a skeptic with a lower-case "s"—he's not really part of the Skeptic community.

According to JREF President DJ Grothe, "Skeptics have little in common with 'moon hoaxers' and other conspiracy theorists because we in the Skeptical community are open to evidence and to changing our minds. Moon hoaxers, Birthers [those who believe Barack Obama is not American], and Truthers [those who believe 9/11 was an inside job] form conclusions from which no amount of evidence can dissuade them."

I ask Jarrah "Grandson of the Apollo Hoax" White about what went on during Savage's lecture. Before he answers, he pulls out a dictation machine from his pocket. He wants to make sure I don't misrepresent his position or misquote him.

We take a seat on a bench and I do my best to type White's exact words as they come from his mouth. He looks over my shoulder, at my computer screen, as I type, which only lowers my accuracy.

"I'm interested in the moon-landing conspiracy," White says. "'MythBusters' did a program where they disproved some of the theories advocated by moon-landing hoaxers—those of us who don't believe we've actually landed on the moon—and during Adam's speech, I pointed out that he botched his exposé."

"How so?" I ask.

"The conspiracy theory is this: The 'astronauts' were filmed on wires, on a film

Adam Savage

set. And then the footage of them on the wires was slowed down. The "MythBusters" disproved the wires and slow motion separately. They never combined the two."

"And you got the mic and said this during Adam's speech?" I ask.

"Right."

"And did he cede that point?"

"Yes."

I can't understand what all the fuss was about. It sounds like White made a simple point and Savage agreed to it.

To see whether there's more to the story, I walk into the green room, and ask Savage himself. Turns out there *is* more to the story.

"My complaint wasn't with what he said during the speech;" Savage tells me, "my complaint was what he did afterwards."

"What did he do?"

"He monopolized me. He kept asking more and more questions, and he saw that there were a hundred people standing around, trying to ask me their own questions and trying to get autographs, but he wouldn't let any of them get a word in. I didn't come to TAM! to appease any one guy."

"Does this sort of thing happen everywhere you go?" I ask.

"That was the first time, actually. I just got my irate-fan cherry busted!"

"And do you think his main point has any merit?"

"Moon-landing deniers claim a hundred different things, and on that list, one is wires, one is slowed-down tape, and one is wires and slowed-down tape. When we shot the show, we made choices about what we'd use to produce a reasonable narrative. We couldn't address all one-hundred moon-hoax conspiracies."

I walk out of the green room and find White still on the bench. A group of Skeptics has gathered around him, and they're debating the specifics of the Apollo video.

One of the Skeptics asks White, "How do you respond to the reflectors?"

"Are you an atheist?" asks another, presumably attempting to judge White's place at the convention.

White says that he is an atheist, and that answer seems to surprise everybody.

After the Skeptics dissipate, I ask White why he flew in all the way from Australia to make this point to Savage. I ask why he spends his life trying to convince people that the moon landings were faked. (White's got a website, a YouTube channel, etc.)

"It's important to get the truth out," he says.

"But you said you're an atheist, too. And a lot of people believe that God exists. So why don't you spend your time on the God issue? Why is the moon one so much more important to you?"

That question gives White pause. (None of my others did). After the pause, he tells me that he wanted to be an astronaut as a kid.

Ah.

See, White never became an astronaut. And now, it's too late for him. So, I could speculate that after White was first told that he couldn't become an astronaut—for this reason or that—he became envious of those astronauts who'd already flown into space and to the moon. I could then speculate that White's emotion led his intellect—i.e., if I can't fly to the moon, then no one can ... *or has* ... and therefore, the moon landing must have been faked.

Any psychologist or trial lawyer will tell you: The heart leads the mind. Of course, the heart can lead the mind to the right place. So even if my speculations are accurate, it doesn't necessarily make White wrong. (What makes White wrong is the fact that we have been to the moon.)

Still, the Skeptics at TAM! respect White's dissenting opinion. Perhaps because they identity with White. Perhaps because they're usually the ones doing the dissenting.

At most meetings, the "crazy" guy is thrown out (or tased) after he asks his "crazy" question or makes his "crazy" point. But not at TAM. What follows White's "crazy" question? Discussion, debate, and civility.

This respect continues throughout the whole conference. During a panel on the paranormal, a man in the audience stands up, takes the mic, and claims that he can "restore normal feelings and sensations" to breast cancer survivors ... by looking at them. He says that he can also cure illnesses over the phone.

I expect the audience to burst out laughing. I expect Randi, who is on the panel, to make some sort of joke at this man's expense.

I am wrong; Randi takes the man's claim seriously:

"This is eminently testable," Randi says. "We'll have to talk to a statistician to see how many cases we need to look into, and we'll have to talk to medical authorities, but we can work out a protocol for this test. We will be in touch."

The audience applauds.

Randi isn't just pretending to take this guy's claims seriously; Randi is taking them seriously. That, I imagine, is the hardest part of being a lifelong Skeptic: Whenever somebody comes forward with an unlikely-sounding claim, you can't dismiss it outright just because you've heard similar bogus claims in the past. Because if you do, if you judge before you investigate, then you're not much better than the guy who believes *everything* he hears.

Ridiculous in a Good Way

This story isn't about Cirque du Soleil clowns. This story is about red-nosed, white-faced, old-fashioned, Ringling Brotherly, Circus Circusian clowns. You don't see too many of them these days—not even at Circus Circus. But they're still around, they're still laughing, they're still tossing pies in each other's faces, and they're still piling into miniature cars. The clowns convened at the Orleans hotel for the 2010 Clown Vegas convention, and I followed them there to discuss comedy, costuming, and coulrophobia (the fear of clowns).

Jim Howle is a clown, but he doesn't look like one. Not today, at least. He's wearing a red T-shirt, blue jeans, black boots, and a Tony Robbins-style microphone. He's lecturing 25 other clowns (also in their civvies) about clown makeup. I'm seated in the audience, between a guy who looks like Santa[25] and a guy named Cricket, who's got a suction-cup propeller stuck to his bald head.

"Some clowns don't like makeup," Howle says. "I hear clowns complain, 'My makeup makes me sweat.' Excuse me, lady, but I don't think it's your makeup; I think it's your giant hat, your three layers of clothes, and your Depends. Don't blame the makeup just because it's your face that happens to be showing the sweat."

Howle brings five audience volunteers to his makeshift stage, and, using putty, fits each of them with a clown nose. Howle manufactures these noses himself. He's got six basic models: The A's are pointed, B's are oval, C's are round, D's are long and tapered, E's are egg-shaped, and Elves are elfin.

According to Howle, "The nose is the center of the clown personality."

He applies pink paint to the volunteers' cheeks ("if you choose not to use base, you're crazy") and white paint above their eyes ("you put white around your eyes because it's traditional"). Howle thrice mentions that you should use clown-specific makeup for this, not "street makeup."

Over the next hour, the audience volunteers slowly transform into clowns. Not fixed-expression perpetual grinners like Bozo or Ronald, but goofy, spritely Dr. Seuss-like Whos.

"The makeup doesn't hide who they are," Howle says. "You can still see their ex-

---

[25] I later found out the guy is a member of FORBS, the Fraternal Order of Real Bearded Santas. He confessed to me that the FORBS members look down upon the other Santa organizations.

| 87 |

Coulrophobia popped up in the news at the start of 2008, back when the Economic and Research Council surveyed 250 kids and found that none of them liked clowns. Many of the teens surveyed felt that clowns were "frightening and unknowable."

---

pressions. You want to put on just enough makeup that you amplify your facial reactions, not muffle them."

That's a good tip, and it goes to the heart of what some psychologists believe is the main cause of the fear of clowns: the covering of the face and the distorting of expression.

Coulrophobia popped up in the news at the start of 2008, back when the Economic and Research Council surveyed 250 kids and found that none of them liked clowns. Many of the teens surveyed felt that clowns were "frightening and unknowable." Other psychologists believe that coulrophobia is a byproduct of the Evil Clown film/book genre. These psychologists cite Stephen King's *It*, and the movie *Killer Klowns from Outer Space* as a cause of the phobia.[26]

After the lecture, I sat down with Howle to discuss coulrophobia. I was afraid to even bring up the subject. I wasn't afraid that Howle was going to go all Joker on me and stick a pencil in my eye; I was afraid of hurting his feelings. Think about it like this: Here's this super-nice guy who became a clown to make people happy, and then, one day after clown college, he wakes up, flips on the news, and hears that some psychopath named John Wayne Gacy dressed up as a clown to murder children. Next thing he knows, the term coulrophobia is in the DSM-IV psychiatric manual and children are crying.

So instead of starting with the coulrophobia question, I begin with a softball:

"Are you a happy clown or a sad clown?"

"I'm a sad clown—a tramp clown."

"Why's that?"

"My theory is, your normal expression is a sum total of your experiences in life. When you become a clown, you don't want to do anything to take away from the

---

[26] I personally cite the episode of Nickelodeon's *Are You Afraid of the Dark?* titled, "The Tale of Laughing in the Dark." It was the only episode that truly scared me.

character that life has given you; you want to bring it out. You want to accentuate what nature has given you. So if you have a severe look in your face, as I do, you take it to the sad side."

"So is that where some of the creepiness comes in—when sad people try to make themselves inauthentically happy clowns?'"

"I think so," Howle replied. "The incongruence is definitely a factor. It's scary whenever something trustworthy turns on you. That's what made Stephen King's book so scary. That's what makes it so scary that certain really bad people have used the clown uniform as an opportunity to lure others … "

"I can't help but notice you avoided mentioning Gacy by name. Do clowns ever talk about him openly? Or is that just too dark for you guys to even fathom?"

"We talk about him. I even joke about him from time to time, but only to relieve tension. It was so bizarre and awful. And yes, it's unfortunate for clowns that the bait he used was the clown uniform."

"So you do 'get' why people are afraid of clowns?"

"I do, but I don't get the extent of it. I just saw this new ad for the post office, and it's got this family acting all leery and terrified, and they're looking at something off-screen, asking the postman to take it from them and mail it, and then the camera pans over and you see that the thing they're so scared of is this cute little clown doll. That's just silly to me. And it's ironic, because I'm much less scared of clowns than I am of somebody going postal."

At the end of our interview, Howle gave me one of his handmade clown noses to take home—a pointy A model. I put it on and looked at myself in Howle's hand mirror.

"Looks good," Howle said.

And he was right. I didn't look scary; I looked ridiculous.

I mean that in a good way.

True Commitment

A tall brunette in a short red dress walked toward me. Most of her skin was exposed, but there was no ink on it.

What's she doing here? Is she media? Is she lost?

The woman walked past me, and I saw that her upper back was covered in tattoos—big, fauvist, *Amazing Technicolor Dream* tattoos. They covered every visible square inch and spilled onto the back of her neck.

Guess she's at the right place, after all.

The Rumjungle DJ took to the mic and shouted into it, "Mario came to town, and he brought 50,000 tattooed motherfuckers with him!"

Everybody cheered.

The DJ was referring to celebrated tattoo artist Mario Barth and his "Biggest Tattoo Show on Earth," which took place at Mandalay Bay the weekend of October 1, 2010.

I'll admit it: When I first walked into Mandalay Bay's Convention Center, I felt intimidated … and very, very naked. I mean, even when I'm naked, I don't feel that naked. See, I don't have any tattoos, and everybody else in sight did—gothic tattoos, Chinese tattoos, Japanese tattoos, Celtic tattoos, Samoan tattoos. The few visibly non-inked patrons were at least wearing tattoo-inspired T-shirts: Affliction, Hyperspace Studios, Ed Hardy.

I chatted with Barth about those brands and about the artists who've tried to cross over from the world of art to the world of tattoos. Here's what he had to say:

"When a painter tries to cross over to the tattoo industry, he runs into problems. You can't paint over, you can't touch up, and every person is a different canvas. Artists aren't used to that, and ninety-five percent of them fail. But on the opposite side, when

Audigier and Aitchison (and Barth) are largely responsible for tattoo imagery's recent pop-cultural boost, but, Barth reminded me, slipping on an Ed Hardy shirt does not a tattoo aficionado make; the real tattoo lifestyle requires more effort.

a tattoo artist goes over to the art world, he often has enormous success. Christian Audigier and Guy Aitchison are great examples of this."

Audigier and Aitchison (and Barth) are largely responsible for tattoo imagery's recent pop-cultural boost, but, Barth reminded me, slipping on an Ed Hardy shirt does not a tattoo aficionado make; the real tattoo lifestyle requires more effort.

"If you see somebody with full sleeves,"[27] Barth said, "you know he's been around for a while and lives a certain lifestyle—distinctive, visual. The sleeves can take seventy to one-hundred hours. It depends on how long a person can sit."

"What's the longest session you've ever done?" I asked.

"I once tattooed somebody for twenty-one hours straight. I did a Viking woman's head across this guy's rib cage, and he had to catch a flight back to Australia, so it was a race against the clock."

What impresses me most about Barth's Australian customer isn't his Mick Foley-like pain tolerance, it's his commitment. When you pay somebody to tattoo a Viking woman across your rib cage, you're not only saying to the world, *I like Viking women*, you're also saying to yourself, *I'm confident I will like Viking women until the day I die.* And that, in my opinion, is real commitment. Law school, home ownership, marriage—that stuff's for rookies.

"Do you think people who get big tattoos like that are better with commitment than others?" I asked Barth.

"You mean romantic commitment?"

"Sure; do you think they're more monogamous?"

"I know that I'm all over the world, but I wear my wedding band every night. And my wife's on my forearm. So, yes, we might be better with commitment—I can see that."

Tattooed Kalamazoo couple Amy and Max Beers could probably see it too. Back in Michigan, they've got a tattoo parlor … and a four-year-old. Max's tattoos, by the way, go across his forehead and cheeks; Amy's run along her scalp. When I approached their booth, Max was tattooing "PINK" onto some lady's calf.

"So," I said to the lady, "you're a big Pink fan?"[28]

"I like that she's herself," the woman responded. "I think she'd be an awesome person to hang out with. She's not afraid to speak her mind, you know? She's not like Britney or Christina."

---

[27] Somebody whose arms are completely covered in tattoos.

[28] Easily the dumbest question I've asked during my *Las Vegas Weekly* tenure.

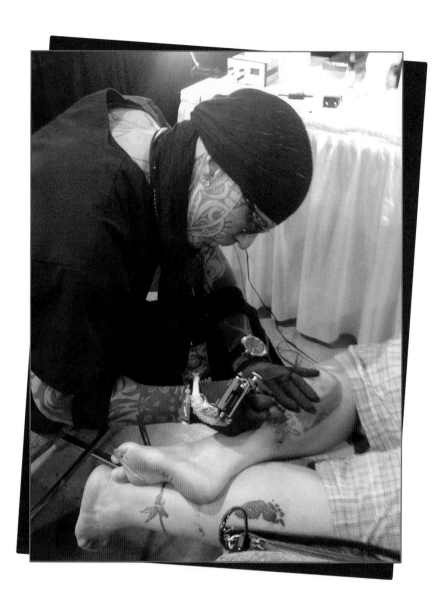

In having "PINK" tattooed on her calf, this lady was not only demonstrating pain tolerance and commitment, she was demonstrating faith—faith that Pink won't release a string of crappy albums, faith that Pink won't say something bigoted on live TV, faith that Pink won't start hanging out with Britney and Christina.

If any of that were to happen, this poor lady would have to change her tattoo … but what could she change it to? PINKY FINGER? PINKEYE? PINKING SHEARS? Could this lady pull a Johnny Depp and chop off a letter,[29] shortening PINK to the self-referential "INK"?

Tattoo cover-ups and alterations are difficult, but not impossible—this according to tattoo artist Robbie Rittenhouse, who told me he once transformed a Satan face into a Jesus face for some born-again Christian. He said he covered the horns up with a crown of thorns.

Rittenhouse, like Beers, Barth, and a lot of the guys at the convention, is covered in tattoos. As I said, these guys intimidated me at first … but only at first. They were all very nice. In fact, I only met one unfriendly guy at the convention, and he didn't even have any tattoos.

He was a lawyer.

Now, I'm a lawyer too, and after I revealed this to the guy, we struck up a legal conversation about the tattoo industry. He mentioned a particular piece of state legislation that interested me, so I pulled out my laptop and asked him to tell me more about it so I could include it in my story. He said that he didn't want to be interviewed (and didn't want to be identified), so I put my laptop away (and won't describe his appearance).

"I'm a lawyer," he said. "You can't be interviewing me. And if you're really a lawyer too, you should know that. You should know better."

I don't remember learning about any rule that says journalists can't interview lawyers,[30] but I also didn't want to start a fight with this guy, so I shook his hand, wished him good afternoon and began to walk away. Before I got too far, he said this to me: "You behave yourself, now—I'm being serious."

I don't know what he meant by that, but I know it sounded like a threat. So, to review, the one intimidating guy at the Biggest Tattoo Show on Earth turned out to be the guy without any tattoos. Rittenhouse, Beers, and Barth were all total gentlemen. Maybe it's time to update my stereotypes.

---

[29] After he broke up with Winona Ryder, Depp had "WINONA FOREVER" changed into "WINO FOREVER."

[30] What I do remember is that my Professional Responsibility professor brought to class Dominic Gentile, the attorney involved in the landmark Supreme Court case that dealt with what an attorney can and cannot say to the press, *Gentile v. State Bar of Nevada*, 501 U.S. 1030. I remember Gentile's guest lecture about this very topic. Basically, Model Rule of Professional Conduct 3.6 forbids attorneys from making certain extrajudicial statements when a lawyer is participating in (or has participated in) a trial or investigation.

The Award Awards

The Oscars are the Oscars of awards ceremonies. Winning one is a really big deal. It gets you more work, gets you laid, secures you an obituary in the *New York Times*—the whole shebang.

But what about winning a Critics' Choice Movie Award? Or a SAG award? Are those awards meaningful? For that matter, how good should you feel about yourself if you're presented with a Marilyn Mozzarella Pizza Rella Pie Parlor Employee of the Week certificate? Very? A little? Not at all?

This Oscar season, I stopped by the Awards & Recognition Association's yearly convention to investigate what makes an award meaningful.

I'm standing in the middle of the Las Vegas Convention Center, and I'm surrounded by awards: gold trophies, silver trophies, plastic trophies, blue ribbons, green ribbons, walnut plaques, diamond-encrusted flasks, laser-cut balsa-wood skeletons, and red-marble obelisks with spherical glass toppers.

If you're not in the awards industry, you're not supposed to see these symbols of achievement back to back like this. Their commonality undercuts their value. These awards are meant to be seen individually, in high school trophy cases and on corner-office bookshelves. They're meant to be presented, one at a time, in public libraries and Italian restaurant banquet halls, by men in nice suits and women in fancy dresses.

At the back of convention hall C5, I come across a booth of giant trophies—the biggest in the room. Trophies that Paul Bunyan might award Brobdingnagians for "Achievements in Giantry." They're distributed by a guy named Jim Seidel.

"I've been selling trophies for thirty-plus years," Seidel, a Gulliver-sized man wearing an open-collar shirt under a gray blazer, told me. "In nineteen-seventy-five I opened up five stores called All-American Trophy King, and in two-thousand-seven, I retired for about two weeks. Then I was recruited by these guys."

Seidel is referring to the people at Venko Trophies, a Brazilian company that manufactures the enormous awards and ships them across the world. The trophies, Seidel tells me, are assembled before they leave the factory. But they're made of plastic, so they're light, and shipping isn't a problem.

"How much would it cost me to ship that big one over there?" I ask, pointing to a six-foot-tall, three-tiered, red-and-gold trophy.

"That one would probably cost thirty or thirty-five dollars to ship. Breaks down into three. Isn't it nice?"

It was nice. And the more Seidel talked about it, the nicer it seemed. And the nicer it seemed, the more I wanted it. Not that I did anything to deserve a trophy of that size. But since when do feelings of entitlement and actual merit equate?

"How much?" I asked.

"Trophies this size are generally for kids," Seidel explained. "And they're not really for individuals; they're for teams. They're meant to go in clubhouses—that sort of thing."

"Oh, I was just joking around," I lied. "So tell me about the biggest trophy you ever received."

"I actually never got a trophy," Seidel said. "Once I won a businessman of the year, award, but it didn't come with a trophy or anything."

I'll leave it to the psychologists to determine whether Seidel's inability to leave the trophy industry connects up with his never having received a trophy himself.

"But who knows," Seidel added, "Maybe this year I'll win a Golden Obelisk."

The Awards & Recognition Association gives out Golden Obelisks. Awards' awards. They recognize achievement in achievement recognition. The awards suppliers

place their trophies on a dozen tables at the side of the convention hall, and the distributors walk past the trophies, pen and clipboard in hand, and rate them.

This year's Obelisk contenders included an engraved wooden cutting board, an engraved-silver soup ladle, a watch-shaped walnut desk accessory, a custom resin of the Four Horsemen from Notre Dame University, and something called a "Shemp-Fest Pie Melee Award" that looked like an explosion of lard held together with wire-hanger pieces.

I cast a mental ballot for the ladle.

I'm standing in the R.S. Owens booth. Owens, a Chicago-based company, manufactures the Academy Awards. I assumed the booth of the company that makes the Oscars would be bigger and flashier than the rest, but it isn't. If anything, it's understated. Maybe its modesty is false, like that of a Harvard grad who says she attended "a small liberal-arts college in Boston." I can imagine an Owens worker telling me, "Oh, us? We do the trophies for this little California-based movie-competition thingy."

One other observation about the Owens booth: You know those Oscar-shaped awards that say things like "Best Dad Award," and "Teamwork Award," and "Rising Star Award"? Well, R. S. Owens manufactures those, too.

I exit the booth and walk towards the registration area. I was all set to interview the man in charge of the entire convention.

Dave Bergeson reminds me of Wolf Blitzer and serves as the executive director of the Awards & Recognition Association. That means he's in charge of the Golden Obelisks, too.

"The Obelisk Awards are very meaningful." Bergeson tells me. "The golds are particularly meaningful, but the clears are significant, too. You'd think that the last thing an award-maker would want is an award. But people love getting Obelisks. Some even cry."

"And what makes the Obelisks so meaningful?"

"It's not about the Obelisk; it's not about the award; it's about the recognition. That's what's meaningful. The awards are just a symbol to capture the recognition."

"I agree," I said. "But that begs the question, What makes a particular recognition meaningful?"

"Let me answer that with an anecdote: My three year old was in a park-district sports program—actually, it wasn't a 'sports' program so much as it was a run-around-and-kick-whichever-ball-is-in-your-way program. Well, on the last day, my son's 'coach'"—Bergeson used air quotes around the word "coach"—"gave him a silly little medal. But Ben—that's my son—showed it to everybody for weeks. He was so proud of it. It was a wonderful feeling for me, too—as somebody in the industry, and as a parent."

Bergeson's point, I assume, is that if a silly little medal awarded for kicking around a ball can be meaningful, then any award can. At the end of the day, it's not about the award; it's about how presenters handle the presentation, and about how the recipient feels.

So let's look back to the question I posed earlier: How good should you feel about yourself if you're presented with a Marilyn Mozzarella Pizza Rella Pie Parlor Employee of the Week certificate? You should feel as good as you damn well want to. You earned it.

4

The Indebted Copperfield Clone, The Reunited Prop Comics, The Evasive Fake Politician, and, Uh, Well, Monti Rock III

I've worked at *Las Vegas Weekly* for three years, and I've had lots of meetings with lots of editors about lots of stories. But one story took up more meeting time than any other, by far.

Was it a potentially libelous, hard-hitting exposé of some undercover casino practice? Was it a controversial opinion piece that had the potential to upset our advertisers? Nope. It was a story in which we ranked the top 50 Vegas personalities.

I'm not saying we wasted time on a frivolous activity; I'm saying that in Las Vegas, we take the business of celebrity seriously. Sure, we take cracks at celebrities, but we never forget that tourists like them … and that tourists are the ones with the money.

Celebrity journalism is huge—just look at a magazine rack—but 99 percent of it sucks. Celebrities are guarded, so they tell journalists the same things again and again, so journalists write the same profiles again and again.

I tried to do something a little different with these:

Steve Wyrick

Steve Wyrick and I have a lot in common. Both of our dads wanted us to practice law, but both of us wanted to practice magic. We both watched David Copperfield on TV, and we both wanted to become the next David Copperfield.

The difference between us is this: Early on, I realized I wasn't Copperfield-caliber material.

Wyrick's failure to realize that cost him dearly. Specifically, it cost him $54 million—that's how much debt he's got, according to a May 17, 2010 bankruptcy filing.

Fifty-four million dollars in debt, $93,000 in assets.

How is that even possible?

Well, Wyrick once claimed to be a better businessman than magician—that should tell you something about his show.

Yes, some tourists paid to see Wyrick's act, but, according to several sources, that's primarily because ticket resellers pushed it hard—because Wyrick reportedly offered the resellers a big percentage of the proceeds to do so. Tourists would hear the resellers' pitch, glance at Wyrick's publicity shots—Wyrick hanging from his helicopter, Wyrick leaning on his Learjet 35, Wyrick sitting on his motorcycle—and think, *Why not?*

Well, here's why not: Wyrick's mediocre at magic. He was only able to achieve (moderate) success and woo investors because 1) He looked like David Copperfield in his publicity shots; 2) The economy was booming; and 3) It's Vegas, baby!

That's what makes Wyrick's tale so unique: It couldn't have happened at any other time, in any other place.

Wyrick accumulated debt after debt and spent dollar after dollar. He surrounded himself with rare magic lithographs (of Alexander, of Carter, of Houdini, of Thurston) and historic neon signs (the "A" from The Algiers, for starters), and he threw extravagant house parties to show them off.

My roommate, a former Folies Bergere showgirl, went to one of these parties.

"The house was amazing," she said. "He had all this expensive art and magic stuff

---

Wyrick accumulated debt after debt and spent dollar after dollar. He surrounded himself with rare magic lithographs (of Alexander, of Carter, of Houdini, of Thurston) and historic neon signs (the "A" from The Algiers, for starters), and he threw extravagant house parties to show them off.

---

on the walls. And he had a big tent set up in front. There were, like, ten red-velvet couches with plush cushions, and a red carpet, and two long tables of food. It looked like there was enough to feed three or four hundred people."

"And how many people showed up?" I asked.

"Less than a hundred."

Another friend of mine dated Wyrick for a couple of months.

"He had the Porsche," she told me, "and he had that huge house, and he had expensive furniture and really expensive magic art—he told me each one was worth two hundred thousand dollars. He took me to Hawaii and stuff like that, but he wasn't always spending. He wasn't one of those guys. He actually liked going to Denny's."

That's a good thing for Wyrick, because these days, Denny's might be the only restaurant he can afford. According to the court filing and other sources, when Wyrick filed for bankruptcy, he had $20 in his pocket, $45.99 in a U.S. Bank account, $5 in a Wells Fargo business checking account, and $5.33 in a Wells Fargo savings account. He's living off checks from his mom, and residing at the home of his former costume/wardrobe lady.

This is the story of the former headliner's fall from fame.

Gale Steven Wyrick grew up in Garland, Texas. As a teenager, he put together a nine-minute manipulation act and performed it at magic dealer Howard Hale's 1985 Magicland convention. The performance had a glitch. Two, actually: 1) Wyrick left his billiard balls—the props he needed for his finale—at home; and 2) He literally fell flat on his ass during the show. Wyrick described the performance to *MAGIC* magazine like this: "It truly was a train wreck!"

In the years that followed, Wyrick performed his act for his senior-class talent show, and spent a lot of time studying Copperfield.

"Every time David had a special on TV," Wyrick told *MAGIC*, "I was there by my VCR. Every time he would come to town, I would have my mom drive me to the back of the theater and I would sit from eight a.m. right up to show time, watching every case come off that truck. The guy was a god to me, and he still is."

With an act and an idol, Wyrick borrowed $5,000 from his mom, and in the early '90s used the money to rent out the 250-seat Owens Theatre in Branson. Wyrick's mom moved to Branson and worked as her son's ticket collector.

What did Wyrick learn from the year he spent in Branson? According to the *MAGIC* interview, he learned that "the more you ask for, the more respect you get."

Wyrick moved from Branson to Vegas and opened a show at Lady Luck called *Sexy Magic*. Ticket sales were poor; Wyrick blamed the title.

But Bill Bennett, owner of the Sahara, believed in Wyrick. Bennett built Wyrick a $56 million theater, and in 1999 signed Wyrick to an eight-and-a-half-year contract.

The show closed after two.

Before it did, though, John Moehring reviewed it for *MAGIC*. It's one of the most scathing reviews the magazine has ever run.

"Quite frankly," Moehring wrote, "it was the perfect time to demand a refund. And it just wasn't due to the fact that good money had been paid to see a really bad show. It was because Steve Wyrick, 'Magician of the Year' at the Sahara Hotel and Casino, had not delivered the show that he had touted."

Moehring writes about how Wyrick botched an illusion and joked about the botch with his audience.

"Apparently," reported Moehring, "something went astray in the performance of the next trick. A white dog is put into a white cabinet and a black dog is loaded into a black cabinet. The two containers are mounted on a trestle-like table, and the canine 'boxcars' are awkwardly tracked onto one another. After some fumbling and prying at the merged cabinets, panels fall open to reveal the dogs are gone or elsewhere (barking continued to emanate from the loudspeakers). Dismissing the canine train wreck, Steve mutters, 'We'll get back to that one later.'" (The dogs were supposed to turn into a Dalmatian.)

According to Moehring, the mistakes didn't end there. Wyrick also flubbed the "Sam the Bellhop" card trick a couple of times.

Moehring spoke with Wyrick after the show, and Wyrick told him, "You caught me with my pants down."

Unlike Moehring, Aladdin CEO Bill Timmins liked what he saw in Wyrick. In 2003, Timmins offered Wyrick a gig at the Aladdin, and then built the magician a $35 million theater, magic shop, and "UltraLounge."

"Quite frankly," Moehring wrote, "it was the perfect time to demand a refund. And it just wasn't due to the fact that good money had been paid to see a really bad show. It was because Steve Wyrick, 'Magician of the Year' at the Sahara Hotel and Casino, had not delivered the show that he had touted."

In January 2004, Mike Weatherford reviewed Wyrick's Aladdin show for the *Review-Journal*.

"It's that talking stuff that's troublesome," Weatherford wrote. "Wyrick never seems sure if he's David Blaine, David Copperfield, or David Carradine." In a later review, Weatherford wrote, "Wyrick is more like an actor running through the cues. He could stay home and hire any magician to play himself."

MAGIC sent Shawn McMaster to review Wyrick's show in 2005. Wyrick's "Sam the Bellhop" trick hadn't improved:

Saying Wyrick was "influenced" by Copperfield would be like saying the Gustav Klimt poster hanging on my dining room wall was "influenced" by Gustav Klimt.

"[H]e had numerous problems doing a one-handed cut," wrote McMaster, "which led him to comment apologetically to the audience about the deck being 'brand new.' He also attempts Zarrow Shuffles during the course of the effect, and 'attempts' is the only word that can be used here, as he never really executes one convincingly. Furthermore, a deficient false shuffle should not be projected onto an eight-foot-high video screen."

I never got to see Wyrick's show myself, but I have seen the YouTube videos. They're posted on a YouTube channel named "InDebtProductions."

Judging by Wyrick's publicity photos alone, I could have told you the guy was a Copperfield knockoff. But I never could have imagined the depth and the breadth of his copying until I watched the YouTube videos with my own two eyes.

Saying Wyrick was "influenced" by Copperfield would be like saying the Gustav Klimt poster hanging on my dining room wall was "influenced" by Gustav Klimt. Wyrick copied Copperfield's tricks, Copperfield's lines, Copperfield's speech pattern, Copperfield's movements, Copperfield's music, and Copperfield's emotionalism.

Wyrick and Copperfield were friends for a while—that's common knowledge among magicians. So there's a chance that in the course of that friendship, Copperfield helped Wyrick with his act. And if Wyrick and Copperfield had entered into some sort of mentor/mentee relationship, it might be unfair to say that Wyrick's Planet Hollywood show was a "copy" of Copperfield's old act. If Copperfield really did help Wyrick, you could argue that Wyrick wasn't unoriginal, but molded.

In 2009, Wyrick planned a Fourth of July publicity stunt of Houdini-like proportions. He called it "Death Drop."

He was going to have his assistants lock him into a box. The box was going to be raised 120 feet in the air by crane, and then moved above 500 flaming spikes. The four ropes running from the crane to the box were going to be set on fire, and Wyrick was going to escape before the ropes burned through and the box dropped onto the spikes.

At least, that was the advertised plan.

A crowd gathered outside Planet Hollywood.

"This has never been done before," Wyrick told them (the entire episode is available on YouTube), "so anything can happen. I'm running on a few hours' sleep."

Wyrick stepped into the box and gave the microphone to his assistant.

"It looks like we're going to chain his hands," the assistant said. "All right. These are for real—the real deal. These are, like, super-heavy duty, uh, Master Locks here. So if anyone is wondering the legitimacy of this, it is absolutely real. Are you guys ready to see him go up?"

The crowd cheered; they were ready.

"This is, uh—these things are real," the assistant continued, "these things are wrapped with some crazy fire stuff—I don't even know."

The assistant was referring to the black curtains going up around the box. He seemed to be saying they were fire-retardant, that they were meant to protect the audience from the fire.

Oh, the irony; a couple seconds after another one of Wyrick's assistants lit the ropes on fire, the curtains went up like tissue paper.

Men in black shirts and black pants rushed the box, fire extinguishers in hand. To extinguish the apparatus' flames, they had to spray for more than a minute.

The booing began.

Then, a short while later, Wyrick appeared on a helicopter—*ta-da?*—but by then, the audience had lost its buzz.

When the curtains caught fire, the audience didn't seem shocked. They must have assumed the fire was part of the illusion. But once Wyrick's assistants opened the box and Wyrick's stage double, Jeffrey Jay, got out of it, the audience realized the trick had been flubbed.

From a magic point of view, the flub was a disaster. Wyrick's assistant had implied that the curtains were fire-retardant—that was their justification, their ostensible reason for surrounding the box. But once they went up like the Hindenburg, it became clear to the audience that they'd been raised to facilitate the switch between Wyrick and his double.

Jay, the double, filed a lawsuit against Wyrick on August 13, 2009, in the District Court of Clark County, in which he claimed he was rendered sick and lame, and received both internal and external injuries, resulting in great pain, suffering, and anxiety.

Nonetheless, in an interview posted on an *L.A. Times* blog, Wyrick said, "I am definitely going to reattempt Death Drop."

∞   ∞   ∞

To the best of my knowledge, nobody has ever questioned Wyrick's résumé until now.

According to one of Wyrick's old press releases, Wyrick "walked away with the top awards at both the International Brotherhood of Magicians and the Society of American Magicians annual competitions." The press release also said, "Once every four years the Olympian-like Federal Congresso de Magica de Spain is held for top magicians from all around the world. Still 15, Steve took ninth place at this largest and most prestigious of all competitions!"

Let's start with the International Brotherhood of Magicians. Wyrick did win first place in their competition, but, according to a 1985 *Linking Ring* article, he won first place in the Junior Stage Magic category, not the main one. People who aren't serious magicians would assume the young Wyrick beat out men and women twice and three times his age.

Next, the Society of American Magicians: When participating in the SAM's competition, Wyrick did enter the adult category, but he didn't win. He took home the second-place "Award of Merit," not the first-place Chairperson's High Score award. So Wyrick got "top honors" in the SAM competition in the same sense that John McCain got "top honors" in the 2008 election.

And what about the Federal Congresso de Magica de Spain—"the largest and most prestigious of all competitions"?

I've never heard of it.

I contacted two magic historians and one acclaimed Spanish magician to ask whether any of them had heard of it.

They said that they hadn't.

Remember, we're talking about what is ostensibly the largest and most prestigious of all competitions—and Wyrick mentioned it in not one, but two press releases.

If the Federal Congresso de Magica de Spain is (or at one point was) the "largest and most prestigious" magic competition, I'd be able to find at least one mention of it on Google, right?

Well, I couldn't find even one.

In reality, the Fédération Internationale des Sociétés Magiques (held every three years) is the largest and most prestigious magic competition, and the only award Wyrick truly deserves is one for résumé padding.

It makes you wonder, if Wyrick could get away with exaggerating his success and with flubbing magic tricks for so many years, what *couldn't* he get away with? Well, there was one thing … the lawsuits. He couldn't get away from the lawsuits. They piled on, one after another.

According to bankruptcy documents, Wyrick didn't pay many of the people who did magic-related work for him.

I spoke with one of Wyrick's debtors—I promised I wouldn't reveal his identity—who had this to say:

"Steve's always been nice to me. Always comped me and my family when we came into town, and he's always been personable. I have nothing against him as a person."

"But as a businessman … "

"My company had a relationship with Steve for a number of years. From the time when he was four-walling that show downtown through his move to the Strip. About eight to ten years, I'd say. Over the course of those years, he'd sometimes pay us up front, and sometimes we billed an open account. He established a relationship with us, and we thought he was credit-worthy—mistakenly, it turned out. And now he owes us a lot—well, not a lot compared to how much he owes some other people, but it's a lot for us."

"So it was a total surprise when he didn't pay you at the end?" I asked.

"I guess it wasn't a total surprise. There were red flags. The fact that the show kept closing and moving. The fact that if you went to his shows or his magic shop, you could see there wasn't a big amount of traffic there. The fact that he was a self-promoter. In my book, any time somebody is telling you how successful they are, how things are going to get better for them, it's a red flag."

The red flags piled up, particularly in the late 2000s. Wyrick stopped paying his rent, and on January 15, 2010, the Miracle Mile Shops took back Wyrick's theater, valued at $16 million. Miracle Mile then got an injunction barring Wyrick from opening the doors to his theater and removing his props.

Wyrick's stage props are very valuable, but they're not worth $54 million. (For starters, Wyrick's LearJet was gutted). So where'd all the money go? To a secret Swiss bank account? To a safety deposit box in Antwerp? No and no.

As best I can tell, it all went into Wyrick's show.

Most financially troubled productions close shortly after they open. Wyrick's didn't. Wyrick was able to keep his show afloat because he kept finding more and more investors, and more and more people willing to work for him without up-front payment—the bankruptcy filing makes this clear.

First there are the big players—the investors who loaned Wyrick cash. Wyrick owes $15 million to developer Stephen Tebo, $7.5 million to Texas businessman Byron Burke Barr, and $5 million to investor/Star Mobile Homes owner Hollis Campbell. Wyrick also owes $6.62 million to the Miracle Mile Shops. None of the above parties returned phone calls for comment.

Then there are the expected expenses: $900 to a scenery company, $686 to a lighting company, $4,000 to another lighting company, $25,000 to a third lighting company, $375 to a storage company, $77.55 to a beverage distribution company, and $1,000 to the City of Las Vegas for parking fines.

Then there are the small and odd expenses: $1,683.15 to Fun City Popcorn, $260 to La Salsa Cantina, $640 to Red Bull North America, $611.51 to Sparkletts, and $1,700 to the county fire department.

When you add up all the figures—the hundreds of thousands owed to various managements companies and law firms, the hundreds of thousands owed to the state of Nevada, the hundred thousand owed to the IRS—it doesn't take long to get to $54 million.

So why did Wyrick keep asking for more and more money? Why'd he keep soliciting work from companies he couldn't pay? Why'd he keep digging himself deeper and deeper into debt? Did he really think he could turn things around financially? Did he really think he could make it back into the black?

Maybe, but that's not the point. For Wyrick, money was never the point. Judging by his own words, the point was becoming the next Copperfield.

Wyrick wanted it so badly that he wouldn't let anything get in the way, including his bad magic act and mounting debt.

☙ ☙ ☙

Early on in the process of collecting information for this story, I tried contacting Steve Wyrick via Facebook. It was just a formality; I didn't expect him to write back.

So you can imagine how shocked I was when I picked up the following message on my voicemail:

"Hey, Rick. This is Steve Wyrick. I wanted to give you a buzz, touch base, and say hello. I received, through an assistant of mine, emails that you had sent, as well as the email on Facebook. I've been out of town. Any inquiries should run through my attorney, who is Zach, and I believe you had left a message for him. Anything else—you'd mentioned that we'd not met, and that is very true. I'd love to meet you. One thing I love to do is talk magic. I love to say hi to all magicians. So if you're going to be around, it's going to be about two weeks, and I'll be back in town. I'd love to meet with you and say hi, and just kind of chat magic, man. Let me give you my cell number as well … "

And then Wyrick gave me his cell number. So I called it.

Before our talk, I didn't understand why anybody in his right mind would give this guy a penny.

But now I do.

The guy is a master of the schmooze. On the phone, he did absolutely everything right. He was incredibly polite, incredibly friendly, and he said absolutely nothing of consequence. You'd never know you were talking to someone who's in such a financial sinkhole.

Wyrick repeated that if I had any specific questions, I should direct them to his attorney. And then he told me, "We should get coffee after your story runs."

"After my story runs," I told him, "you're not going to want to have coffee with me. I don't want to be coy; this story is very critical. A lot of people have very negative things to say about you. And that's why I was hoping you could answer some questions, to maybe set the record straight … "

"The story's going to turn out great," Wyrick assured me. "You're in touch with some great people who will be able to give you a lot of great answers. And I see that you're a digger. So here's what I'll say: Turn over all those rocks, man, because I think you'll find a lot of interesting stuff."

I submitted numerous questions to Wyrick's attorney (e.g., Why can't I find any evidence of the Federal Congresso de Magica de Spain?), but I didn't hear back. So I sent an email to Wyrick's attorney asking for confirmation that the questions had been received. Didn't hear back. So I called his attorney's office to ask for confirmation. No response. So I sent the questions to Wyrick via Facebook and told him that he could have some extra time to answer them. Didn't hear back.

I'm guessing coffee's off.

Postscript: The Wyrick story came out, and I became the Bob Woodward of magic. Most magicians had positive reactions to my story—I got lots of phone calls from lots of big names—but a couple had negative reactions.

Take L, a magician who used to have his own show on the Strip. L compared my story to shooting Steve Wyrick in the head. And as L made that comparison, he pressed his body up against mine in a threatening manner. This conversation, by the way, took place at a dive bar, at midnight. L was looking for a fight, and I asked him to curb the physical confrontation.

"If I were being confrontational," L replied, "I'd knock you out."

"Please don't threaten me with violence," I said.

"I didn't threaten you," he went on, "I said, *if* I were being confrontational, I *would* knock you out. If you understood the English language, you'd see that that wasn't a threat."

Sounded like one to me.

"Why are you here?" L asked, referring to Boomers, the dive bar that plays host to Gary Darwin's magic club.

"I've been coming to Darwin's magic club ten times as often as you," I pointed out.

"How long have you even been doing magic?" L asked, changing the topic.

"A long time," I said, not feeling the need to defend myself with specifics. (If L's Wikipedia page is accurate, then the answer to the question is, I've been doing magic for nine years longer than L has.)

"Show me a trick," L demanded.

"I don't perform magic when I feel challenged," I replied.

I was done defending myself.

"It's not a challenge. I just love seeing magic," he claimed.

According to two of my friends, after I left, L said, "I should have knocked him out" a couple of times. L also tried to turn my friends against me, arguing that I shouldn't be welcome at Darwin's magic club because I was "hurting the brotherhood." Apparently, L also told everyone that I "couldn't even show [him] a single trick."

L's show closed and he moved away from Vegas. Apparently, he owes some people some money, too.

Carrot Top and Gallagher

Carrot Top has been the butt of more jokes than Tonya Harding, Monica Lewinsky, and Brooke Hogan combined. But he's still standing, still inventing, and still performing prop comedy to sold-out crowds at the Luxor.

Only one other prop comic has ever reached (and arguably surpassed) that level of success: Gallagher. Back in the 1980s, Gallagher's watermelon-smashing TV specials catapulted him into that league of stand-up comedians who, for a brief period of time, were bigger than stand-up comedy (e.g., Steve Martin, Andrew Dice Clay, Dane Cook).

On June 20, Gallagher performed at Boulder Station, and afterward, he hung out with Carrot Top. It was the first time the two prop comics had spoken to each other in nearly 20 years. The following is the story of their falling out and their reconciliation.

ᴗᴗ   ᴗᴗ   ᴗᴗ

Three weeks ago I caught Carrot Top's show at the Luxor's Atrium Showroom, a theater pimped out with vibrating seats, police lights, and foam machines. At breakneck speed, he showed off his dog-poop picnic plate (so the flies stay off your food), his feet-shaped shoes (which you don't have to take off for airport security), and nearly 200 other comedic inventions. Every 15 minutes or so, he paused to let the audience catch its breath. Aside from that, the night was filled with laughs.

"I'm attacked every second of the day," Carrot Top (whose real name is Scott Thompson) told me after the show. "But it's getting to the point where it's hack to pick on Carrot Top. Today, people are like, 'He got through twenty years, let's give him a break.'"

Unlike Thompson and Gallagher, most prop comics who reach the two-decade mark are reclassified as something other than "prop comics." Example One: In the 1970s, Steve Martin wore bunny ears, Groucho glasses and an arrow through his head. He made unrecognizable balloon animals and performed nonworking magic tricks. But after he got big, nobody thought of him as a prop comic. Example Two: Harpo Marx performed gags with hats, canes, peanuts, scissors, sausages, and bike horns. But today, nobody remembers Harpo as a prop comic; we remember him as one of the Marx Brothers.

Most comedians who use props in their acts (Demetri Martin, The Amazing Johnathan, Rip Taylor) shy away from the term "prop comic." Perhaps they do so in response to the comedy world's sentiment that prop comics wouldn't be funny without their props. What's ironic is that Thompson, one of the few comedians who doesn't

mind the title "prop comic," never set out to do props. For Thompson, the visuals are just means to an end: laughter.

"I try to hit the audience with everything," says Thompson, "jokes, musical soundbites, visuals—the visuals are just different ways to incorporate a punch line."

Thompson understands why his act works. He understands his strengths and his weaknesses: "I love Dennis Miller and Bill Maher. I love watching smart comedy, but I can't pull it off. There are a lot of dumb jokes in my show—like the one about Mr. Clean dying of pneumonia—and I deliberately throw those in so the show works on different levels. George Carlin did that too; he'd talk about abortion for 15 minutes, then he'd pause and say, 'You ever fart on a plane?'"

Thompson mentioned Carlin's name several times during our interview, but he mentioned Gallagher's twice as often. Like a lot of young comics, Thompson was deeply inspired by Gallagher's act. Thompson actually grew up down the road from Gallagher's then-manager, Gary Propper. As a teen, Thompson would hang out backstage with Gallagher, and one of Thompson's proudest moments was when Gallagher asked to hear a joke.

"Here's the one I told [Gallagher]: 'In California, it's legal to start a fire in the woods, but not on the beach. But on the beach, you're ten feet away from sand and water—that's the shit that puts it out!' Gallagher asked me if he could use that joke, and I was like, of course you can use it; you're Gallagher!"

Gallagher's relationship with Thompson turned sour in the early '90s.

"I'm playing comedy clubs," Thompson explained, "and then I get the call about 'The Tonight Show,' and all of a sudden I'm legitimate. And then Gallagher stopped talking to me. Maybe he thought I was a threat? Things got ugly between us, which is a shame, because I'd love to have a guy like that as my mentor. Gallagher took this genre, prop comedy, and turned it into a franchise."

I told Thompson that I was going to be speaking with Gallagher the following day, and he replied, "Tell him I still think he's the best, and that I'll go to my grave thinking that."

"Will do," I said.

꘏   ꘏   ꘏

I called Gallagher at 3 p.m. I admit, I was nervous. Like Thompson, I grew up watching Gallagher's TV specials—watching Gallagher pick apart the English language ("Why do they call them 'apartments' when they're all stuck together?") and logically deconstruct the world around me ("Why do cowboys wear a spur on each boot? If one side of the horse moves, the other side moves with it"). Of course, I best remember Gallagher from his Sledge-O-Matic infomercial parody. Gallagher wasn't the first comedian to satirize infomercials (and he certainly wasn't the last), but like many great parodists (Gilbert and Sullivan, "Weird" Al Yankovic, Stephen Colbert), Gallagher respects the art form out of which he's taking the piss. You get the sense that if things had gone differently, Gallagher could have found success as a legitimate infomercial pitchman.

Like Thompson, Gallagher never set out to do props: "It's not that I'm a prop comic," Gallagher told me. "I just used so many props on those TV specials because I understood that television is a visual medium, and if you're doing a TV show, you should be visual. The comedians at the time weren't using the medium effectively."

Today, Gallagher focuses the bulk of his comedic efforts on more traditional (i.e., non-visual) stand-up bits, like this one: "Why is it that every time we want to be fancy, we speak French? We don't have a 'fancy room'; we have a 'suite.' We don't have a 'report'; we have an 'exposé.' We don't have 'fancy sex'; we have a 'liaison.' That's not 'crap' on the floor; it's 'debris.'"

But Gallagher still does props, too, and this, according to him, is the reason why: "If you do same thing again and again, an organism will habituate. It becomes numb in that area, and anything more you do in that area will not get a response. But if you go from talking to showing an object, you can get an audience's interest, and keep it."

Unfortunately, these days it's tougher and tougher for Gallagher to do props. "When you have a truck and a soundman and sound system, and you sell a hundred T-shirts before each show, you've got the freedom to bring around large objects. But I'm not doing two-thousand people anymore. So now I come into town, go to Walmart, and spend three-hundred dollars. About two-hundred dollars of that is on food items to smash. Then I buy men's underwear and a hula hoop for two other bits. And I buy a shirt, too, because during Sledge-O-Matic I take my shirt off like a rock star and throw it into the audience. That way, I don't have to wash anything after the show."

Like Thompson, Gallagher never set out to do props: "It's not that I'm a prop comic," Gallagher told me. "I just used so many props on those TV specials because I understood that television is a visual medium, and if you're doing a TV show, you should be visual.

Gallagher brought up Carrot Top before I had the chance to relay Thompson's message. "The problem with Carrot Top," said Gallagher, "is that he has very few things in his little trunk that are funny, and a lot of those things can be purchased—like his lights around the toilet seat. I've seen that one online."

I told Gallagher that I had caught Carrot Top's show the previous night and that I'd spoken with him afterward, but before I could pass on Thompson's kind words, Gallagher asked, "Did Carrot Top tell you the story?"

"What story?" I asked.

"Carrot Top came to my shows as a young kid. In Fort Lauderdale, he lived down the street from my promoter, Gary Propper, and his wife Ruth. Gary Propper and I had an argument one day, and Gary said, 'I'm going to go and get the kid down the street [Carrot Top] to copy your act.' So I said, 'If you do that, then I'm going to get your wife.' And we both did what we threatened to do. Carrot Top got my manager, my bus driver, and my soundman. And he went around with a striped shirt, a microphone around his neck, and a box full of props."

I got the sense that Gallagher hadn't seen Thompson's act in a long time. I told Gallagher that Thompson doesn't wear a microphone around his neck anymore, and that he doesn't wear striped shirts, and that he definitely has way more than one "little trunk" of props. That he doesn't do any gags with toilet lights. And that none of his props are available on the Internet (to the best of my knowledge). That gave Gallagher pause. Then I told Gallagher all the nice things Thompson had said. Gallagher went silent.

The following day, Gallagher's PR person told me I could give Gallagher's phone number to Thompson, which I did. Thompson called Gallagher a few days later, and the two arranged to meet up. Gallagher's PR person told me they didn't want media (i.e., me) at their reunion.

Thompson's manager described their meeting as "two friends catching up." Gallagher's PR person said, "Gallagher and Scotty did get together, and had a great talk. Thank you for your help in putting this together."

There's no denying the similarities between Carrot Top's act and Gallagher's. But Carrot Top is the first to admit that he was inspired by Gallagher's work, and sometimes the line between inspiration and imitation is a tricky one to pin down. But it sounds like Carrot Top and Gallagher are willing to try, and for that, you've got to give both of them props.

Scott Ashjian

Part One: The Back Story, Which You Have to Read Before We Can Get Into the Juicy Stuff

I donated $35 to Tea Party of Nevada Senate candidate Jon Scott Ashjian. No, I'm not a Tea Partier; I'm a journalist who thought it'd be a good way to get an "in" with the campaign.

Six hours after I made the donation—this was back in mid-March, 2010—I got a personalized email from Ashjian saying, "Richard, Thank You!! I will fight for you!!"

I replied with an email applauding Ashjian for opposing tort reform, and asking him what I could do to help his campaign.

No reply.

Maybe he was busy. Back then, Ashjian was appearing on *Fox News*, drawing double-digit support and posting fiery Facebook status updates: "Harry Reid is pushing this Health Bill!!! Obama will sign it for sure!!! Reid must GO!!!!! The only candidate that can stop him is ME! Scottashjianforsenate.com! I will Stop the madness come November 2010!!!!"

But Scott Ashjian had one small problem … and it wasn't his painfully juvenile overuse of exclamation points; it was legitimacy. Prior to the campaign, he'd demonstrated no involvement with the Tea Party whatsoever.

Nobody had heard of the guy.

The media speculated that Ashjian was a secret liberal who'd entered the race to split the conservative block, siphon votes from the Republican candidate, and get Harry Reid reelected.

To prevent that from happening, the conservative PAC Our Country Deserves Better/TeaPartyExpress.org spent $18,400 opposing Ashjian's campaign. And the conservative group Independent American Party of Nevada filed a lawsuit to get Ashjian's name off the ballot.

Ashjian won that lawsuit, maintaining that he was a legitimate Tea Party candidate who was "one-hundred percent sure" he could win the Senate race "by a large margin."

And then, predictably, Ashjian's poll numbers dropped, along with his public profile. By late June, it seemed as though the Scott Ashjian narrative had come to an end.

But where I was concerned, it hadn't; things were just getting interesting.

Part Two: The Man Behind The Curtain

In early July, a question popped into my head: What happened to my $35 donation?

I emailed Ashjian and asked how my money had been used.

Again, he didn't reply.

It wasn't the first time a journalist had asked Ashjian about campaign finance. On *Face to Face*, Jon Ralston asked Ashjian whether he had put his own money into the race. Ashjian responded, "I have put my own money into it. I will continue to put my money into it."

"How much of your money are you willing to put in?" Ralston asked.

"Whatever it takes," Ashjian answered. "I believe that with friends and family and supporters, we can put enough money into this race to beat Harry Reid."

How much did Ashjian spend and receive? I wondered.

So I went to the Federal Elections Commission website and pulled up Scott Ashjian's financial disclosure page. Under the heading "Contributions Made by This Candidate's Committees," I found this message: "No Contributions Have Been Made by This Candidate's Committees." Under the heading, "Individuals Who Gave To: ASHJIAN, SCOTT," I found the message, "The query you have chosen matched zero individual contributions."

But that's not true; I donated $35 myself!

Ashjian didn't necessarily violate FEC reporting requirements; maybe his campaign was so incredibly slight that it hadn't even triggered his reporting responsibilities.

The Campaign Guide for Congressional Candidates and Committees says, "An individual triggers registration and reporting responsibilities under the Act when campaign activity exceeds five-thousand dollars in either contributions or expenditures."

So, is it possible that the man who put his own money into the race, the man who vowed to spend "whatever it takes" to win, the man who promised he'd get enough in donations from "friends and family and supporters" to win, the man who appeared on national TV, the man who was "one-hundred percent" certain of victory, didn't even spend or receive $5,000?

Ashjian clearly wouldn't answer that question for me, so I contacted the man who used to be behind the curtain: Ashjian's attorney and longtime friend Barry Levinson.

Levinson is listed as the secretary of the Tea Party of Nevada, the group that Ashjian made up to get his name on the ballot. That means Levinson is the guy who reports to the Secretary of State on behalf of the Tea Party of Nevada.

During my brief phone interview with Levinson, the local attorney did everything he could to distance himself from the Tea Party.

"I'm not a Tea Party guy," he told me, "I am exactly what I registered as. I vote for whoever I want to vote for. All these freaks think I'm a Tea Partier or Tea Bagger, or whatever. But I'm a Democrat, and I vote for who I want to."

So, just to be clear, the secretary of the Tea Party of Nevada is "not a Tea Party guy."

"And what's going on with the Ashjian campaign?" I asked.

"I know about as much as you do," Levinson replied.

Article Five, Section Six of the Tea Party of Nevada Constitution says the secretary's role includes "recording, keeping, and reporting the minutes of the state central committee and executive committee, safeguarding the non-financial records of the TPN, [and] seeing to the handling of a state party correspondence." It sounds like the secretary's job is to keep abreast of the goings on of Tea Party of Nevada.

So if Levinson is "not a Tea Party guy," and isn't even following Ashjian's campaign, then why did he go to so much trouble to help Ashjian get his name on the ballot?

Well, he didn't go to that much trouble at all. It was easy …

Part Three: The Magic Number

Let's say you lived in Alabama. And let's say you were a political independent or third-party candidate (like Ashjian). To get your name on the ballot for U.S. Senate, you'd need to collect about 40,000 signatures. In North Carolina, you'd need about 85,000. If you lived in Arizona, you'd need about 20,000. In Maryland, you'd only need about 10,000. And in Colorado, you'd need a mere 1,000.

Pretty low, right?

Wrong. Colorado ain't nothin'; in Nevada, Ashjian needed only need 250 signatures to get his name on the ballot.

And how'd he get the "Tea Party" name with no Tea Party credentials? Simple: Nobody stopped him. According to Nevada Secretary of State Public Information Officer Pam duPre, "There are no restrictions in state law on political party names; individuals forming the party must simply file bylaws and constitution as required by state law."

Would you like to be the "Sin City Republican Party" Senate candidate? Two-hundred-fifty names. Hell, why not run as the "Barack Obama Party" candidate or the "Oprah Party" candidate? People like those two!

According to Nevada Secretary of State Public Information Officer Pam duPre, "There are no restrictions in state law on political party names; individuals forming the party must simply file bylaws and constitution as required by state law."

It's not hard to imagine that, in picking the "Tea Party of Nevada" name, Ashjian made a calculated decision. He heard "Tea Party" in the media every day, he saw Tea Party favorite Sen. Scott Brown take the Massachusetts special election and he struck while the iron was hot.

Was that the first time Ashjian made a calculated name-picking decision?

Maybe not …

Part Four: The Counterfeit Boss

Back in 1994, Ashjian started the Nevada business A&A Asphalt Paving Company. That was seven years after Claude Winegard started the Nevada business AA Asphalt Sawing & Patching. Much like the Nevada Secretary of State, the Nevada State Contracts Board had no law stopping Ashjian from using the similar name.

According to Las Vegas trademark attorney Ryan Gile, "The Nevada Secretary of State, which issues company charters for corporations, LLCs, and other business entities, does not make determinations about whether a particular name is confusingly similar under trademark law."

But how can that be? I mean, I can't open up a hamburger joint called McDonalt's or sell a soda called Pipsi—right?

"From a trademark-law perspective," Gile explains, "the scope of protection afforded to a name like AA Asphalt Sawing & Patching is somewhat limited. The letters AA at the beginning of the company name would receive relatively weak protection given the large number of businesses that use A prefixes in their names in order to be the first listed businesses in phone directories. Consumers recognize that many different companies will use A, AA, AAA, AAAA prefixes along with some descriptive business name. Accordingly, consumers are likely to view the two company names A&A Asphalt Inc. and AA Asphalt Sawing & Patching as two separate companies."

But did customers see the companies as separate?

According to AA Asphalt, no.

I called AA Asphalt, and the man who picked up introduced himself as AA Asphalt owner Michael Walters. Walters had a lot to say about Ashjian and A&A Asphalt. He told me that lawyers mistake AA Asphalt for A&A Asphalt all the time.

"I just talked to the Marquis & Aurbach attorney today. This is the third time we've been involved with a complaint that was supposed to be directed at A&A Asphalt. Happens the same way every time: We get the paperwork, and it takes a year or two to get it all unraveled. We get sued for something, and once we get the contract, we see the job was done by A&A on Rainbow."

"Did the businesses ever get mixed up before the lawsuits?"

"Sometimes," Walters said, "we would receive his bills."

"Is that it?"

"A couple times, he'd get our checks. And he actually cashed them."

That's a damning charge, so a few days later, I called AA Asphalt back to ask for verification.

The man who picked up the phone introduced himself as AA Asphalt General Manager Vern Peden.

I asked Peden if he could confirm what Walters had told me about A&A wrongly cashing AA's checks.

"Absolutely," Peden replied. "At a minimum, I remember it happening twice."

But when I asked Peden if he remembered the names of the companies that sent the checks, he said that he didn't. And when I asked Peden if he kept any documentation of the transactions, he said he didn't.

I told Peden to have Walters call me back, and he assured me that Walters would.

I got a phone call 10 minutes later, but it wasn't from Walters. It was from Peden. And what Peden said shocked me.

"Mike Walters and his brother are the owners of AA Asphalt. You haven't talked to either one of those people. I'm the general manager of AA Asphalt. And all the info you've got is from me."

"You mean, you were pretending to be Walters?"

"I'm surprised you didn't recognize my voice."

"I'm surprised you pretended to be your boss."

"I felt guilty there for an instant, and I want to set the record straight. I do have a little bit of ethics. That's why I called you back. And I have been with the company since its inception—it's not like I just fell off a turnip truck—so I might have misled you on who you were talking to, but that's it, everything I told you is the truth."

A couple days later, I spoke with AA Asphalt controller Dave Sterns, who explained why Peden had pretended to be his boss.

"Vern tried to represent that he was Mike because Mike asked him to."

"Mike asked him to?"

"Well," Sterns replied, "not in that particular situation. But we get a lot of calls from people who say, 'I want to talk to the owner,' and usually they got something to sell, and Vern will say, 'I'm the owner, I'm not interested.' It's what we consider a nuisance call."

Sterns then sent me an email in which he fleshed out the charges made by Peden.

"Bardon Materials, subsidiary of Frehner Construction & affiliated with Southern Nevada Paving, on numerous occasions, invoiced AA Asphalt for material or services belonging to A&A Asphalt Paving Company in error. Bardon Materials, when notified, always corrected the errors on a timely basis ... We also experienced this problem with Wells Cargo on more than one occasion ... Our accounting department advised me that on more than four occasions (approximately nineteen-ninety-five thru nineteen-ninety-seven) our customers sent checks due to us to A&A Asphalt Paving Company in error. In each instance A&A Asphalt Company deposited our checks in their account or held them without notifying anyone ... "

I sent a message to Ashjian about this, and got no response.

I told trademark attorney Ryan Gile about the alleged confusion, and this was his reply:

"While the trademark protection afforded to a company that calls itself AA Asphalt Sawing & Patching is somewhat weak, that does not preclude the company from enforcing what limited trademark rights it has in order to prevent consumers from being confused. And according to what you told me, there has been evidence of actual confusion—this favors AA Asphalt."

Of course, an *AA v. A&A* lawsuit is purely hypothetical. AA Asphalt doesn't have the evidence necessary to mount a lawsuit, and the statute of limitations has surely passed, and, well, Ashjian doesn't have the money to be sued.

In February, the Nevada State Contractors Board revoked Ashjian's license for "failure to establish financial responsibility" and "fraudulent or deceitful acts." The board had received five complains about defaulted payments, totaling $37,000. Ashjian didn't respond to the board, and he didn't attend the board hearing at which the complaints were supposed to be discussed, so he now faces an additional $2,648 in fines and investigative costs.

That's only the tip of the iceberg. Ashjian was served with a $200,000 IRS lien two years ago; three of his properties were served with default notices, and Ashjian's family trust failed to pay its homeowners association dues; Ashjian's property debts have nearly hit the $1 million mark; and the University of Iowa is trying to get out of a deal it made with Ashjian's energy drink company, TNT Energy Productions.

Ashjian, though, says, "We haven't had financial problems and we haven't had any situation that we haven't been able to resolve."

So, what's really going on?

I needed to find a straight shooter who could tell me what, exactly, was really going on with Scott Ashjian and his Senate campaign.

Let me introduce you to the man I found.

Part Five: The Pitchman Steps In

On July 31, Ashjian finally got in touch with me—by returning one of my Facebook messages.

"Hi Ricky. Please contact my new campaign manager Gene Burns … He will get your questions to me and get you some answers!"

Burns is a real-estate guru—an infomercial pitchman minus the infomercial. His website's homepage features a blog post from March 2007 titled, "If You're Not Investing in Real Estate With Me Now, You'll Hate Yourself Later." According to the post, real estate is "A Fail Safe Investment Strategy" that will give you "A HUGE Return on Your Investment, Guaranteed to make you smile like a Cheshire cat."

I mentioned that Burns wrote this blog post in 2007, yes?

I contacted Burns, but not to make an investment; I contacted him with questions about the Ashjian campaign. I asked him about campaign finance, the candidate's relationship with the Tea Party, and the allegedly wrongly cashed checks.

Burns's first email to me: "Hi Rick, I will get these to Scott!"

His second: "I am pushing him."

His third: "I am trying to get you answers by this evening."

His fourth: "I am pushing hard to get your answers."

His fifth: "Man … I will call him."

His sixth: "He told me to wait."

His seventh: "Ok. Can talk tomorrow."

His eighth: "Rick, can we do this over the phone, or do you want a face to face?"

His ninth: "Can I get you a sit down on Monday?"

His 10th: "I will see him in one hour and try to set this up for you."

His 11th: "I will push for this!"

His 12th: "Scott will talk to you today and address these issues."

His 13th: "Yes. I will get back to you at the best time for Scott today. Thanks for being flexible!"

Burns never got back to me with that time. And something tells me he never will.

Is Ashjian really a secret Harry Reid supporter who's trying to split the vote? Let's look to Ashjian's own words.

1.) When Jon Ralston asked Ashjian whether he was a Reid footman, Ashjian replied, "I've never met Harry Reid. Don't plan on meeting Harry Reid. Don't like Harry Reid. Never have seen Harry Reid in person."

The fact that Ashjian hasn't met Harry Reid, doesn't plan on meeting Harry Reid (irrelevant speculation), and has never seen Harry Reid in person (means the same thing as "hasn't met") proves nothing. A lot of Reid supporters have never met Reid. And a lot of people who oppose Reid *have* met him.

2.) When "Fox News" asked Ashjian whether he was concerned about splitting the vote, Ashjian responded, "I don't think that splitting the vote is even an issue."

Sure, vote splitting isn't an issue with the Ashjian campaign; *it's the only issue*. Ashjian was playing dumb. And as of August, Ashjian is done playing dumb on this issue. He then admitted that vote splitting *was* an issue. An August 10 Ashjian campaign press release reads, "Scott remained quiet to allow [GOP challenger] Sharron [Angle] to muster everything she had to demonstrate she could beat Harry Ried [sic] in November without the distraction of a third candidate. He wanted to see if Sharron could dominate Reid in the polls and not try to split the conservative vote."

Those two statements are incriminating, but far from conclusive. They don't prove that Ashjian is a secret Democrat or a Reid footman.

My theory? I think Ashjian entered the race to distract Nevadans from his financial woes and troubled business dealings. I think he didn't want to be known as the guy who couldn't pay his bills; he wanted to be known as Nevada's third-party senatorial candidate. I think when Ashjian first entered the race, Barry Levinson was the only one who realized the incredibly important (and incredibly obvious) vote-splitting implications of Ashjian's bid.

But what matters isn't why Ashjian entered the race; what matters is that Ashjian is in the race. He's still claiming to represent the Tea Party.

True, Ashjian probably won't get many votes in November. But neither did Ralph Nader, back in 2000—and we all know how that one turned out. So if Harry Reid wins the election by fewer votes than Ashjian receives, then Scott Ashjian won't go down in history as the guy who couldn't pay his bills, the guy who had his business license revoked, or the guy who stole the Tea Party name; he'll go down in history as the guy who gave Nevada's 2010 U.S. Senate election to Harry Reid.

Monti Rock III

Monti Rock is not a has-been. Monti Rock *was* a has-been, decades ago, but now he's something else, something transcendent. It's hard to say what.

It's easier to say what he's done. Monti Rock (born Joseph Montanez Jr., in 1942) sold seven million disco albums, appeared on "The Tonight Show Starring Johnny Carson" 84 times, and had a cameo in *Saturday Night Fever*.

But Rock's not a singer or an actor—he admits this much. So what is he? A personality? A punch line? A parody? A VH1 "Celebreality" show waiting to happen? What does he do?

Earlier this month, at Hennessey's Tavern on Fremont Street, Rock answered that last question: He performs. No, he doesn't do it as often as he used to, but you don't have to perform to be a performer.

Rock didn't perform on his own; he was the special guest of Derek David and The Platters, who play regularly in Hennessey's. They do a dinner show targeted at Baby Boomers. Rock joined the show, for one night only, for a very specific reason.

He told me this reason a week before he took to the stage. He told me that it was "very important," several times, so I'd be remiss if I didn't share. Here goes:

Recently, Rock auditioned to play a gay hitman in an independent film. For the audition, he chopped off his trademark ponytail. Now, he's worried that his fans will think he "pulled a Britney Spears," and he wants "to show them that [he's] not Britney Spears."

I hope that clears up any confusion.

A couple weeks back, I attended Rock's Hennessey's performance. I was seated at a tiny dinner table, next to a couple who reminded me of my parents. In fact, everybody in the room reminded me of my parents.

As the servers brought out the cheesecake, The Platters sang a catchy arrangement of Jackie Wilson's "Higher and Higher." The audience ate it up—both the cheesecake and the song. But I couldn't envision them going for Rock.

Monti Rock is an acquired taste. I know that because, before his gig, he called me so often that I had his number memorized. And only after several of our chats did I feel as though I "got" him. At first, he just seemed odd.

After I "got" him, though, I grew protective of him. I didn't want to see him bomb. I didn't want the audi-ence to reject him—I didn't think he'd take it well. So I grew nervous as hell for him. And then, one of the Platters called him to the stage.

"He's a legend in his own time, in his own mind. You know how they say James Brown is Soul Brother Number One? Well, Monti Rock is Disco King Number One. Ladies and gentlemen, Monti Rock!"

Rock entered from the back of the room. He wore a white suit, white beads, and a white tallit. His eyes sparkled, his lapel sparkled, and his rings sparkled. He carried a stuffed white cat that he referred to as "my pussy." He walked to the stage belting "On Broadway" and tossing white carnations into the audience. A man followed behind, video camera in hand.

The man at my table asked his wife, "Who is this guy?"

And for the next 25 minutes, Rock answered. That's the genius of Monti Rock's act (if you want to call it an "act"): He knows people have questions about him, and he answers each and every one. (Whether his answers are fully accurate is up for debate.)

What was his childhood like?

"When I was thirteen, my mom found out I was gay and threw me out. I sold my body on Forty-Second Street, and made every trick a John, and every John a producer."

How did he get started in acting?

"One of my husbands was murdered in a pool. I got indicted for the murder, so I went to Mexico, and there, a man asked me to be in the movies."

How did he build a following in Las Vegas?

"People came to see me because I had no talent, and that upset people. I'm not a singer. I'm not an actor. What I am is somebody who believes so much in myself that I can make you believe."

Rock put on a white cowboy hat and white feather boa. He sang two more songs (one in Spanish) in a wavering baritone. He moved about the stage like an aged Scott Hamilton, directly and indirectly asking for applause. And every time, he got it. Against all odds, the audience loved him. They were shocked, amused, confused, and delighted. And after 15 minutes, they all believed.

Rock concluded by singing his 1975 hit single "Get Dancin'." Well, he didn't sing it so much as he strutted around the stage and fiddled with the microphone as the background track played.

But the audience loved it.

Whatever it was.

Monti Rock inhabits the space between Andy Kaufman and Tony Clifton, between Rip Taylor and James Brown, between Andy Warhol and José Eber. It's a gray area, but it's got sparkles.

I don't know if Rock really has a TV deal, a book deal, and an album deal in the works, as he claims. And I don't know why he calls me so frequently—I mentioned that I know his number by heart?—but I do know that the guy can still put on a great show and that Las Vegas is lucky to have him.

Who is Monti Rock? He's the man for whom the phrase *je ne sais quoi* was invented.

5

Nightlife

For a while, I told my friends that nightlife writing was a "tricky balance."

"You have to get drunk enough that something crazy happens," I'd say, "but not so drunk that you can't remember the crazy thing the next morning."

I suppose that's true, but for me, it's not an issue. I never get so drunk that I can't remember things. For me, the biggest challenge in nightlife writing is making dull nights sound exciting. Making ordinary nights sound extraordinary.

The second-biggest challenge is keeping the Vegas Nightlife Tone going, even when I'm in a crappy mood. Everybody's getting crazy, everything's wild, the party never stops—even if I just got a ticket and got sick and got dumped.

The following stories move quickly and blend together. They're punctuated by fleeting moments of triumph and euphoria. Such are the nights on the Vegas Strip.

These stories are intended to be read and instantly forgotten:

The Strip Club Date

I'd never ask a girl on a strip-club date. But when S asked me, I said yes.

We weren't the only couple at the Spearmint Rhino that night. Apparently, strip clubs are semi-popular Vegas date destinations. But why is that? Don't strip clubs intimidate women? Make them self-conscious about their bodies?

"I actually felt less pressure than usual," S told me after our date. "At a nightclub, I feel like I have to compete with the other girls for men's attention. But when we went to the Rhino, it was a given that the guys would be gawking at the strippers. So I didn't feel bad that I didn't get many looks."

I had another theory as to why S didn't feel self-conscious: She's very attractive.

I asked her, "If you thought the dancers were more attractive than you, would you have had such a good time?"

"If that were the case," S replied, "I probably wouldn't have gone."

Guys: Unless you're with a girl who's got superhuman self-confidence, don't ask them to a strip club.

Also steer clear if you want a future with your girl.

"If I met a guy, and he proposed taking me to a strip club," S told me, "it'd be obvious that our relationship was going in the sexual direction and that we wouldn't have longevity. If you start off with something so sexual and intense, where do you go from there?"

The main upside of taking a girl to a strip club is that it might turn her on. But the odds are slim—S says it didn't—and the potential for disaster is high.

So, I say, wait until she asks you.

The Geeks at LAVO

In celebration of National Nerd Day, LAVO brought Dustin "Screech" Diamond to the Palazzo, and brought this question to the nightlife forefront: Can a hot girl be a nerd?

I vote no.

I hate going through drop-dead-gorgeous girls' social-networking profiles and seeing, "I'm such a nerd!" *Really? Do you watch* 'MythBusters'*? Did you play Magic: The Gathering in middle school? Do you know how much mana you have to tap to play an Ornithopter? (Trick question; the Ornithopter has a casting cost of 0.) Then take off those thick-rimmed, taped-up glasses and admit that Honey Horneé (Garth Algar's girlfriend in* Wayne's World 2, *as portrayed by supermodel Kim Basinger) has no real-world counterpart!*

Well, hot female nerds might not exist in reality, but they sure existed at LAVO—hot girls sporting "KICK ME" signs, hot girls in pigtails, hot girls dancing like Peewee Herman. They were all there. One of them even took home the $1,000 costume prize. And while I wish the money would've gone to a guy, I'll get over it. After all, LAVO's event was a genuine celebration of nerddom, not a mockery, so I approve and applaud.

I'm sure Melvin Nerdly and Maxwell Nerdstrom would, too.

On a Scale From Ten to Zero, He Got a Ten For Looking Like De Niro

Last weekend, TAO gave away $15,000 to the best '80s celebrity look-alikes. When the club asked me to serve as the evening's celebrity judge—"celebrity" in the absolute loosest sense of the word—I jumped at the chance. First, because I love judging people (in non-moral contexts), and second, because I'd heard that club contests are rigged, and I wanted to find out for myself.

Turns out they're legit. At least, this one was.

Over 65 look-alikes entered the field. They were dressed as icons like Michael Jackson, Madonna, Rick James, and Cher. But none of *those* celebs, in my mind, truly exemplify the '80s. Their careers were longer, spilling over into the '70s and '90s, too.

Same goes for Indiana Jones, who called TAO beforehand, in character, to ask if he could bring in his whip. When he arrived, Jones filled out his application by Zippo light, which won him some points, but not enough to eclipse his non-resemblance to Harrison Ford. He looked like Harry Anderson from "Night Court;" he should have come as Judge Harold T. Stone.

I was less impressed by the guy who showed up in blackface saying he was Sho'nuff from the 1985 movie *Shogun of Harlem*. And was Sho'nuff the slightest bit embarrassed when requesting a contest application form from TAO Group marketer Jillian, who's black? Course he wasn't.

We let Sho'nuff compete, but we had to draw the line at Austin Powers. His first movie didn't come out till '97. Inside TAO's Opium Room, Pee-wee Herman had an impromptu dance battle against one of the Rick Jameses, as the Terminator (T-800) watched from afar, unflinching.

Using four criteria (resemblance, '80s-ness, audience reaction, sexiness), the other judges and I narrowed the field down to six. I fought against Pam Anderson (too '90s) and Robert De Niro (not '80s-specific enough), but I eventually buckled. I couldn't deny Pam's sexiness or De Niro's striking resemblance and strong audience reaction.

The finalists—Pam, Bobby, Pee-wee, Whitney Houston, Terminator, and Rodney Dangerfield—took to the main stage and the audience made its decision clear: De Niro would walk away with the big check. I'd have picked Pee-wee, but I respect the democratic process. Which is just one of the many reasons TAO should invite me back to judge their next girl-on-girl kissing contest.

The Porn Pool

The most shocking thing about Hard Rock's XFANZ Outdoor Porn Expo was how much it resembled any other afternoon at a Vegas casino pool. I'm not saying XFANZ wasn't sufficiently pornographic—it was; there were over 100 starlets in attendance—I'm saying XFANZ revealed, by comparison, how pornified the Vegas pool party scene has become.

"The purpose of the XFANZ expo," event organizer Kristen Kaye told me, "is to give guys the chance to interact with the porn stars. At the AEE, the girls are behind the counters, but here, they're out talking, swimming, and interacting with the fans."

I can attest to the bit about interactions in the pool. Cliché as it might sound, "scandalous" is the only way to describe them. Well, "oral sex" would work, too.

The Sticky Bra

Recently, I visited Deuce Lounge at Aria with my lovely roommate and three of her friends: Tala (one of Matt Goss's Dirty Virgin Dancers), Kat (a freelance dancer), and Kat's friend Jared, an inked club host.

Our drinks were comped because we're young(ish) and pretty, so I went for the $25 Deuce-Tini. The girls all went for Raspberry Lemon Sorbets. After the first round of drinks, Kat showed us her Sticky Bra.

A Sticky Bra, I learned, is composed of two sticky teardrop-shaped breast covers, which fasten together at the center. That's the whole bra. No straps, no wraps, no nothing. Of course, to properly display the bra, Kat had to lower her tank top. Enough to disrupt the $100-limit blackjack table, but not enough to get us kicked out.

Tala was debating whether she should celebrate her 30th birthday with a pillow fight or with a Dirty Santa party. Big question.

But the bigger question was: *What does one do when they turn 30 in Vegas?*

The Bagel Ball
and The Matzo Ball

Sure, American Jews like Chinese food and movies, but we visit Golden Wok and AMC every Christmas Eve is because nothing else is open. This season, though, Vegas' eligible Levites had other options.

The night before Christmas Eve, the Jewish Community Center of Southern Nevada held its annual Bagel Ball at Blush. The place was packed with nearly 300 single Semites, ranging in age from 21 to 86. How religious was this group? I didn't see any kippahs, but I did see a leopard print pimp hat. That answer your question?

"We held the event tonight," JCC Executive Director Neil Popish told me, "instead of tomorrow, Christmas Eve, because tomorrow is Shabbat. I don't think a lot of people will show up to the Matzo Ball for that reason. Honestly, there's no competition."

Popish was half right. Only 70 people showed up to JDate's December 24 Matzo Ball, held at Blue Martini. But what the event lacked in numbers it made up for with a giant, badass, ice Menorah.

A chosen UNLV law student, Jeff, recognized me and my date from the previous night's Bagel Ball. "I'm here on the Sabbath, breaking the holiest of holy days, looking for love," he told us.

By the end of the night, he was still looking. Oh well, Jeff, Tu Bishvat parties are right around the corner.

The A-Minus Dance

I've been out of law school for two years, but I remember it like it was yesterday. Like a war, a wedding, or a divorce, law school isn't easily forgotten.

The most nerve-racking part of law school, of course, is grades. In most classes, your entire grade is based on your final exam performance, and you don't get your scores back until several weeks after you've taken your tests.

Well, the UNLV Boyd Law School 1Ls just got their grades back. So if you've noticed random shrieking and crying throughout the valley, you now know why.

My new 1L friends Emily and Lisa did really well, so we headed to Cosmo to celebrate with cocktails. First at Chandelier Bar, then at Marquee. (We were planning on drinking either way, we just didn't know if we'd be drowning sorrows or toasting triumphs.)

Marquee was a madhouse. From the line, you'd assume they were giving out crack. The place was packed with pretty patrons, prettier go-go dancers, and equally pretty bartenders. So much pretty it hurt. So much pretty it made me want to run back to the Midwest and admit defeat.

Now, I'm rarely surprised on a dance floor, but, I admit, when Marquee's mammoth gusts of frozen air ripped through the dance floor, I was surprised. Never felt anything like that before. Well, not inside.

At 3:00, my posse moved up to the Library room for further cocktails. A bouncer gave us a copy of *The Big Butt Book* to peruse, and Emily and Lisa did just that for at least 20 minutes.

Can't blame 'em; come next week, when classes resume, they won't have time for free reading.

But, if I remember law school correctly, there's always time for cocktails.

How to Be the Guest of Honor

Las Vegas Weekly threw me a book release party for my latest memoir, *Fool Me Once: Hustlers, Hookers, Headliners, and How Not to Get Screwed in Vegas*. The event was a great success, largely because I followed these rules:

1. Look better than everyone else. If you're going to be the center of attention, you better give everybody something to look at. So go out and buy that Technicolor belt buckle or unicorn skin tie you've had your eye on.

2. Take as many pictures as you can. This ensures your party will live on in Facebook albums for years to come. Make a special

effort to take pictures with the people who don't like to be photographed. They'll probably make the picture their profile shot, for lack of other options.

3. Don't have fun. Think of your party as a gig. Your objective is to chat with everybody in attendance for at least two minutes. Your fun will come the following day, when everybody starts calling you and emailing you and telling you what an amazing time they had.

How to Throw a House Party

No line, no cover, no dress code—house parties are great. If you're thinking about throwing one this spring, here's some vital intel:

1. Hide your valuables. Especially if you're expecting randoms or friends-of-friends-of-friends. Better in the safe than sorry.

2. Skimp on food. Your friends are there to drink, not dine. Take the money you were going to spend on snacks, and invest in Goldschläger and Sambuca.

3. Make it a red-carpet affair. With a couple yards of red flannel duct-taped to your front hallway, your friends will feel like movie stars. Or, at the least, they'll wipe their feet.

4. Take lots of pictures, but only post the best 15 percent on Facebook. That way, when your "friends" who "couldn't" make your party because they were "feeling under the weather" click through your Facebook photo album, they'll kick themselves for ditching your once-in-a-lifetime soirée.

5. Consider a theme. Everybody loves dressing up in costume! Well, except for the many, many people who hate it. But you don't want those people at your party. They're no fun. In fact, even if you're not actually planning to throw a costume party, you should still claim that you are in order to keep these uninspired downers away from your bash.

6. Put on a show. Got a friend who can juggle? Another who can put her feet behind her head? One who can juggle while her feet are behind her head? Put them to work for you. A short, informal performance will give your guests something to talk about the following day, aside from how terrible Goldschläger tastes.

7. Put cleaning off for a day. When you wake up the following morning at 4 p.m., don't start cleaning up right away. You deserve a break. So drive to IHOP and grab breakfast. Trust me, the mess ain't going anywhere.

Rick Lax's Birthday Party at Marquee's Library Room

Mid-Gaming

This is one of those clubs that has a bar in every corridor. There's a bar when you enter, a bar by the dance floor and a bar by the stage. Spending a night here without buying a drink is kind of like spending the day at Disney World without going on any of the rides.

Here's how I did it: When my date—we'll call her "S"—asked me if we should order some drinks, I replied, "Sure, but can we step out of the club for some fresh air first?" Now, if S had been here before, she might have known that the place has outside access. She might have suggested that we go up there, order drinks, and kill two birds with one stone. But S didn't know, so she followed me out of the club without protest.

Pre-gaming, n., a bonding ritual in which college students drink large quantities of cheap alcohol before hitting up the bars (e.g., "We were low on cash, so we pre-gamed until midnight. Then we headed to McFadden's and had another round there").

Mid-gaming, n., a penurious, miserly method of drinking for free while visiting Vegas nightclubs (e.g., "I would never date a mid-gamer; I have standards").

I found a penny slot machine, fed it a dollar, and started betting the minimum: One cent. Before long, a cocktail waitress came by and asked if we wanted drinks.

"Should we just order our first round here?" I asked, as if I hadn't been planning on doing precisely that from the moment S and I had parked.

"Why not?" S replied.

When our drinks arrived, I tipped the waitress, cashed out my 65-cent ticket and slipped it into my wallet. S and I strolled back to the club, and by the time we arrived, we'd cleaned out our glasses. (Total amount spent: $2.35.)

I walked S to the dance floor, and after 30 grinding minutes, I sensed that S was about to ask for another cocktail, so I preempted her request by suggesting we "go back and play the slots for a few more minutes."

And that's how we got our second round of drinks.

S didn't say anything about our coming and going, so I assumed she didn't process what was going on. I further assumed that if she did pick up on it, she'd be secretly impressed by my cleverness and economic savvy, by my technique for beating the system and fighting the Man and all that. I assumed that she'd reward my cleverness later on that evening in one way or another.

I was wrong.

The following day S revealed to me that she knew exactly what I was doing. Turns out she wasn't thrilled about it: "[Women] want to feel like someone is trying to impress us—especially at the beginning. We want to feel like we're worth a $10 drink at the least, you know?"

"But the drinks cost more than ten dollars," I suavely pointed out.

"I started to wonder if you were even having fun with me or if you wanted to be drinking and gambling by yourself."

"Of course I was having fun with you!"

"Well, you didn't show it. You weren't very considerate last night. All that walking

back and forth and back and forth … did you even notice how high my heels were? Five inches, Ricky."

One could argue that mid-gaming is no different from pre-gaming. One could point out that it's not technically illegal. But I can't imagine that any major moral philosopher (aside from Nietzsche) would give mid-gaming his stamp of ethical approval. No matter how you slice it, mid-gaming is a grifter move.

Still, if you're not concerned with impressing the person you're with, and if you're confident that your friends can keep a secret, perhaps mid-gaming is for you. Desperate times call for desperate measures.

At least, that's what I keep telling myself.

How Society Works

If you asked your friend, "Do you like sociology?", he might reply, "Why do you ask? You think you're better than me?"

More likely, he'd say, "Not really."

He'd be wrong. *Everybody* likes sociology; it's the *word* "sociology" that people don't like.

Once I realized this, I wrote as many sociology pieces as I could. Pieces about crime, about religion, about the sex industry, about the service industry—the topics that people discuss when they gather around the proverbial water cooler. Hopefully, these stories will give you some water cooler fodder:

How I Spent Passover

We're not going to get into whether the Jews killed Jesus.

I realize this omission is itself moderately controversial. I realize that a lot of Jewish people would tell me, "You have a responsibility to inform your readers that the Romans killed Jesus, not your ancestors." And I realize that those who believe the Jews did kill Jesus—those who quote Matthew 27:25 ("His blood be on us and on our children.")—will see that omission as a de facto admission that the Jews did kill him. As if I were in a position to make this sort of admission just by virtue of the fact that a) I'm Jewish; and b) I'm writing about the subject.

I'm not qualified to discuss the intricacies of Jesus' death. Before watching the East Vegas Christian's Center's Passion Play, most of my knowledge of the crucifixion came from the first half of a single sentence on the first page of *The Hitchhiker's Guide To The Galaxy*: "And then, one Thursday, nearly two thousand years after one man had been nailed to a tree for saying how great it would be to be nice to people for a change … "

So we're not going to get into it.

They're called passion plays, and they're performed around the globe, from New Jersey to Sri Lanka. The most famous one has been staged since the early 1600s in a small Bavarian town called Oberammergau. Even sin-soaked Las Vegas has its own Passion play, with six pre-Easter performances at the East Vegas Christian Center.

Passion plays have a rocky history. *The Christian Science Monitor* says, "Historically, productions have reflected negative images of Jews and the longtime church teaching that the Jewish people were collectively responsible for Jesus' death." So in the late '80s, the U.S. Bishops' Committee for Ecumenical and Interreligious Affairs published "Criteria for the Evaluation of Dramatizations of the Passion"—criteria that included, Don't stereotype the Jews, and, Don't use problematic lines like, "His blood be on us and on our children."

Passion plays have a rocky history. *The Christian Science Monitor* says, "Historically, productions have reflected negative images of Jews and the longtime church teaching that the Jewish people were collectively responsible for Jesus' death."

Then, in 2003, Mel Gibson released *The Passion of the Christ*, and all my friends and my family freaked out, though none of them actually saw the movie. I know I didn't see it.

So on March 25, 2009, when I drove across Las Vegas to watch the Christian Center's penultimate rehearsal, I had no idea what I was in for.

I enter the church, and climb up the stairs. I walk into a beige room with a stack of folded blue gym mats in the far corner. At the front of the room, a woman strums a guitar, and sings, "Oh Lord, you're beautiful. Your face is all I see."

A group of 35 sings along. They raise their arms, just like on TV. Some palms face up, some face forward.

"Lord, we have a city that desperately needs you," the singer prays. "We see the shining lights, but hidden in the shadow are those who are broken. We pray that you will bring those people to a place where they're confronted with the Gospel. And we pray for those on stage."

I look around the room and wonder, *which one of these guys is Jesus?* The skinny guy with the brown beard is the obvious choice, only he'd introduced himself to me as JT the PR guy, not an actor.

The woman with the guitar introduces extremely red-haired director Coey Humble, who, in turn, introduces me to the Passion players. They applaud.

"We can show the city, through drama, the sacrifice that Jesus made for all of us," Humble says.

Her idealism is quickly superseded by tangible concerns. A woman in the back raises her hand and says, "I still don't have my headdress!"

Humble says she's on it. The costumes and the props will be ready by show time, she assures the group. To demonstrate this point, she brings out one of the just-made props: a Seder plate.

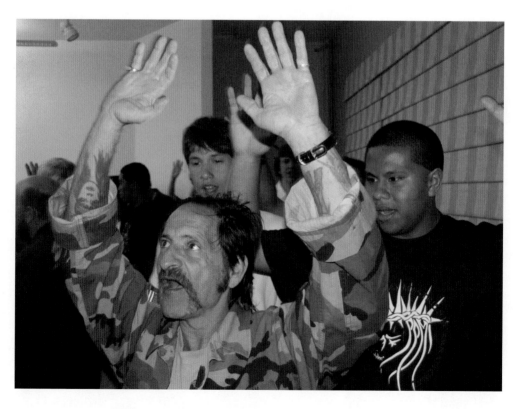

"Who doesn't know the symbolism of the Seder plate?" Humble asks.

Pretty much every hand goes up … except for mine. I might not know the story of the crucifixion, but I know the Seder plate like the back of my yad (Hebrew for hand).

Coey picks up each object on the plate and tries her damndest at pronunciation. She says the "cha" in charoset, the way I say "cha" in "charcoal." (You're supposed to make the "cha" sound by clearing phlegm from your throat with the letter H.)

She picks up the hardboiled egg and says, "I'm not even going to attempt to pronounce this one. Does anybody know how to say it?"

I keep my mouth shut. I'm not eager to reveal to the group that I'm Jewish, but this says less about the group than it does about my insecurities.

The Seder plate also has a piece of ostensibly unleavened bread on it. I'm pretty sure it was a Mama Mary's miniature-pizza crust, though.

The group moves out onto the second-floor balcony, and for a few seconds we stare at the city glowing in the distance. There's a large gulf of darkness separating the Strip from the church. The question on everybody's mind is: *Come Easter, will Las Vegas cross that buffer to watch the Gospel unfold, to pray, to repent?*

The Passion players have been rehearsing 11 weeks in the New Horizon church. This is their first rehearsal in the actual performance space.

"I want the merchant women to come up the center!" Humble shouts. "Like this! Like this!"

Nobody's listening, so assistant director Patty Murphy blows her whistle.

It takes the group 45 minutes to block the opening entrance. I flip through the program. First I read the back, which features a reprinted article, "The Passion of the Christ from a Medical Point of View," written by Dr. C. Truman Davis.

According to my Google search, Davis is a theological one-hit wonder. He's famous for his detailed description of Jesus' suffering. Here's a couple sentences from his hit single:

"The legionnaire drives a heavy, square, wrought-iron nail through the wrists and deep into the wood. The left foot is pressed backward against the right foot, and a nail is driven through the arch of each, leaving the knees moderately flexed … As He slowly sags down with more weight on the nails in the wrists, excruciating, fiery pain shoots along the fingers and up the arms—the nails in the wrists are putting pressure on the median nerves."

I look up from the program and see that Humble and Murphy are trying to get everybody's attention once again. Apparently Humble confiscated Murphy's whistle because people were getting annoyed. Humble gives them their motivation: "It's Passover week, and you heard that Jesus is coming! You've got goose bumps!"

Children shout, "Jesus is coming!" and then Jesus comes. Turns out JT isn't just the PR guy; he plays Jesus, too.

"We love you, Jesus," one of the kids tells him.

JT overturns the money tables and exits stage left.

Having heard most of the actors speak, I can tell you that the U.S. Bishops' Committee for Ecumenical and Interreligious Affairs has little to worry about with respect to stereotyping Jews. These actors couldn't pass as Jewish to save their lives. Not the black guy, not the Asian guy, not the guy with the Southern accent, and certainly not the guy who sounds like Don Knotts.

During the scene change, I talk with producer Garry Knight. He was responsible for bringing the Passion Play to Vegas 15 years ago.

"One of the toughest scenes for the cast," Knight tells me, "is when they have to yell, 'Crucify him!'"

These actors couldn't pass as Jewish to save their lives. Not the black guy, not the Asian guy, not the guy with the Southern accent, and certainly not the guy who sounds like Don Knotts.

It sounds like a silly concern, but it's not. The passion players aren't professional actors, so they're not used to saying things they don't mean. And they love Jesus, more than I can imagine. For Christ's sake, they're in a Passion Play.

"The scourging scene is tough, too," Knight says. "They've got to act drunk and whip JT without really hurting him. The scourge is made of rope, but still, by the end of the season, JT is pretty beat up."

They use a gimmicked cross, too. There's a ledge for JT to stand on, and the hand nails work like the old arrow- through-head gag.

Later, as I prepare to leave, the Passion players ask, "Will we see you on Monday?" Knight asks me.

"God willing," I reply.

The sun is going down, and it's the first night of Passover. I should be at a Seder, like my parents or President Obama. Instead, I'm heading back to church.

About 200 people, including 50 children, have shown up to watch the first show. The toddlers fidget, the babies cry, and they don't stop until Jesus is crucified. That gets their attention. At times I'm bored—particularly during the musical numbers,.

But things get exciting toward the end. Like when the soldiers taunt and scourge Jesus. They may have struggled with the scene internally, but it looked great. When they're through with Christ, he turns around and reveals the bloody whip marks on his back. It's a prosthetic. It's a good one.

When the soldiers nail Jesus to the cross, he lets out three cries. After a few minutes, he says "It is finished," and dies.

Then we applaud, which feels weird.

The last scene is the best. Peter, played by Eddie Conover, steals the show as he asks who will resurrect Jesus. (It's a rhetorical question; the point is, only Jesus can perform resurrections.) Peter leaves and returns with good news: After three days, Christ is alive and well.

And then resurrected Jesus, now wearing a shiny white robe, steps out onto the balcony. As he does, he hits his head on a fluorescent light hanging from the ceiling. It swings back and forth for 20 seconds and then the lights go dark.

I don't think the Jews were stereotyped in this Passion Play. On the other hand, the performance *did* include the problematic line, "His blood be on us and on our children," so perhaps this version wouldn't get the U.S. Bishops' Committee for Ecumenical and Interreligious Affairs' blessing.

The subtext of the play is clear: *See how much this guy is suffering? Well, he's doing it for you. Now what are you going to do for him?* In a sense, it's about guilting people into following the church.

I don't have a problem with that.

I'm not a Christian. I don't think Christ can save me, in part because I don't think I need to be saved. But I appreciate that a lot of people—people like Coey, Patty, Garry and JT—do. They believe that I'm destined to burn in hell for all of eternity if I don't change my beliefs. So I don't fault them for trying to change my beliefs, even if they use guilt or fear in their attempts. I'm much more offended by those who believe I'm headed for eternal damnation but don't do anything about it.

Tipped Off

Glen doesn't view serving as a job, he views it as a profession. He's nearly 60, and he's been waiting tables most his life. He works at a restaurant at Town Square, but he asked me not to say which one because he doesn't want to get fired. He also asked me to make up a fake name for him, so I picked Glen.

Glen, you see, isn't supposed to be discussing tips with customers, let alone with journalists.

"See those four over there?" he said.

I peered over my shoulder and saw four older, well-to-do diners finishing their entrées. Two men, two women, a dozen stuffed shopping bags surrounding their table.

"I can tell you right now, they're going to leave me ten percent. Now, a lot of serv-

ers would take that as an insult, but I don't. I understand that it's a cultural thing. Those four are English, and over there, ten percent is standard."

"How often do you get stiffed?" I asked.

"All the time," Glen replied. "But again, it's usually by foreigners, by Orientals. They're not acclimatized to our tip system. In their countries, the tip is built into the check. Of course, I'm not allowed to explain to them that over here, it isn't."

Every place has its own tipping customs. For instance, in a Vegas casino, you're encouraged to tip your dealer. But in a Tasmanian casino, if you tip your dealer, you might find yourself in jail. Over there it's considered bribery.

Every place has its own tipping customs. For instance, in a Vegas casino, you're encouraged to tip your dealer. But in a Tasmanian casino, if you tip your dealer, you might find yourself in jail. Over there it's considered bribery.

"I don't want to get too specific," Glen went on, "but even over here, there are certain groups of people who don't tip as much as they should. I'm not talking about foreigners now; I'm talking about people who know better. Or, at least, people who should know better."

He left me the check; I left him 20 percent.

Like Glen, a lot of Las Vegans make the bulk of their income from tips. And when these food servers, cocktail waitresses, bottle attendants, bartenders, dealers, bellmen, cab drivers, casino go-go dancers, and strippers get together, they discuss tips the way the rest of us discuss the weather. But, as Glen pointed out, they're not allowed to talk about tips with the rest of us, so we never hear these conversations.

Until now.

John at the bar is a friend of mine. He doesn't get me my drinks for free, but he is quick with a joke—and I'm confident that if I smoked, he'd be quick with a light, too. He's almost 40, and for the last four years he's worked at a bar in a casino on the Strip. I promised him I wouldn't reveal which one.

When the economy turned south two years ago, his tips followed.

"Sometimes, if I'm working the walk-up daiquiri bar, I'll get two customers per hour. And at the walk-up bars, people don't always tip. So when it gets that slow, I'll go to the manager and say, 'Do you really need me here?' See, because of tip compliance, I'm losing money at that point."

John explained tip compliance:

"The IRS understands that I make tips, so I get taxed on them. But they don't track my individual tips; they set a per-hour fee. So if I'm not getting customers, I still have to pay taxes on the tips I'm not making."

The state of Nevada requires employers to pay bartenders minimum wage, so that's what they do—usually not a dime more. By comparison, most states allow employers to pay tipped employees far less than minimum wage. Either way, if a bartender isn't getting good tips, he isn't living the good life or anything close to it.

So begins the hustle.

"The number-one unethical thing I see," John told me, "is over-pouring—making drinks that are too stiff. When you do that, you're cheating the company you work for. You're stealing from them. Same thing with giving customers extra shots—throwing 'em in and not ringing 'em up. I see that all the time. The customers obviously never say anything to management, and they usually leave a bigger tip."

John says that he never over-pours, but he does admit to doing other things for extra cash.

"Every now and then, somebody will offer me money to do something silly. That's the kind of place I work. And as long as it's not a health-code violation, I'll do it. Whip off my top off for fifty bucks? Sure. Pretend that I'm doing something nasty? Sure."

"Don't you feel demeaned when you're doing that stuff?" I asked.

"Mildly, but that's my job. Bartenders work to make people happy, and people pay us for it. So it's not just me, personally; in a sense, all bartenders are whores."

That's a novel line, but not a novel observation. John isn't the first one to compare service industry workers to sex workers. In the book *On The Make: The Hustle of Urban Nightlife*, University of Pennsylvania sociology professor David Grazian writes, "dining service is surprising similar to lap dancing, insofar as both require the worker to quickly yet accurately predict what kind of experience their client desires, and immediately respond in an appropriate manner."

And when you think about it, it's not just servers and bartender who make money by attempting to give their customers the kind of experience they're after; it's all workers.

In that sense, we're all whores.

The state of Nevada requires employers to pay bartenders minimum wage, so that's what they do—usually not a dime more. By comparison, most states allow employers to pay tipped employees far less than minimum wage. Either way, if a bartender isn't getting good tips, he isn't living the good life or anything close to it.

Sonia is a dancer—a trained dancer. She's been in shows on and off the Strip, and she currently works as a casino go-go dancer. She works behind the blackjack tables, alongside the pit bosses.

"How's business?"

"This one guy—a regular, a high roller—tipped us six thousand dollars in the past two months. We all get so excited when he comes in, and he really likes us, too. But recently, some girls got in trouble for hanging out with him at the table. To me that's crossing the line; that's going into stripper territory. And it makes me wonder what the guy thinks about us."

"You mean, what he thinks about the nature of your relationship?"

"Exactly. Why is he giving us so much money, you know?"

To me and to Sonia, it's obvious that the dancers' relationship with the high roller is purely business. And I'd bet the high roller realizes this, too … but I wouldn't bet my life on it. A lot of patrons (particularly men) delude themselves into believing that their servers (particularly female ones) are their friends. According to Grazian, "[Customers] take pleasure in what they interpret to be the authenticity of their encounters with service staff, particularly when they are of a desirably intimate or sexualized nature." And when customers "take this pleasure," they tip more. Any stripper will tell you that the guys who believe their strip-club interactions are authentic are the ones who tip the most.

Assuming the high roller doesn't come in, how much can Sonia make in tips at that gig?

"It's really hit or miss. Depends on the night. Some nights I'll walk away with no tips; some nights I'll get up to three hundred, three fifty. What happens is, as soon as the first person calls me over and gives me a tip, the other gamblers get the idea that it's okay to tip the go-go dancer, and then they all start calling me over and giving me tips. Unlike strippers, I'm not allowed to have dollar bills hanging out of my underwear, so people don't know to tip me. I think I'm going to ask my friends to start coming by and giving me fake tips, just to get the ball rolling."

The trick is letting customers know they can tip you without explicitly saying it. Sonia figured this out after a few months, but not from her go-go gig. When she's not dancing, she dresses up in a costume—I promised her I wouldn't say what kind—and walks around the casino, taking pictures with tourists. She's not supposed to take tips, but she does. Everybody does.

"I figured out this trick that boosted my tips like a hundred percent," she told me.

"As we see somebody coming up, I'll give a dollar to my friend, as if I'd just gotten it but don't have a pocket to hold it. Or we'll act like we're divvying up a tip from the last group tourists. We do this even if nobody has tipped us. And then, when somebody new sees us, they see the money in our hands, and they think I guess I should give a tip, too. I guess that's what people do."

It's all about expectations. If a guy thinks you're expecting a big tip from him, he's more likely to give you one. At least, that's what my friend Sandi told me.

Sandi is stripper and a psychology student, and she applies what she learned in class to her work.

"When I first approach a guy, I'll say, 'I can tell you're a high roller,' regardless of how well he's dressed. Maybe I'll hold his watch and say, 'This is such a nice watch. I can tell it costs a lot.' So then, when it comes time for him to give me a tip, he thinks that I think that he's rich, and he doesn't want to burst my bubble and admit that he's not, so he gives me a big tip to keep up the misperception he thinks I have. It's not about what he thinks of himself; it's about what he thinks I think about him."

If a guy doesn't object when Sandi tells him that he's high roller, it's as if he's confirming her assertion. And the longer he goes without objecting, the stronger his implicit confirmation becomes. So when it comes time to leave a tip, he thinks to himself, I led her on. *I led her to believe I'm rich, so at this point it'd be wrong of me to not to give her a big tip.*

But that's not her number-one trick.

"Number one is neuro-linguistic programming—subliminal messages."

How does that work?

"If a guy tells me that he's flying home tomorrow, I'll say, 'Let me give you a big tip about the Vegas airport.' That phrase—'Let me give you a big tip about'—I find a way to work it into our conversation a couple times, no matter what we're talking about. And it stays in the guy's head to the end, even though he doesn't know why it's in his head."

Monika is a cocktail waitress. She's served drinks for eight years, on and off the Strip. Right now she works off the Strip, and she says tips are good. She attributes this to her big smile and big personality. I've seen her work a few times, and I agree.

"It's not like most servers are happy to be at work," Monika admits. "We're like anybody else in that respect, but we have to seem happier. The girls who get the biggest tips are the ones who come across as genuinely liking people."

"Can you tell if you're going to get a big tip ahead of time?"

"No, but I know when somebody is going to give me a bad tip. They mumble, they don't make eye contact. Going into it, they know they're not going to give a good tip, so they feel uncomfortable in their own skin."

"And what do you think of these people who leave really small tips or no tips?"

"What goes around comes around."

That sounds ominous.

"What do you mean?" I asked.

"If people do the right thing, nothing bad is going to happen. If you do the right thing, people aren't going to mess with you. But if you think you're going to screw the waitress, she'll screw you over in ways you don't want to imagine."

Monika was right; I didn't want to imagine. But I had to ask.

"How can they screw with me?"

"Back when I worked on the Strip, I saw this a lot: A customer would get drunk, give his credit card, and then forget to take his customer copy. So the server would just change the amount on the merchant slip. There are all kinds of ways you can alter a slip: You can change numbers, you can add a number, or you can just print out a new set of slips and forge the signature. The customer isn't going to remember how much he left, and if he does, he didn't keep the customer copy, so what's he gonna do about it?"

Note to self: Always keep the customer copy.

"Do you think servers who do that are unethical?" I asked.

"Let's just say, I understand why they're doing what they're doing."

In the opening scene of *Reservoir Dogs*, Mr. Pink (Steve Buscemi's character) defends his no-tipping policy like this:

"I don't tip because society says I have to. I'll tip if somebody really deserves a tip. If somebody really puts forward the effort, I'll give them something extra, but this tipping automatically is for the birds. As far as I'm concerned, they're just doing their job."

When Mr. White (played by Harvey Keitel) brings up the tip-compliance issue, Mr. Pink responds thusly:

"Hey, I'm very sorry that the government taxes their tips. That's fucked up. But that ain't my fault. It would appear that waitresses are just one of the many groups the government fucks in the ass on a regular basis. You show me a paper that says the government shouldn't do that, I'll sign it. Put it to a vote, I'll vote for it. But what I won't do is play ball."

You don't hear many people echoing that sentiment. But the question is: Do people think it? Before you say no, keep in mind servers get stiffed every day, and the ones doing the stiffing must have some justification for their action. Ignorance on the part of those visiting the country can only explain so many of the bad tips servers receive.

Tipping your server is undoubtedly the "right" thing to do. Assuming your server did her job, you'd be wrong to stiff her. But how wrong would you be? And just where does the moral obligation to leave a tip come from? That's what I asked UNLV ethical theory professor David Forman.

"As soon as you give your order to the waiter, there's an implicit agreement that there'll be a tip at the end. If you don't like that agreement, then you shouldn't be

Interview with UNLV ethics professor David Forman

RL: Is it ever okay to stiff a waitress?

DF: If she breaks your implicit contract—for instance, by refusing to honor some reasonable request of yours without any justification—then it seems to me you're not required to tip her.

RL: Would any major moral philosophers be okay with me stiffing a waitress?

DF: Maybe you could push a Utilitarian like Peter Singer in that direction. Singer tells us that we should be giving more money to support Third World countries. One might reason that the money you are contemplating giving as a tip would be used for greater good by UNICEF than by your waitress. Then again, you probably should have given your money to UNICEF instead of paying sixty bucks for the fish at Bartolotta Ristorante di Mare. Applying the Utilitarian calculation only after your bill arrives is pretty self-serving …

RL: Do I have a moral obligation to tip my blackjack dealer or my plumber?

DF: That all depends on expectations. I've never played blackjack, but if I did, I suppose I'd first ask about what everyone else does. In this case, a kind of moral relativism is entirely appropriate. There's an underlying universal moral principle here: You should keep agreements—even agreements that are not legal, and even agreements that are merely implicit. The relativism comes from the implicit agreement you enter into when you sit down at a blackjack table or call for a plumber—it's relative to the culture you're in. In this case, "When in Rome" is a valid, universal moral principle.

in a restaurant—at least not in a place like the U.S., where a tip is expected."

"But what if you're a conscientious objector, like Mr. Pink? What if you disagree with the implicit-agreement theory and don't want to further it with your participation?"

"That's still no excuse for not tipping. If there were no tipping, the wait staff would be paid more, and this would be reflected in the price on the bill. But if you don't tip, then you're benefiting from the institution of tipping without contributing yourself. So you're not only stiffing the wait staff; you're cheating all the tippers."

Forman was arguing, essentially, that when it comes to tipping, you can't be a conscientious objector, only a de facto thief.

And what do we do with thieves? We punish them. So maybe Monika's former coworkers—the ones who altered the slips—weren't hustlers, after all; maybe they were just vigilantes.

A few months back, I went to local bar and ordered Dragonberry lemonade. The drink cost five bucks, and I handed the bartender $10. She handed me back $5, and I handed the bill right back to her to ask for change (so I could tip her a dollar). But before I could get the words out, she snatched the five from my hand, stuffed it into her tank top, said, "Thanks, dear!" and walked to the far end of the bar.

At first, I let it slide. After all, I didn't want to shout, "Come back, Miss! I didn't mean to tip you that much!"

But then I realized I was being hustled. I realized that the bartender knew I didn't mean to tip her the full five bucks. I realized that she assumed that I would never embarrass myself by asking for my money back.

She was wrong.

I got off my stool, walked to the far end of the bar, flagged her down and said, "I wasn't offering you the five as a tip. I was asking for change, dear."

I ended up tipping her a dollar for the performance. Still, I was pissed.

But after talking with Glen, John, Sonia, and Monika, I'm a little less pissed. I don't forgive the bartender entirely, but I appreciate where she was coming from.

The (Imaginary) Enemy at the Gate

I live in a gated community. That might sound prestigious, but I assure you it isn't. I count among my neighbors the uneducated, the unemployed, and the criminal. From my front door, I've seen flashing squad car lights, hovering police helicopters, tearful arrests, and dramatic drug busts.

Aren't gated communities supposed to be exclusive suburban safe havens? Surely *all* my homeowner's association (HOA) dollars aren't being spent on those noisy leaf blowers that only show up when I'm asleep. Surely the slow-moving aesthetically unpleasing iron gate erected between my condo and the rest of Las Vegas does *something*.

The question is, what, exactly, does it do?

Since 1991, murders per 100,000 residents have dropped from 12 to six, burglaries from 1,400 to 830, larcenies from 3,550 to 1,750, and vehicle thefts from 650 to 470.

The history of gated communities ties into the history of HOAs, and the history of HOAs ties into racism. Prior to the 1950s, property owners kept black people out of their neighborhoods using racially restrictive covenants. But when the Supreme Court struck this practice down in *Shelley v. Kraemer* (1948), white landowners moved from de jure racism to de facto.

"HOAs were a direct response to growing diversity," says UNLV urban politics professor Kenneth Fernandez. "They created rules to keep out minorities and other unwanted social classes. In place of racially restrictive covenants, HOAs used high fees and evictions."

Taking the segregation one step further, many HOA neighborhoods erected gates. And then, in the '60s and '70s, neighborhoods without HOAs began erecting them, too. "The gates," Fernandez says, "were a response to the rapidly growing crime rates from the sixties to nineteen-ninety-one."

In most of the country, crime rates have declined significantly since then. Nevada is no exception. Since 1991, murders per 100,000 residents have dropped from 12 to six, burglaries from 1,400 to 830, larcenies from 3,550 to 1,750, and vehicle thefts from 650 to 470. But only now are Nevadans and Americans beginning to grow aware of these declining crime rates. Accordingly, since 1991, the number of gated communities has risen.

Gated communities are not only the product of consumer demand, they're also something that's been marketed to us. Says Fernandez, "We've been sold this idea that gated communities are what you should want, that gated communities are safer."

But are they?

I can't believe nobody's broken into my condo yet. No idea what I've done to deserve such good karma. Did I rescue a bus of orphans while I was asleep? Really, each

morning I wake up pleasantly surprised that my Wii and my laptop are right where I left them.

My community's gate couldn't be easier to subvert. My HOA hasn't changed the four-digit code since I moved in two years ago. My roommate and I have given this code to nearly every pizza-delivery guy and repairman in Las Vegas. And I'm sure everybody else in our condo complex has done the same. Oh, and if you want to get into my neighborhood and don't know the code, just pull to the side of the gate and wait for somebody else to punch in the code for you. Shouldn't take more than three minutes.

The truth is, most gated communities are not safer than their non-gated counterparts. As Officer Marcus Martin of the Las Vegas Metro Police Public Information Office points out, there's a big difference between a gate that has guards and a gate that doesn't. The former provides some protection, the latter doesn't. Martin urges those who live behind gates without guards not to adopt a false sense of security. "We can never seem to make people diligent enough to lock their front doors," he says. "A lot of home invasions begin with people just letting themselves in through unlocked doors." Even those who live behind gates with guards should remain vigilant as many of these guards are untrained and poorly paid.

The Metro PIO and Henderson Police Department don't have ready-to-go statistics on the crime rates in gated communities versus non-gated communities. But professor Suk-Kyung Kim published a paper at Texas A&M focused on that very issue. Kim's research found that residents in gated communities felt safer than residents in non-gated communities, but also reported more crime. In other words, the gates offered a psychological boost, but not a warranted one.

How can this be? How can gated communities be less safe than their non-gated counterparts? Maybe it's a product of gated community residents' false sense of security (unlocked doors, unlocked cars, open garages). Maybe criminals are targeting gated communities (like the thieves in Atlanta who got to 90 homes in gated communities before getting caught). Or maybe the statistics are off; the city of Miami reported that gates actually deterred car thefts and reduced the burglary rate. Then again, even Miami admits the deterrence was slight—and temporary.

America's love affair with gates is waning. HOA fatigue is setting in, too. People are sick of the restrictions and sick of the fees. More and more buyers are choosing homes because they're *not* part of HOAs. And some buyers seek to avoid gates.

Take Midwesterner Amber W. She recently moved into Pacific Trace, in Green

Valley Ranch. Pacific Trace has a gate, but not a guard. "The actual gate is just a heavy, prison-bar looking thing painted forest green," Amber says. "It is entirely unembellished and reacts sluggishly to my gate clicker. It doesn't make me feel safer. If anything, it makes me feel impatient."

Amber didn't want to live behind the gate; she picked the home based on location, size, and price. "I felt a bit embarrassed about the gate. To me, gates are to a housing development what the Greek system is to college: an effort at exclusion that neither elevates those on the inside nor serves to endear them to those on the outside."

As the months went by, though, Amber began to notice some positives about living in the gated community. "Perhaps it's that our community is very condo-like, with small lots and narrow streets, but I feel an increased sense of closeness to my neighbors. I know more of my neighbors here, and I see them more frequently."

This benefit, of course, has an equal and opposite cost. Gated communities might increase intra-community interactions, but they surely decrease inter-community interactions. And for many sociologists, these two things don't balance each other out; when you interact with different communities, you expose yourself to people of different races, income levels, and life views. This decreases racism and increases social capital.

So maybe it's time to tear down these swinging metal walls. Their security benefit is minimal and their sociological cost is clear. I don't know about you, but I'd rather be safe than feel safe. And while we're at it, I'd rather spend time I waste waiting for my gate to open on sleep.

If those damn leaf blowers would even let me.

A Tale of Two Tables

Magicians are honest deceivers. Unlike crooked politicians, slick salesmen, and unfaithful spouses, a magician doesn't just trick you—he tells you he's tricking you.

Except for when he doesn't.

With a little practice and a straight face, a magician can use his skills in deception to mimic mediumship (pretending to talk to the dead) or beat the dealer. And when some magicians can't pay their bills, they do just that.

On the other hand, magicians are usually the first to expose fraudulent mediums and card cheats. In their stage shows, Penn & Teller, and Derren Brown replicate and reveal the mind-reading tricks of "psychic" Sylvia Browne and crossover-er John Edward. Sleight-of-hand experts Steve Forte and Jason England help Vegas casinos catch card cheats.

The following is the story of two magicians who use their powers of deception for good. They've taken two illusions—table illusions, to be specific—from the fields of mediumship and card cheating, and they've ushered them into the world of magic. These might be the most interesting tables you'll ever read about.

Dead people can't talk, play trumpets, ring bells, move Ouija boards, or levitate tables, but that didn't slow down 19th century medium Eusapia Palladino. She had a fantastic, sprawling, decades-long career. She won the confidence of author/physician Arthur Conan Doyle, as well as Pierre Curie and many other scientists. She got them all believing in life after death. How'd she do it? By floating a table in the air.

First, Palladino would ask her audience to sit in a small circle around the table. Then she'd dim the lights. She'd ask the people on either side of her to place their feet on her shoes so she couldn't raise the table with her feet. And, slowly, the table would begin rocking. Then, it would start floating.

How'd Palladino do it? With her feet, of course. She had hard, gimmicked shoes, which would stay in place when she slipped out of them. Then she'd slide her feet under the table legs and lift.

Cute trick, right?

Wrong. This wasn't presented as a trick. Palladino told her spectators that their dead wives, husbands, and children were moving the table. And then she took their money.

That's how it worked with mediums. They performed a magic act and presented it as proof of life after death. Then they accepted people's checks and moved to the next

town. Many charged exorbitant fees, and many of the people paying those amounts were emotionally crippled grievers.

So, ethically speaking, the floating table has a dicey history. Today, though, one magician is reviving the illusion on firm moral ground.

Dirk Losander looks like a magician. Not a Lance Burton-type magician, but a Harry Potter-type magician. He's got long blond hair, he wears flowing jackets, and he often carries a staff. He surrounds himself with bubbles, flames, and New Age music.

"Eighteen years ago," Losander says, "I had a corporate gig for a fryer company. They wanted me to float the inside of a two-foot-by-one-foot fryer, to show how easy it was to clean or change the oil. I designed a method, and I performed it at the convention. It was a huge hit. When the convention was done, I started thinking about how I could use the secret technique I'd developed to float something else. After two weeks, I decided on a table."

If you watch Losander float a table, you'll notice two things: 1) The trick looks like real magic, and 2) The trick is really hard to figure out. The table doesn't use strings, doesn't use magnets, doesn't use electronics, and, unlike the Palladino version, doesn't use feet.

"I did a show in a German airport," Losander recalls, "for the opening of a new terminal. My son had a book that made an airplane sound when you pushed a button, and I wanted to incorporate that into the performance. So when the table began to fly, my son would push the button. After the show, a couple people told me, 'That's a nice trick, but you have to do something about the engine—it's too loud.' They thought I had a gasoline-powered table."

Losander's method is entirely different from Palladino's. But the thing that most distinguishes his performance from hers is what Losander is trying to accomplish. Whereas Palladino floated tables to extract money from the vulnerable, Losander floats tables to inspire.

"The main purpose behind my magic is showing people that anything is possible. I want people to see my table, and then think about their own lives, and realize that just because something seems impossible doesn't mean that it can't happen later. Change is possible."

If Arthur Conan Doyle and Pierre Curie were alive to see Losander's trick, who knows how they'd react. Who knows what they'd guess Losander's method to be. They'd probably believe whatever he told them. In fact, a lot of people would do the same. And if Losander were a different man, he could probably make a lot of money with his trick. But he's no fraudulent medium; he's just a magician with a really good table trick.

In the 1970s, Ray Carson lived in Henderson. He worked as a pit boss at the Horseshoe casino and as a security supervisor at Caesars.

Oh, Carson had a third job, too: designing gambling devices for card cheaters.

Carson, who passed away at 102, grew famous for his prism blackjack shoe, which allowed crooked dealers to glimpse the next card to be dealt, and then deal the card beneath it. But the prism shoe was Carson's passion project; Carson's bread and butter was the holdout table.

A holdout table looks like a regular card table, but when you sit at just the right spot and push in just the right place, it sucks up a playing card or spits one out. You cover the sucking and spitting from the other players with your hands or with your other cards.

One of Ray Carson's most deceptive holdouts is a 32-inch-by-32-inch folding card table with a wood top, felt inlay, and metal legs. It looks like the kind of thing you'd buy at Walmart or Target. It looks thin, cheap, and completely nondescript. Of course, it might be the most distinctive folding card table in history.

Its secret is a springboard concealed beneath the felt inlay. When you press on the right spot, the spring pushes a card through the part where the felt center meets the wood.

According to sleight-of-hand master and cheating expert Jason England, "The Carson table was most likely used for gin. In gin, a single good card, like an ace, seven or eight, could be very useful. And if you're playing in a big game, where $25,000 or $50,000 might change hands, a single good card could be really useful."

Who knows how much money illicitly changed hands atop the Carson table. The one thing we know for sure about the table is this: It's going up for auction in late January. The starting bid is $1,500, and it's expected to go for $3,000-$5,000.

The table is at the Chicago-based Potter & Potter Magic Memorabilia auction house, and the man bringing it from the back rooms to the spotlight is auctioneer/magician/magic historian Gabe Fajuri.

Fajuri has been doing magic since he was six. He's performed at kids' birthday parties, and at restaurants like Max & Erma's, and Bennigan's. At 17, he lectured at the Magic Collectors Weekend in Chicago, and since then he's established himself as one of the world's foremost magic scholars.

"Ray Carson definitely built this table for crossroaders—cheaters," said Fajuri. "But we're selling it for entertainment purposes only. It will probably go to a magician or to a collector who can show it off. It's not our goal to arm Legion of the Night with tools of their trade."

Holdout tables like Carson's, Fajuri says, aren't often available to the public. "This stuff trades privately," he said. "It's rarely available by auction. You can count the number of times these things have come to auction on one or two hands."

But isn't there a danger that a magician would acquire the table and then use it for evil?

Unlikely.

"Most magicians," Fajuri explained, "don't have the balls to be card cheats, let alone use a holdout table. If you secretly palm a card or do a shift or second deal and get caught, there's no real evidence against you. But if you get caught using a holdout table, it'd be hard to deny."

Thanks to Fajuri's efforts, a powerful tool for criminals is being transformed into the ultimate magician's show-and-tell piece.

Both Fajuri's Carson holdout table and Dirk Losander's floating table illustrate the possibility of positive transformation. Think back to Palladino's floating table. Think of how she used it to take God knows how much money from God knows how many grieving widows and parents. And now, think about how Losander uses the exact same trick to inspire and delight.

Just because a trick or an object has been used for nefarious purposes doesn't mean it always will be. Like Losander said, change is possible. Even in the seemingly most rigid of things.

Dress Up: Playing and Paying

Every November 1, a couple of my Facebook friends pose this question as a status update: "Why do girls wear such slutty Halloween costumes?!?!" And every November 1, I vow to answer it.

My research typically ends a minute after it begins, when I find myself clicking through some online photo gallery of women in sexy Halloween costumes: sexy nurses, sexy Harry Potters, slutty Harry Potters, slutty hookers—you get the idea. After a couple dozen of these pictures, I forget about the question that brought me to the gallery in the first place, and I don't think about it again until the following year.

Well, I've resolved to break the cycle once and for all. So I began this year's research before Halloween.

Fool-proof plan?

One of the few sectors not affected by the sagging economy is the Halloween industry. It's up 50 percent over the past four years. Americans now spend $6 billion every Halloween.

Far from it; the Internet is flooded with a deluge of recent research-inhibiting photos, many of which were taken at Blush and Eve's "Halfway to Halloween" events.

The Blush event drew more than 1,000 costumed partiers. It was meant to feature women, but as the photos showed, the guys got in on the costume action, too. They came dressed as superheroes, boxers, Army sergeants, Jesus. Everyone in attendance had clearly put a lot of time, effort, and money into their outfits. Maybe they were hoping to win the $5,000 prize—the money went to four girls dressed as the four seasons (the temporal construction, not the musical group or the hotel chain)—or maybe there was something more going on.

As it often happens, my "research" didn't lead to an answer; it led me to more questions: What kind of people put so much effort and money into their costumes, and why do they do it?

Star Costume & Theatrical Supply is kind of like Halloween USA, but with fewer severed feet. They've got the monster masks and the fake blood, but they specialize in period costumes, novelty disguises, dancewear, and sexy outfits. Apparently, there's big money in false mustaches and chain bikinis; Star Costume's security system—with its two extra-giant flat-screen TVs displaying 16 different security-camera shots—rivals that of a small casino.

Clay Miller started working at Star Costume right out of high school. He worked the cash register, he sold, he restocked, and he stayed with the store for 14 years. Now he's the manager.

"These days," Miller told me, "we do our biggest business with out-of-towners—conventions, weddings, that sort of thing. Earlier this month, we did a Greek wedding where we rented out seventy-five Elvi and thirty-five Marilyns. We had them email their sizes over from Greece so the costumes were ready when they got here. We always get the sizes in writing."

"Why's that?"

"People lie about their sizes."

"So you had seventy-five Elvis costumes lying around, ready to go?"

"Actually, we've got one-hundred-twenty-five. They're really popular with Asians."

Miller walked me around the store. He showed me the gold boots favored by our city's go-go dancers and the Kryolan TV Paint Sticks popular with our city's female impersonators.

"The sticks are thicker than regular makeup," Miller explained, "so they hide stub-

ble and other imperfections. The cast of *Divas* is in here all the time; Derrick Barry, the Britney impersonator, is in here all the time. [Female impersonators] probably buy a third of our makeup."

"Who else comes in the store?" I asked.

"Actually, the FBI was just in here. They weren't buying costumes or anything; they were telling us that because the economy is so bad right now, a lot of people are robbing banks, so we should be on the lookout for people coming in, asking about our wigs and moustaches, acting strange. We're supposed to take down their license plate numbers and give 'em over."

The FBI isn't being overly paranoid. In April in Ohio, 30-year-old, white male Conrad Zdzierak allegedly used an incredibly realistic African American mask, manufactured by SPFX, to rob four banks in one day.

Ironically, one of the few sectors not affected by the sagging economy is the Halloween industry. It's up 50 percent over the past four years. Americans now spend $6 billion every Halloween.

Moving from economy to erogeneity, I asked Miller about the sexy Halloween costumes.

"Vegas is a party town, and Halloween is a party holiday," he said. "Halloween is all about sex, and in my experience, anything sexy will move."

I wondered whether Miller was exaggerating. Could he actually move a sexy garbage man costume? Sexy Janet Napolitano? Sexy Alan Greenspan? He probably could and charge a lot for them, too. These days, even a skimpy costume can run you a fortune.

Let's say you want to be a sexy schoolgirl for Halloween. And let's say you want to get your costume from the Los Angeles-based Trashy Lingerie. Well, Trashy Lingerie's "Reform School Waist Trainer" will run you $250, their "Reform School Pleated Skirt" costs another $150, and the suggested accompanying "Nicole Bra" will set you back another $70. The "Reform School Collar"? That's $35. Pair that getup with a pair of sexy shoes and stockings, and you're looking at a $600 price tag.

Of course, you get to keep the costume when you're through. By comparison, some folks go to Star Costume and spend $500 on a rental.

Clay Miller walked me beyond the mask wall, through the curtains and into the rental area. I'd never seen so many hangers in one room. You could take a Nordstrom salesman, a dry-cleaner owner, and a hanger manufacturer into the back of Star Costumes, and they'd all walk away saying, "Whoa, this guy's got a lot of hangers back here!"

In this hypothetical, "this guy" is Bob Love, Star's rental inventory manager. When I met him, he was ironing his way through a heaping pile of blue ruffled shirts. Judging by the size of the heap, I sensed he'd be ironing long after I left.

"I don't add an item to my inventory unless it can be used at least three different ways," Love told me. "Like these shirts here. They can be used for seventies costumes, for Victorian-era costumes, for eighteenth-century costumes (if you turn the collar up and press the collar points down), and for *Dumb & Dumber* tuxedoes."

"I want to know about the expensive stuff," I said.

"Two years ago, Marc [Salls], the owner, bought five extremely expensive costumes—they cost thousands of dollars apiece, five-hundred to rent for a weekend. You don't come across too many people who want to spend that much for a costume rental, but here in Vegas, you do. We've already rented them out a few times."

"Who rents them?"

"High rollers, guys who go to the Playboy Mansion, guys who throw high-end costume parties. There's this bar owner in town, a young man, who rents from us all the time. He rented out some our most expensive pieces: our Genghis Khan, our Black Warrior, our Elven Knight, our Attila. Now, I respect him because he's as picky as I am, and he's very specific about what he wants. But he's kind of a narcissist; he likes perfection. Guys like that go for the elaborate costumes. They come in here every Halloween."

I left Love to his pile and Miller to his mustaches, and asked UNLV sociology professor Michael Borer to analyze what I'd heard at the shop. First, I inquired about guys who put so much time and effort into their costumes.

"Even though costume parties are supposed to be fun," Borer said, "they can also lead to stress for the more competitive types. While costume parties can be opportunities to 'try on' different identities and forget about one's social status, the status of costumes—their presentation, their construction—can become part of an emergent status hierarchy. Temporary, yes, but real."

Next I asked Borer about the girls—the million-dollar question: Why do women, especially those hitting the Las Vegas Strip, wear such sexy costumes on Halloween?

"Like I said, traditionally, Halloween functions as a ritual of reversal. These practices were used to relax the 'normal' power structures during the ritual event, where paupers would act like kings and vice versa. But today, the 'normal' rules of behavior and codes of conduct are softened, allowing people the freedom to play with their public presentations and performances of self. 'Dressing up' as something they're not—whether it's a zombie, a pirate, or even a prostitute—gives you a chance to express a part of yourself that isn't normally appropriate or acceptable."

Women tend to opt for slutty costumes on Halloween, in other words, because they can. Sure, they might have to put up with a judgmental Facebook status update or two, but they won't be branded a slut for life. (Speaking of which, I just had the best idea for a postmodern Halloween costume: sexy Hester Prynne [the woman from *The Scarlet Letter*]. Now there's a costume Clay Miller could move!)

I ran Borer's theory by my roommate, an expert on skimpy costumes as of last Halloween, when she wore the skimpiest costume I've ever seen. Really, if you crumpled this thing up, it would fit into one of those colored plastic eggs that come out of gumball machines. Technically, it was a sexy nurse outfit, but practically, it was a series of interconnected red and white bandages.

"It started out as a box lingerie thing I got from the Halloween store," she explained, "but I added a belt, stripper shoes, white stockings and then anklets and earrings, which I made myself."

"Why'd you put so much effort into it?" I asked.

"I was going to the Beaux Arts Ball, and I knew that everyone else was going to put a lot of effort into their costume, so I didn't want to let everyone down and look lame."

"And why'd you go for something so skimpy?"

"I was actually trying to make fun of all the girls who think that Halloween is about dressing slutty. I was trying to take the piss out of them by dressing extra-extra-slutty. But in retrospect, I don't think anybody got the joke. Most people just stared."

After talking with my roommate, Prof. Borer, Bob Love, and Clay Miller, I've realized that there is no one reason many girls dress slutty on Halloween. And there is no one reason certain people put so much time and energy into their costumes. Some do it as self-expression, others do it because it's expected of them, others do it for social status, and some, apparently, do it as satire.

So, Facebook friends, remember: This Halloween, if you see a girl wearing a pleated, nine-inch, plaid skirt, a midriff-baring T-shirt, thigh-high boots, and pigtails, remember: She might be making the exact same social critique you plan to make the following day. She's just doing it in her own way.

It's Not Us; It's Them:
The Moral History of
America, Starring Sin City

I'm not sure whether this strip club, just north of the Stratosphere, has a name. The marquee outside says, "STRIPPERS" and "NUDE DAILY," but there's nothing approaching a proper noun.

Below the marquee, in the middle of the parking lot, are two grotesque mannequins. The first one—the one that's crying and yelling at the same time—is wearing a Marilyn Monroe dress and wig. She's standing on a low-power fan, which is kicking up the tiniest corner of her dress. Like a flopping fish. It's the second least-sexy thing I've ever seen.

The #1 least-sexy thing I've ever seen is the other mannequin—the one wearing the plaid schoolgirl skirt and riding the creaky mechanical bull. Well, technically she isn't riding it so much as she's tied to it with a rope. On the bull's unmanned control panel is a bumper sticker: "FUCK ALL Y'ALL," it reads.

I walk past this torture-porn nativity scene and through an equally depressing tiny sex shop. The condoms are cheap, the lube is cheap, and the bargain-bin VHS cassettes are going for $2. They might be Betamax, actually—those cases are huge. I try to stay away from hypotheticals, but I'll allow myself this one time: If a sex shop could get away with selling used sex toys, this place would do it.

The older shop worker is bragging to the younger one about how he just 86'd some black guy from the strip club in back—he mentioned the man's race several times—for getting fresh with one of the girls.

And then, all too soon, I'm at the club's entrance.

I'm not alone, by the way. I'm with my friend Valerie. She's a stripper, and it's her off-night, and I've somehow convinced her to join me.

This strip club is different from most in that it's a "nude" club. What's the difference between regular strip clubs and a nude club? Well, vaginas. At most clubs, the dancers have to keep 'em covered. Here, they show 'em. Technically, dancers don't *have* to show their vaginas, but the patrons expect it of them—that's why men patronize all-nude clubs in the first place. So if the dancers don't bare it all, they're prudes by default.

Most strip clubs don't go all-nude because once they do, they can no longer serve alcohol—let's call that *Law A*. But because all-nude clubs can't serve alcohol, what they *can* do is hire 18-to-21-year-old dancers. (Regular Vegas strip clubs are 21 and older,

for patrons and workers.) Let's call that *Law B.* As a result, most of the girls who work the all-nude clubs are under 21. As soon as they hit 21, they move to a 'regular' clubs because that's where the money is.

Now let me connect the dots, if you haven't already connected them yourself. The practical effect of *Laws A* and *B* is that in Las Vegas, *only* teenage strippers have to show their vaginas.

Way to go, legislators. Way to think that one through. You've done your churches proud.

Back to the nameless club. I actually thought about backing out at the last minute. I'm not a prude; I'm just con-

cerned about desensitization. I don't want naked women to become commonplace for me. The next time I'm having an intimate evening, I don't want to think to myself, *Hey, this is just like that one time at the HoochHut!* (My apology; fictitious strip clubs names are the lowest form of comedy.) Like standup comedian Mitch Hedberg, I don't want to taint my life's romantic experiences.

Oh, here's the pertinent Mitch Hedberg joke:

> Some songs have a special meaning for a man, in regards to a special woman. But this can backfire because maybe the song had a deeper meaning to begin with, but now it's been cheapened: *"We are the world. We are the children. We are the one's who make a better life, so let's keep on giving."* Remember that song from the night I fucked you in the pet cemetery?

I share my concern with Valerie, and she tells me I'll be fine. She says a single visit to an all-nude strip club won't ruin me for life. And she turns out to be right, for an unexpected reason: There are no strippers in the club. Two patrons, zero strippers. I mean, there's a girl in the entrance hallway, wearing shorts and a tank top—possibly the girl the sex shop worker was referring to?—but she isn't actually in the club or dancing or naked, so I'm not counting her.

The place looks like a conference room that was turned into a strip club overnight. It's the opposite of *La Cage aux Folles. Quick! The writer is coming! We have to make this place look like a sleazy dance hall!*

In the club's defense, it's Monday night, 6 p.m. That's hardly primetime for small strip clubs. So Valerie and I walk across the street, to another club. A bigger, topless club (i.e., no vaginas). There are 10 people in this one, including two dancers and two waitresses. We take a booth six or seven yards from soccer mom-type giving a lap dance to a guy with long hair.

"She'll make twenty bucks from him," Valerie says, "but she had to pay a hundred to work here tonight, and she's got to tip out her manager and the deejay. So at this point, she's in the red."

Valerie used to work at this place.

"Only one shift, though. I had to be my own security here. At most places, when you're giving a guy a lap dance and he touches you, security will step in and stop him. But here, I had to do it myself. And when you do that, the customers start calling you a bitch."

"How often does that happen?" I ask.

"The touching? All the time, especially in Vegas, because here, everyone feels anonymous. When guys are from out of town, tourists, they're not worried about running into people they know, so they act like assholes."

Valerie sees asshole behavior on a nightly basis, and patterns emerge from it.

"I start with a guy who's about to get married, about to make the biggest commitment of his life, and he claims that he would never cheat, and when I'm done with him, he's begging to cheat. He's begging me to go home with him."

"How often does that happen?"

"More often than not. Eighty-some percent of the time. If there's enough conversation. Even the guilty guys go for it. They start out saying, 'I shouldn't be doing this, but I love it'—that sort of thing. They're married or they're in a relationship, but by the end, they want to take me to their rooms. The taken guys are actually the most desperate sex beggars."

Okay. Let's stop here and run a thought-experiment. Let's imagine that Valerie went on a cable news show and said what she just told to me. Let's say the topic of discussion was "Moral Decay in America," and let's say she was paired up with an older, right-wing talking head. How would he reply?

I'll tell how he'd reply—It's easy to put words into the mouths of imaginary people! He'd say, "If you look the way you do, and wear what you wear, and if you throw yourself at a man (figuratively and literally), and if you start rubbing up against him and do … whatever it is you do"—In this hypothetical, the old right-wing guy is pretending that he doesn't know what goes on at a strip club. Cute, huh?—"then *of course* the man is going to want to sleep with you. You've sexually entrapped him!"

Imaginary Right-Wing Guy's argument is true, but it's also distracting from the bigger point, and the bigger point is this: *Men visit Vegas strip clubs.* The supply isn't the 'problem'; the demand is.

Las Vegas isn't the disease, it's a symptom.

I watch a lot of cable news shows, so I'm familiar with the moral history of America. In case you don't and you aren't, allow me to enlighten you:

Jesus gave George Washington the Constitution in 1776, and for the next century or two, good Christian men spent their days farming, building cars, and staying faithful to their wives. But then, in the 1960s, everything changed. The country split in two: the heartland and the coasts. The heartland stayed on track, but the coasts—Massachusetts, New York, San Francisco, Los Angeles—strayed far from God's original vision of America. And nowhere is this moral divergence more apparent than in Las Vegas.

Next, let's hear the non-satire version of that argument, made on the "Wake Up America, Inc" website:

"America is incrementally and systematically Rejecting God. As a result, our nation is experiencing unparalleled moral decay. National immorality flourishes when the hearts of a nation's citizens reject God and His principles. Simply stated, Spiritual decline leads to moral decay!"

Next, let's address the argument. Specifically, let's address the assumption that America was a moral country in the first place. Old people are constantly telling me about "the good 'ol days." You know, that time when men were men (does that mean not gay?), and deals were done by handshake, and you could leave your front door unlocked.

Jesus gave George Washington the Constitution in 1776, and for the next century or two, good Christian men spent their days farming, building cars, and staying faithful to their wives. But then, in the 1960s, everything changed.

The old people who tell me about this magical time are always white, by the way.

Now here's the real moral history of our country: First we had slavery, then emancipation and de jure racism, then Jim Crow laws, and then de facto racism, and now we have, well, whatever it is we have now. (Things aren't perfect, but after we elected a black president, it's hard to argue we're not at least moving in the right direction.)

I focus on the racial component of America's moral history not only because it's hugely important, but because I want to discuss civil rights novelist James Baldwin. Just as Valerie has a unique view of America's moral landscape, Baldwin had a unique view. He wrote about it, too, in his book *The Fire Next Time*. It came out in 1963, exactly 100 years after the Emancipation Proclamation.

"White people in this country," Baldwin wrote, "will have quite enough to do in learning how to accept and love themselves and each other, and when they have achieved this—which will not be tomorrow and may very well be never—the Negro problem will no longer exist, for it will no longer be needed."

It's the same argument I made 400 words back—the one about how Vegas isn't the disease, but the symptom. Baldwin saw racism as a symptom of white people's internal problems. He believed that once white people became more accepting of each other, they wouldn't have so many problems, and they therefore wouldn't need to use black people as scapegoats. Similarly, if you're in a good marriage, you're not going to be visiting strip clubs. Not because your wife forbids it, but *because you don't want to.*

And back to Baldwin:

"Negro servants have been smuggling odds and ends out of white homes for generations, and white people have been delighted to have them do it, because it has assuaged a dim guilt and testified to the intrinsic superiority of white people."

The analogy continues: When Vegas newspapers reported that Paris Hilton got arrested for cocaine possession at the Wynn, that Bruno Mars got arrested for cocaine possession at Hard Rock, that Vince Neil got arrested for drunk driving near the Strip—three examples among many—the rest of the country smiled. Stories like that reaffirm Vegas' negative stereotypes, and people like seeing their stereotypes reaffirmed. (On that note, those who believe all lawyers are two-faced will be thrilled to hear that Clark County District Attorney David Schubert, who prosecuted Bruno Mars and Paris Hilton for cocaine possession, was recently arrested for cocaine possession.)

Now, here's where the analogy gets deep. Baldwin wrote, "I have seen and heard and endured the secrets of desperate white men and women, which they knew were safe with me, because even if I should speak, no one would believe me. And they would not believe me precisely because they would know that what I said was true."

Similarly, married men share their darkest desires with Valerie, and they do it with confidence that if she were to ever repeat what they'd said, no one would believe her. After all, to believe a stripper is to acknowledge that at the end of the day, all men are animals, and most people can't handle that.

Let's end the analogy here. Baldwin wrote, "[I]t can almost be said, in fact, that [black people] know about white Americans what parents—or, anyway, mothers—know about their children."

Las Vegans know more about the heartland than the heartland knows about itself. Because we see heartlanders at their drunkest, their horniest, and their weakest.

It ain't pretty.

"Sin City" is an organically developed marketing strategy—one that we can't even take credit for. We're not the only city to promote ourselves with booze, sex, gambling, and drugs. And we're definitely not the first. Bangkok, Macau, Ibiza, Berlin, Shanghai, Amsterdam, Rio de Janeiro, New York, Chicago, New Orleans— we're all in the same boat.

Sometimes, when tourists visit Las Vegas, and when they sin, they feel self-conscious about it. And that hurts our bottom line. (The more self-conscious tourists feel, the less they drink/gamble/spend. So we encourage them to sin by acting like we're all sinners ourselves. We play dance music 24/7 and we join them for a shot, as if none of us have kids or mortgages.

"Sin City" is an organically developed marketing strategy—one that we can't even take credit for. We're not the only city to promote ourselves with booze, sex, gambling, and drugs. And we're definitely not the first. Bangkok, Macau, Ibiza, Berlin, Shanghai, Amsterdam, Rio de Janeiro, New York, Chicago, New Orleans—we're all in the same boat.

The concept of a sinful city goes all the way back to the Bible. But there's a fundamental difference between Sodom and Gomorrah, and Las Vegas: *We're a tourist town.* We don't do the sinning ourselves; our visitors do.

We also can't take credit for being the first ones to spin perceived moral decay into a selling point. Credit goes to the *fin de siècle* artists (French artists painting at the end of the 19th century), who were called "decadents" by their critics (who saw a moral decline in the artists' work, compared to those of the Romantics), but then co-opted the title for themselves, the same way the Fauvists and the Cubists did. (Art Critics: Stop thinking up names for the artists you hate! It's going to backfire!) And once the *fin de siècle* artists acknowledged their moral decadence, they became harder to criticize.

Similarly, once our mayor started moonlighting as a Bombay Sapphire Gin spokesman and Playboy photographer, the heartland eased up on us. *You think calling us* *"perverts" and "drunkards" is going to hurt our feelings? We picked a pornographer/booze pitchman to **lead** us.*

Oh, who am I kidding: Heartlanders only eased up on us because they've got bigger fish to fry. Namely, men having sex with each other. By comparison, our heterosexual debauchery is like a Disney movie. (Maybe we should run with this. Maybe the Las Vegas Convention and Visitors Authority should advertise our city with, "Vegas: A century-long track record of by-the-book heterosexuality" or, "Vegas: Hey, at least we're not having butt sex here."

And if that won't work, I have a backup plan. A plan for what we can do about our reputation as a morally decayed city: *Nothing*. I know the truth, and Valerie knows the truth, and you know the truth—that it's *the rest* of America that's so messed up—but our city's reputation puts food on our tables, so let's all take a page from Godfather Liberace's playbook and cry our way to the bank.

Love and the City

If you're a female between the ages of 21 and 40, and if you meet me at a bar, and if you ask me what I do for a living, and if I describe my job to you, you're going to reply, "Oh, so you're like a male Carrie Bradshaw!"

Essentially, you'll be right.

The *Sex and the City* writers got so much right in the Carrie Bradshaw character: The incessant questioning, the charmless analysis, the tricky life/work intersection management—they nailed it.[31]

Unlike Carrie, I don't write many relationship stories. But I do write about the search for love. Las Vegas is the perfect place to do it. After all, if you can find love here, you can find it anywhere.

---

[31] Except for Carrie's financial situation. Carrie writes a single weekly column for *The New York Star*, yet somehow has enough money to 1) live at an upper-Eastside brownstone,* 2) eat and drink at trendy Manhattan restaurants *every single day*—we're talking lunch and dinner, people, and 3) wear the most expensive clothing on earth.

*Okay, the Internet tells me that Carrie's apartment was rent-controlled. But apparently this wasn't addressed until far into the series.

Lovehunting

My friend Kelly says that Las Vegas is a bad city for dating. But my friend Rachel says the same thing about New York, and Sylvia says the same thing about Chicago, and Hanna says the same thing about Los Angeles. So maybe the city isn't the problem.

"The city *is* the problem," Kelly insists. "The standard of beauty here is impossibly high, and I feel like I can't compete with it."

"You're the one setting the standard," I reminded her.

Kelly, you see, is a *Jubilee!* showgirl, and she's very pretty. But you wouldn't know it from the things she says.

"It doesn't feel like I'm setting the standard. All I know is, the guys here in Vegas treat me noticeably different from the way the guys treated me back in Omaha. In Omaha, I was a catch. Even in New York, when I'd walk down the street, I'd get catcalls and that sort of thing. But that doesn't happen here."

Kelly told me this at Starbucks. I'd invited her there, along with our mutual friend Sheena (another *Jubilee!* showgirl) to discuss the dating scene in Las Vegas. Here's what Sheena had to say:

"It feels like a lot of the guys I meet moved to Vegas for money or for sex. Vegas is so consumed by those things. And when you move here looking for that stuff, you're not in the right mindset to have a committed relationship."

You can't refute the truth of the premise on which Kelly and Sheena's arguments rely. Las Vegas does have a high standard of beauty,[32] and the city is fixated on sex.[33] But does a sexual fixation really impede a committed relationship? A month back, I wasn't so sure. But I was sure of where I could look to find out.

On January 9, I attended the Adult Video News awards—the porn Oscars. My thinking: If I can find one instance of true, committed, romantic love at a ceremony that glorifies the glorification of casual sex and its glorifiers, then there's hope for the rest of us. In other words, I was looking for the exception that disproved the rule that sexual preoccupation impedes committed, loving relationships.

Twenty minutes before the awards began, I entered the Pearl Theater at the Palms, and propped myself against the wall by the downstairs bar. I saw a small, blond woman in a small, royal-blue dress get off the elevator, and then I saw a giant guy intercept her with his giant right arm.

"Fuck, you look hot tonight," he said, as he put his left hand on the small of her back.

"Gross!" she said as she threw his hand off her body and walked away. The guy turned to his friend and said, "Bitch never remembers me. We fucked in two movies two years ago, and I was always so nice to her."

I took my seat in the balcony, among patrons who'd paid $300 to attend. I watched porn star Erik Everhard (get it?!?) present Sasha Grey with the award for Best Oral

---

[32] Las Vegas attracts a disproportionately large number of attractive females from all across the country. It's no secret: If you're female and you're pretty, you can make a lot of money here. When it comes to separating tourists from their money, promotional models, Pleasure Pit dealers, and bottle-service girls are our front-line warriors. And even if you don't patronize the businesses at which these women work, you still cross their paths at the gym, the grocery store, the mall, and the dog park, so they still play into your standard of beauty.

[33] For business purposes, of course. I appreciate that the vast majority of the women who work as convention models, burlesque performers, and strippers aren't actually looking for an endless string of casual sex partners*, but for business purposes, they have to act as if they are. And remember, men across the country see only the projection (through TV shows, movies, Vegas vacations), and they move to Vegas hoping to get in on the (largely nonexistent) action.

*One of my good friends, a stripper, identifies as asexual.

Sex for her work in *Throat: A Cautionary Tale*. Grey, 21, has been the toast of the San Fernando Valley ever since she scored the leading role in Steven Soderbergh's *The Girlfriend Experience.* She's the closest thing to Sally Field the world of porn has, so the bar for her acceptance speech was set pretty high.

And here was her speech:

"Can somebody out there please remind me which guy was in this film with me?"

The only evidence I saw of a committed relationship in the world of porn came from the acceptance speech of the guy who won "Best Ethnic-Themed Series—Black." He said, "I want to thank my wife for allowing me to make porno and then come home without getting in trouble."

Thanking your wife for not punishing you after you sleep around isn't exactly Danielle Steel material, but it's moving in the right direction. Then again, when Sheena talked about a "committed" relationship, she presumably meant an exclusive one.

As I understand it, the general sentiment in the psychology community is that open relationships don't work because one partner will inevitably find somebody who he/she prefers to his/her initial partner. And even though this preference might be temporary, its effects are not.

But maybe the psychologists have it wrong. Maybe it is possible to stay in a committed, open relationship. After all, there is one porn star who, in recent years, has grown famous for having a solid, loving marriage, despite being in the industry: Tera Patrick.

So I knew that before I came to any conclusion, I'd have to hear what Patrick had to say.

Tera Patrick's book, *Sinner Takes All: A Memoir of Love and Porn*, tells the story of how she and *Oz* actor Evan Seinfeld met, married and managed to survive, despite her involvement in the industry. According to the book jacket, *Sinner Takes All* reveals "how love and marriage fit into the triple-X world."

Writes Patrick, "I really did know that Evan would be my husband on that first night together. I never believed in that until it happened to me. With Evan, I just knew it."

Writes Patrick, "Nobody believed in us in the beginning, but that only made our bond even stronger. It felt like Evan and me against the world, and I liked that."

Writes Patrick, "[Evan was] the one solid thing I could always count on for all my needs."

So I read all that, and then I read the book's afterword, which goes like this:

"Over the course of putting together this book over the past year, a lot has changed. And the biggest change is that I am no longer with Evan … He was looking for his entry into porn and he got it through me. So, yeah, I do feel used to some extent … "

So maybe the psychologists have it right, after all.

Patrick, who was in town for the Adult Entertainment Expo—the porn convention—came to Borders bookstore at Town Square for a book signing. After the event was through, I met her for an interview in the back office. She introduced me to her mom, and then to her sister, and to her friend. Then she said she was ready to start the interview.

"In here?" I said. "In front of your whole family?"

"Sure. Why not?" Patrick asked

Uh, because I plan to ask you, among other things, about the time Erik Everhard tore your vagina. And even if you feel comfortable discussing this in front of your mom, I don't.

"Can we just go to the next room?" I said.

We walked to the kitchen and sat across from each other. I jumped right into the topic of *Island Fever 2*. In *Sinner Takes All*, Patrick describes the filming: "I was in cowgirl position on top of [Everhard], and all of a sudden something in him snapped. He started fucking me violently, so hard that I bled everywhere. He actually tore my vagina. It was embarrassing and violating … he was pounding the shit out of me and it hurt. I was so tired of working at this point that I just shut off my emotions, turned that 'switch' on, and went through with my job."

"Tell me about the switch," I said.

"I learned early on how to turn on and off my sexual side," Patrick replied. "For me it comes from early traumatic sexual experience. But I think all women have this inside of them. When women say, 'How do I be sexy?' I tell them, 'It's inside of you.'"

"So you're saying 'the switch' is something you turn *on*? That you're turning *on* your sexual side? Because in the book it sounded like you were turning something *off*. It sounded like you were turning your emotions off … "

"The two are connected," Patrick explained. "I turn my personal emotions off and my professional mind-set on."

"And you can flip the switch at any time?"

"Right."

"So you were torn, you were bleeding, you were in pain, you felt violated … but you could still flip the switch?"

"Right."

I suspect Patrick believes that her experiences during sex are just as intense of those of everyone else (until she flips the switch). But to me, Patrick's ability to flip the switch suggests that her emotional experiences during intercourse are not as intense as those of most people. I don't see how any emotionally healthy person could flip off his or her emotions in a situation like that.

Anyway, if you're still keeping score, my chat with Patrick and my observations at the AVN awards both confirmed the hypothesis that sexual fixation impedes committed relationships.

But if that's true, and if Las Vegas is so fixated on sex, then how do any local couples make it longer than a week? After all, a lot of couples do. Some even marry—and what's more, they do it in non-drive-thru/non-Elvis chapels. White gown and all.

So how do these women in white transcend the lust?

Well, they don't.

♥ ♥ ♥

Men: The Bridal Expo at Mandalay Bay is a great place to pick up women—way better than the porn convention. Think about it: 90 percent of those in attendance at the porn convention are male, and 90 percent of those in attendance at the Bridal Expo are women.[34] And not all of the women are brides.[35] Many are jealous/available/vulnerable sisters and girlfriends, in desperate need of your companionship.

Women: When it comes to convention lust, you're just as guilty as we are. The Bridal Expo is kind of the like the porn convention, but for women. The women walk around from booth to booth, lusting after what they see. They don't

---

[34] A similar line of reasoning should tell you that Coyote Ugly and Hawaiian Tropic Zone are terrible bars to meet girls. Any place that culls patrons using beautiful women is going to attract mostly guys.

[35] I know this because the brides were all wearing red-and-white stickers that say "BRIDE" on them.

lust after people, they lust after wedding objects. Winged bridal gowns, opulent three-tier cakes, Bellagio-caliber floral arrangements. They lust after the perfect wedding.

That last line is more than liberal linguistics; it's really important. Obsessing about your wedding is like buying a puppy because you like puppies. Just as the puppy will grow into a full dog faster than you can say, "Mr. Popsicles shat on the bed," weddings become marriages faster than you can say, "If you wanted to remodel the den, then maybe you should have thought twice before you ordered those gold-leaf panda-skin wedding invitations!" And just as the dogs are around for a lot longer than puppies, marriages last a lot longer than weddings. And you can't drop a marriage off at the front door of a shelter in the middle of the night.

Easy for me to say, right? I'm a guy, after all, and weddings are marketed to women.[36] But I've got an expert—albeit a male expert—to back me up:

Dr. Paul Dobransky wrote the book *The Secret Psychology of How We Fall in Love*, and he runs the website WomensHappiness.com. I interviewed him over the phone, and here's what he had to say about what I'd witnessed at the Bridal Expo:

"There's a lot of talk about the objectification of women, but men get objectified, too. And you might have seen that in play at the Expo. One way to objectify a man is to see him as a placeholder in marriage. For some women, marriage can become an acquisition, rather than an honorable joining of individuals. The perfect wedding with

---

[36] Even the items at the Wedding Expo that were ostensibly marketed towards grooms were actually marketed towards brides, as groom pacifiers. Case in point: Gimme Some Sugar Cake Design's "Groom's Cakes"* (i.e., "This way, I can get the cake I want, and you can have a separate cake in the shape of a football for you and your friends.").

*According to the very exciting Gimme Some Sugar brochure, the Groom's Cake is "An old tradition that has become a hot new trend! The bride has the glamorous cake she's been dreaming of, and the groom gets his own personalized cake beside it! Also known as compromise!" Can somebody get the Gimme Some Sugar brochure some lithium?

the perfect cake and the perfect dress can become the end goal."

"So might that be more problematic than the objectification of women—like when a guy watches too much porn?"

"They're both problematic. Yeah, watching too much porn can make a relationship difficult, too. For a relationship to work, you need attraction, and then friendship, and then commitment—those three things. But if a guy is immersed in porn, he'll have trouble making it to that second stage, let alone the third."

Dr. Paul seemed to be supporting Sheena's theory, and before we were through, he also supported Kelly's—the one about Vegas' high standard of female beauty impeding romance:

"Las Vegas glorifies the female body. The stage shows, the burlesque shows—they set expectations very high. A big sector of the Vegas economy involves promoting this ideal, the perfect woman with the perfect female body, and that ideal is impossible for any person to measure up to."

That explains why Kelly feels like she can't compete in Vegas: She's not actually competing against the other women in the city; she's competing against the ideal that they (and she) promote.

So basically, all is hopeless.

Sorry to be such a downer, but all my anecdotal observations—from the AVNs to Patrick, from the bridal expo to my chat with Dr. Paul—only confirm Kelly and Sheena's initial assertion: that Vegas is a bad city for dating.

Okay, I guess *all* isn't hopeless. There are 10 words that make the situation a tiny bit less depressing—10 words that not even Kelly and Sheena can deny. So if you've got nothing else to do, why not take five minutes and repeat them as a mantra? Dr. Paul shared them with me at the end of our interview, and I'll pass them on to you now:

"Despite all that, you've got to remember, it only takes one."

I'm So Excited. I'm So Sad

Foreword: This story is a downer. You should probably skip it. The accompanying picture is pretty, and the subject matter is exciting, but I promise you the excitement ends there. The text is quite depressing.

Think about it like this: If I were your friend, and I came to you and said, "I'm really depressed, and I want to talk about it," you'd be socially obliged to hear me out. But you and I aren't friends, so you've got no obligation here. Moreover, I have no way of knowing whether you actually read this story, so by going through it, you're not doing me any favors.

Walking from the Venetian parking garage to the Sands Expo & Convention Center, I passed dozens of distinguished-looking reporters in expensive-looking suits. Their hair was coiffed and their shoes were shined. They were surrounded by men holding top-of-the-line video cameras. These guys were pros.

Of course, they weren't going to the Adult Entertainment Expo porn convention, like I was; they were boarding shuttle buses and heading to the Consumer Electronics Show at the Las Vegas Convention Center.

The reporters in the AEE pressroom, by comparison, wore rumpled T-shirts and tattered jeans. On the plus side, standing next to the guys who run TheHermaphro Blog.com and *Taint Monthly*—I assume these things exist—I felt like Brian Williams.

But the saddest thing about my AEE assignment was that it wasn't an "assignment" at all. The story wasn't "handed to me," and I wasn't "stuck with it." I had asked for it. If my editor had said no, I would have begged.

Is it just me, or has Larry Flynt gotten lazy about thinking up pornographic parody titles? At this year's AEE convention, Hustler was promoting both *Not Married With Children*, and *This Ain't Saved by the Bell*. What's next? *This Film is Not the Major Motion Picture Titled Avatar—Rather, It is a Pornographic Parody of That Film*? I always figured the main reason porn studios made so many parodies was that they're so much fun to title.

Still, a "Saved by the Bell" parody is a "Saved by the Bell" parody, and I respect anybody who makes one. I said as much to her, the girl who played the porn version of "Saved by the Bell" character Jessie Spano. I found her walking around the Hustler booth in a neon-pink dress and dark-blue Uggs.

"Did you watch 'Saved by the Bell' as a kid?" I asked.

"Religiously!" she replied.

I can't tell you how happy her answer made me. I'm somewhat embarrassed about how much "Saved by the Bell" I watched … but standing right across from me was a girl who proudly declared that she'd watched the same amount.

"What was your favorite episode?" I asked.

"The one where Jessie takes the pill and goes crazy," she said.

Red flag.

For those of you not familiar with "Saved by the Bell", the "pill" to which she was referring was not birth control; it was a caffeine pill that Jessie took to help her study. Because the episode "Jessie's Song" contained the melodramatic line, "I'm so excited! I'm so excited! I'm so … scared!," it's become the most popular and most quoted "SBTB" episode. So saying that you're a fan of "SBTB" and that "Jessie's Song" is your favorite episode is kind of like saying that you love Billy Joel and that your favorite song is "Piano Man." It's suspicious.

"What's your second-favorite episode?" I asked.

"It's hard to pick an episode," she said, "They were all so good."

"You already picked the one. I'm just asking for a second."

"It's so hard to choose from all of them. I mean, they were all so good."

"Okay, what are your top five?"

"I like all the ones where Zack gets in trouble."

To continue the earlier analogy, saying that your favorite "SBTB" episodes

---

**The attraction is a one-way street. The starlets
all have stock lines about how great their fans are,
but the starlets aren't sexually attracted to their fans.
Not even close.**

---

are the ones where Zack gets in trouble is kind of like saying that your favorite Billy Joel songs are the ones where he plays the piano and sings.

She wasn't the "Saved by the Bell" fan she claimed to be. Like a B-list actress starring in a comic-book adaptation, she was just another hot girl claiming to be dorky to attract fans.

And she did have fans. Hundreds and hundreds of them. They stood in line to get her autograph and snap her picture. Many of these guys flew across the country and paid hundreds of dollars to do precisely this. They really, really like her. And Kayden, and Sasha, and Bree, and Jesse.

Now, this both goes without saying and bears repeating: The attraction is a one-way street. The starlets all have stock lines about how great their fans are, but the starlets aren't sexually attracted to their fans. Not even close.

And that's why I felt so depressed at the AEE convention. Standing around men who were willing to go to such great lengths to have such fleeting interactions with women brought me back to high school. It made me think about all the girls I had strong feelings for—the ones who barely knew I existed—and about how much effort I was willing to exert to fashion the most insignificant interactions with them.

But you've changed, I told myself. *You're not in line with these guys. You're here on an assignment. You've got a press badge that says so!*

I kept telling myself that, that I'd changed, again and again and again, and it made me feel better … until I saw this starlet at the Digital Playground booth and instantly fell in love with her. She was young and pretty and pale, and she didn't look like a porn star; she looked like somebody I might meet at XS. Nonetheless, she was a professional pornographic actress, and if I wanted to talk with her, I'd have to wait in line like everyone else.

So I got in line.

Maybe things haven't changed, after all.

I came to my senses, got out of line, and got ready to leave the convention. But before I walked out, I came across a woman who looked even sadder than me. She also (if informal Internet research serves) had the world's second-largest breasts. She was sitting by herself, behind a tiny foldout plastic table, peddling DVDs. But nobody was buying. Nobody wanted a picture or a signature. I wanted to walk up to the woman and give her a hug.

Obviously, logistics barred that.

The saddest part of the AEE isn't what happens at the convention; it's what's going to happen afterwards. It's what's going to happen when the attendees fly back home and start comparing the porn stars they just met to the real women in their lives. Suddenly the real women won't seem so attractive and so sexy.

Guys tell me they can "separate" strippers, call girls, and porn stars from the "real women" in their lives, but I bet most evolutionary psychologists would disagree. The human brain can't help but compare, and when men compare, the "real" women come up short. Not because porn stars are always more attractive than men's significant others, but because porn stars act exactly how men want them to act: provocative, interested, charmed, and aroused. They always act this way. It's their job.

But what's the alternative? You can avoid AEE, but you can't avoid desirable women altogether. And you can't force all attractive women to walk around in Snuggies all day (though certain cultures have tried variations of this plan). So either way you're screwed.

So to speak.

Afterword

Since writing the first draft of this piece, two encouraging developments have occurred:

1) I was able to talk my way into the Consumer Electronics Show.

2) I ran into the Digital Playground starlet at the Palms the following night, and we talked for 10 or 15 minutes. I didn't have to wait in line or anything. Just walked up to her and started talking. She seemed like a nice girl, and she's a local. And now we're Facebook friends.

Putting Aside the Pick Up

Do you think it's okay to break up with somebody over Facebook?

Before you form a response to that question, you should know that I don't care about your answer. In fact, the question isn't even a real "question"; it's an *opener*—an innocuous line that Pickup Artists use to begin conversations with beautiful women.[37] I learned Facebook Breakup from the LoveSystems Super-Conference held at the Hard Rock last month. Cost of attendance: $3,850.[38]

I know what you're thinking. You're thinking, *Any guy who would fly across the country and pay such a large sum of money to learn how to ask women scripted questions is a desperate loser at best, and a sex offender at worst.* You're thinking, *These guys shouldn't have to work so hard to meet women; it should come naturally; if these guys would just "be themselves" everything would fall into place.*

Here's the reason you're thinking that: You haven't been rejected as much as they've been rejected. You think you have, but you haven't. So I kindly ask that you wait until you've finished reading this article before you make fun of us—er, *them*. Make fun of *them*.

---

[37] Specifically, it's an opinion opener. Common opinion openers include, "Who lies more, men or women?" "Do you think spells work?" "Do you think David Bowie is hot?" "Did you see the two girls fighting outside?" "If you're dating a guy but kiss somebody else, is that cheating?" and "Do you floss before or after you brush?"

[38] $3,850 buys students a "Gold Level" pass, which includes "Infield Training" sessions in "Vegas VIP Clubs." For $950, though, students can purchase a "Silver Level" pass, which gets them into the daytime lecture rooms only.

I'm sitting in a gray banquet hall at the Hard Rock Hotel & Casino with 100 other guys. There's a projection screen set up at the front of the room, and it's playing a pre-taped episode of "The Tyra Banks Show." Tyra's guest is LoveSystems CEO Savoy,[39] the man who organized the Super-Conference at the Hard Rock. When Tyra says that some men pay Savoy "thousands of dollars … *thousands of dollars*" to learn how to pick up women, her audience gasps.

I find an open seat next to Michael from Australia. He's 36 and describes himself as a "PUA dinosaur." He's right; most the guys in the room appear to be in their mid-

---

[39] Every Pickup Artist has a "handle," a seduction nickname that reveals something about his character. Savoy's real name is Nick Benedict.

20s. They're mostly well-dressed, and largely good-looking. So based on appearances alone, you wouldn't guess that these guys had trouble attracting women. But, as any pickup artist worth his weight in feather boas would tell you, it's not about how you look; it's about how you make women feel.[40]

Oh, there are a lot of bald guys in the room, too. And there's a guy behind me with a handlebar mustache and a red-and-black bandana. And there's a guy to my left with at least one filled-in ear (it's got no hole). And then there's a long-haired guy in front of me who's got to be at least six-foot-five—that's Savoy.

My tablemate Michael looks around the room and offers me this assessment: "Some of these guys are incredibly insecure—can't even talk to girls—and some of them are James Bond. And some of them are in the middle."

"Where are you?" I ask.

"I'm in the middle. You?" Michael asks me.

"Hard to say," I reply. "Ever since I moved to Vegas, people tell me I'm Bond-y, but most of the time I feel like I'm still in middle school—insecure."

"I hear ya," Michael says. "I went through a long insecure phase. I was always the nice guy, the guy who helped his friends meet women. Basically, I was too scared to tell my girl—I mean, my friend who I wanted to be my girl—how I felt. And when I finally did tell her that I loved her, she told me that she didn't love me back."

"So she LJBF'd you?" I ask.[41]

"She did, and I swore on a thousand Bibles that it would never happen again."

Savoy takes the stage, welcomes everybody to the Super-Conference and emphasizes the importance of active participation: "There are beautiful women in this very casino. So use this stuff right away. One thing we're experts on, aside from picking up women, is how to learn. So listen to me when I say you should take lots of notes."

At that instant everybody in the room cracks open their LoveSystems folder (leath-

---

[40] The general PUA wisdom goes like this: Good looks a foot in the door, nothing more.

[41] LJBF stands for Let's Just Be Friends, and can be used as a verb. Now, the fact that I 1) know this acronym and 2) am able to use it correctly in casual conversation probably has you wondering whether I identify as a Pickup Artist. I do not.* Before writing this story, I'd never attended a Pickup Artist convention, and had never been active in a Pickup Artist lair. But, that said, I am friends with several guys who identify as Pickup Artists, I've read several books by Pickup Artists (including, though not limited to, *The Game: Penetrating the Secret Society of Pickup Artists*, by Neil Strauss; *Mystery Method: How To Get Beautiful Women Into Bed*, by Mystery; and *The Layguide: How to Seduce Women More Beautiful Than You Ever Dreamed Possible*, by Tony Clink), and I've put what I've learned to good use.

*I'm pretty sure I give off Pickup Artist vibes, though, because when LoveSystems sent its press release to everybody at the *Las Vegas Weekly* office, a couple of editors forwarded the emails to me two seconds later.

Admitting that you need help with women is embarrassing and emasculating. In most cases, the decision to attend a LoveSystems bootcamp is not motivated by libido; it's motivated by loneliness.

er, complimentary) for the first time and begins writing. Shortly thereafter, Savoy introduces to the stage the "Number-one-rated instructor from last year: Soul."

Soul, a soft-spoken, self-assured Sri Lankan guy, puts to words what's on everybody's mind:

"It's a scary thing, spending your weekend learning to meet women. It's humbling. We don't want to admit that we need help, but we're here because we've reached a point where our regret has built up and we said, 'No more!' So I know you're feeling nervous, and I know you're feeling weird, but I want you to know that this is a good place to be. When you stop getting nervous about your life, that's when your life gets boring. Okay, a show of hands; this is the first pickup event for how many people in the room?"

Half of the guys in the room put their hands up.

"And how many of you told your friends you were coming to the Super-Conference?"[42]

Ten hands.

"Who feels uncomfortable about being here?"

Almost every hand goes up.

"Yeah, the first experience is weird," Soul admits. "Four or five years ago, I got together with a group of Pickup Artists in London. On my way over, I remember thinking, I'm about to meet up with some guys I don't know to approach women and recite scripts I found on the Internet. What am I doing?"

The thing to take from Soul's comments is that you don't need to make fun of Pickup Artists because they're uncomfortable enough as is. Admitting that you need help with women is embarrassing and emasculating. In most cases, the decision to attend a LoveSystems bootcamp is not motivated by libido; it's motivated by loneliness.

---

[42] All the instructors were very good about calling the conference a "Super-Conference."

I'm standing in the "Breakout Room." It's another gray conference hall, but there are no tables in this one. There's a raised platform at the front of the room, and there are four chairs on it, and there are four instructors sitting on the four chairs. There's a tall, blond guy, there's a guy wearing an Abercrombie & Fitch shirt, there's an Asian guy, and there's a guy with a backward baseball cap. They're leading a session on "Approaching & Transitioning."

"There are different types of openers," Blond Guy explains. "Some lines open easily; some lines are more rewarding. 'What time is it?' will open 95 percent of sets,[43] but where are you going to go with that? I mean, where's your transition? On the other end of the spectrum, 'Want to go to my room to fuck?' is not likely to open many sets, but if it does open, well … you're probably in luck."

The instructors split us up into four groups so we can practice delivering "mid-spectrum openers." We're told to keep our tone strong and deep, and to keep our body position nonthreatening (facing slightly away). We're told to "be real," and "sell the line."

My group instructor, the guy with the backward baseball cap, asks the two guys to my right to pretend to be attractive women. Then he tells me to try to pick them up.

I walk past them and then turn back at the last minute, as if I've got an afterthought.

"Can I get your opinion on something?" I say. "Is it okay to break up with somebody over Facebook?"

"Dude," Backward Hat says, "you're being way too serious. You've got to say the line with a little smirk that lets your target know you're going somewhere with this."

I know this is going to sound silly, but Backward Hat's note hurt my feelings. It's not every day that somebody tells you you're bad at talking.

Next, Backward Hat has the student to my left try out the same line.

"Let me ask you two a question," the guy to my left says, but he says it too quietly; the students pretending to be women act as if they didn't hear him. So he beings to repeat himself:

"Can I ask—"

"Let's stop right there," Backward Hat interrupts. "When you repeat yourself you lose value. And you've got to be the one with the higher value; you're the prize; don't put the pussy on the pedestal."

---

[43] A set is a group of people that contains at least one target. And yes, a target is a girl a Pickup Artist is trying to pick up. If you don't like the terms—and a lot of Pickup Artists don't—take it up with Mystery. They're his, and they caught on.

Yes, Backward Hat actually said that, and yes, it was misogynistic. But ladies: I don't want you to go away from this article thinking the average Pickup Artist is more sexist than the average guy. I want you to know that if anything, the opposite is true. I want you to know that I hear misogynistic comments like that all the time, especially in the locker room and at the poker table.[44]

After the session is through, I wander into the hallway, and I come across a table with a dozen iPhones on it. LoveSystems, I learn, is beta-testing an iPhone pickup application, LoveSystems Mobile. The guys at the Hard Rock are waiting for the maiden upload.

Mahipal Raythattha, the application programmer, hands me his phone, and I open the LoveSystems Mobile application and click on "Openers." A list of pre-written conversations pops up. "Rich Girl," "Female Roommates," "Text Message Breakup" (a variation of Facebook Breakup, I presume), "Horse Girl," "Sorry I'm Late," "Dead Best Friend"—they're all there. I click on "Horse Girl."

"The blue text," the programmer tells me, "is the dialogue—what you're actually supposed to say. The pink is the response you can expect [e.g., 'Break up over Facebook? How long have you been dating her?'], and the white text is tips from the Love-Systems instructor.

"Once you've tried a couple out," the programmer continues, "there's a function that allows you to rate the routines based on how much success you've had with them. And we track the community ratings, so if everybody is rating a routine at five stars, then new users can begin with those."

The programmer's iPhone starts to ring. The iPhone has a photo caller ID, so I can see that the caller is young and blond. Her picture resembles the cover of Britney Spears' ... *Baby One More Time*.

The call, it turns out, is fake; the Britney look-alike is part of the LoveSystems Mobile software. LoveSystems users can program their iPhones to receive fake calls from imaginary pretty girls. The hope is that the real girl you're trying to pick up will see the fake caller, get jealous, and want you more.

Before Raythattha can load the application onto my iPhone—I bet you dollars to

---

[44] First example to come to mind: Two days ago I was playing poker at The Mirage, and the guy to my left, upon seeing an attractive woman at a neighboring table, said this to me: "Just how I like 'em: blond and drunk."

doughnuts that fake caller-ID thing works—Savoy exits the Main Stage room and tells me he's ready for our interview.

Here's how journalism works: I want Savoy to say something weird or strange; Savoy wants to promote his business. And here's what happens in our interview: Savoy wins. Let me explain: As we sit down on the couch for the interview, an obese attendee wearing an Affliction T-shirt walks by.

"That guy had an amazing night last night," Savoy tells me.

I tell Savoy that I want to hear about it, so he calls the guy over. Here's what the guy has to say:

"Last night I went to Tryst. It was my fifth-ever time in a nightclub—keep that in mind. It's two a.m., and I've been talking to these two girls for an hour, and then my coach, Tenmagnet, tells me I should ask them if they want to go to breakfast, and they say they'd rather go to a sex shop. I'm freaking out, because nothing like this has ever happened to me before, so I just nod. We go, we buy two … then we come back over to Wynn, and we go up to their room, and first the girls … and then we all …."

The guy takes out his digital camera and shows me a picture.

"These girls are really cute, for a guy like me," he says.

"That's one of the most rewarding things about this job," Savoy says. "I get letters and phone calls all the time. Wedding pictures, too."

"How many students have sent you wedding pictures?"

"About a dozen. We have a wall at the office where we put up stuff like that."

Here's how journalism works: I want Savoy to say something weird or strange; Savoy wants to promote his business. And here's what happens in our interview: Savoy wins.

The big guy's pictures look legit, but they alone are not enough to validate his whole story. And that raises the question, is he lying or exaggerating? And what about the rest of the guys in the hallway? A lot of them have told me stories about all the wonderful things that ostensibly happened the previous night. Are they lying or exaggerating?

I have to find out, so that night I follow the guys to see for myself.

When clubgoers head to XS on Saturday night and see that the line stretches all the way back to the Danny Gans Theatre, they walk over to Tryst. That, I presume, is why the line at Tryst is so incredibly long. Luckily, I've brought my S and my roommate with me (both attractive women), so we don't have to wait very long.

We descend the stairs, order cocktails and position ourselves near the Pickup Artists' table. After 15 minutes, one of the guys approaches my roommate.

"My sister made me up to look Asian tonight," he tells her. "Do you think it worked?"

"Sure ... " my roommate replies, tentatively.

The guy is Asian, by the way.

"So what is it?" he continues. "The shirt, the pants, the face?"

"It's ... "

"She's a racist!" the guy calls back to his friend. "She's a racist!"

Now, I've got a creative mind and a rudimentary understanding of psychology, but for the life of me I can't figure out what that guy is going for. But I don't view his pickup attempt as a failure. Turns out the guy has never before approached a girl in a nightclub. So the point isn't that he struck out; the point is that for the first time he swung.

As the hours go by, more and more students approach my roommate, my girl S, and every other woman in sight. Whatever the pickup coaches told the students is working; they're finding more and more success. One of the guys brings a girl over to the Pickup Artist table, and when she gets there, she sits down on his lap. A couple of minutes later, they're making out. Another student chats up my roommate and takes her to the dance floor. I see him snapping a couple of photos that he can take back to Nebraska or Ohio or wherever he's from, show to his friends and brag.

I'd say the students got their money's worth.

At 2:30 a.m., S and I walk back to the parking garage. When I start the car, the fuel tank warning light comes on. I'm nearly out of gas. Luckily, I have a spare fuel canister.

I pop the trunk, take out the canister ... and realize that I have no clue how to operate it. Seems like it'd be a straightforward procedure, but the nozzle is too short, and the gas isn't flowing out of it properly ... and I spill some on my pants.

That's when two men walk by. They're coming from the casino, heading back to their car.

"What the fuck are you trying to do?" one of the guys says.

"Trying to get gas into the car. Do you know how?" I ask.

"Yeah, it's called a gas station."

They both laugh.

Assholes.

Even though they're 50, they remind me of every guy who ever made fun of me in middle school—the ones who dated the girls who didn't know my name.

"Seriously," I say, "if you guys know how to work this thing, could you please help me out?"

"Figure it out yourself, fag."

Now, I'd like to think these guys were jealous. After all, it was 2:30 a.m. on a Saturday night, and I was going home with a beautiful woman … and they weren't. They were probably feeling bitter about it, and probably looking to make themselves feel better by bringing me down. But even that realization, along with the absurdity of the guy's particular insult (I was the one with the girl), didn't change the fact that when the slur left the guy's mouth and arrived in my ears, I felt like I was back in middle school.

So why did the comment so deeply affect me? Why couldn't I just shrug it off? Why couldn't I just say, "I've got a girl, you guys don't, so piss off," and leave things at that? Same reason the Pickup student wanted some photos of himself with my roommate. Same reason Pickup Artists remain active in the Pickup community even after they've mastered the skill: It's not about getting laid; it's about social acceptance.[45]

So, ladies, the next time a guy asks you whether it's okay to break up with somebody over Facebook, consider answering the question. Consider playing along. He's not a loser; he's just a little insecure. He might be after social acceptance, but who isn't? Give the guy a chance. I'm sure Savoy will clear off some space on the LoveSystems bulletin board for your wedding pictures.

---

[45] Rolling Stone writer Neil Strauss drives this point home in his book, *The Game: Penetrating the Secret Society of Pickup Artists* (also known as "by far the most entertaining book I've ever read in my life").

"Some guys play the game because they have an isolated work life," Strauss told me over the phone. "Some guys are there because they had issues with their parents growing up, and for some guys it might be social ostracism. So what they think they want might not be what they actually want; they might think they're after sex, but ultimately they learn that what they're really after is social acceptance."

"So that's how people get into the Pickup Artist community," I said. "But how do they get out? How did you get out?"

"I think of the PUA community as something I went through, like college. It was a place I visited for a higher education on social skills … and then I moved on. Now, I'm working on other parts of my life. I do a seminar about once a year, but that's about it. It can be a trap; you've got to move on from it. It's not a place to stay forever."

Vegas Escape

I've got to get out of here.

Seriously, Las Vegas is fucking with my head. When you spend as much time on the Strip as I do—three or four nights a week—you start to believe the hype. You drink the Kool-Aid because it's the only thing they're serving.

Cosmo, Aria, Wynn, Venetian, Bellagio. Everybody's young. Everybody's pretty. Everybody's rich. Everybody's spending. They're spending $50 on miso-glazed salmon, $500 on bottles of Grey Goose, and $5,000 on Tom Ford suits.

Everywhere I look.

I blame my job. As a writer for *Las Vegas Weekly*, I spend a ton of time on the Strip. But unlike most locals who work there (bar backs, housekeepers, dealers, security guards, cab drivers), I rarely get to see behind the curtain. The opposite, actually; I'm the one for whom the curtain was erected. Aside from the high rollers, the journalists and the critics are the ones hotels and casinos most want to impress.

I frequent media events (hotel openings, club anniversaries, show milestones) with white tablecloths, red carpets, top-shelf booze, and celebrities. The hotels running these events hire professional models to serve me crab claws and miniature tiramisu cups. Sure, the "regular" hotel servers are incredibly hot themselves—they were hired based on their looks—*but*, the hotels figure, *why not spend a couple thou to turn the 10s into 11s for a night*?

Intellectually, I know that the Las Vegas Strip is like one big media event: It's a carefully created, heavily managed construct. The Strip is an entertainment destination, not an actual way of life. Intellectually, I know that not everybody in America is young and pretty and rich. I see the statistics—the rising median age, the rates of obesity, the average household income—but I never see those statistics played out. What I see is a self-selecting group. I see the extra-pretty locals who were hired to dazzle tourists with their beauty. I see the tourists who are rich enough to fly to Vegas for the weekend and stay at the Bellagio villas or the Palazzo suites.

Like Ed Harris said in *The Truman Show*, "We accept the reality of the world with which we're presented."

Intellectually, I know that the Las Vegas Strip is like one big media event: It's a carefully created, heavily managed construct. The Strip is an entertainment destination, not an actual way of life.

Of course, unlike *The Truman Show*, the Vegas Strip wasn't imposed on me. I sought it out. I moved here from the Midwest because I wanted to. I jumped at the chance to write for *Las Vegas Weekly*. I volunteer consistently for stories that bring me to the Strip. And I love media events.

So, unlike Truman, I have nobody to blame for this existential mindfreak but myself. And yes, I use the word "mindfreak." Not just in my writing, but in casual conversation.

Like I said, I've got to get out of Vegas.

Recently, I went back to the "real world"—West Bloomfield, Michigan. My hometown. Everything seemed drab, slow and pedestrian. By the time I got up and headed out of the house, shops and cafés were closing for the evening. One night, around 9:45 p.m., I went to a restaurant I used to frequent, but the server told me the kitchen was closed for the night.

"At nine-forty-five?! That's ridiculous! Why do you close so early now?"

"Now?" she replied. "We've always closed down at this time."

Oh.

Spending 20 hours a week at high-end casinos messes with your head, but it teaches you a lot about life, too. About men, about women, about ego, about desire, about heartbreak, about sex, about deception, and about authenticity. Patterns emerge. Friends tell me stories. Most of my friends in this town are women, and most of them work in the "industry" (meaning they're promo models, dancers, servers, bartenders, and strippers), and most of their stories are about men. In almost every tale, the man is the sucker. The punch line.

Will that be me one day?

I hope not. I hope I'm the guy who beats the system—the guy who keeps his money, loves his wife, and only visits Vegas for the gourmet food and the Justin Bieber Cirque show.

But I'm scared of forgetting everything I now know to be true. I'm scared of growing foolish with age. So here's my plan: before I move away and forget what I've learned, I'm going to take notes. The following letter is a good starting point. It's meant to be read, by me, during my mid-life crisis, right before the Vegas vacation part. Here goes:

Dear Rick,

Or is it "Richard" now? Or maybe "Dick"? Dear God, I hope it's not Dick.

Congratulations on not dying! Your mom was pretty worried about that, especially after you told her you were moving to Vegas. And a lot of people (but mostly Glenn Beck) were worried the whole world would fall apart. But if you're reading this now, it means you're alive and well and planning a trip to Las Vegas. Maybe you're a bachelor and traveling alone. Or maybe you're bringing the wife and kids. Or maybe you're traveling with your robot, Kevin. Regardless, I urge you to take the following advice to heart:

Lesson One: Cocktail Waitresses Aren't Real

Neither are strippers or go-go dancers or that club employee you've got your eye on. Sure, she's real when she's not working, but you've only seen her "in character." She doesn't actually act that way or dress that way or smile at you that way when she's not being paid to do it. In fact, she hates having to dress that way and hates having to act that way.

Don't compare the women in your life to her, because the women in your life will always come up short. This girl is a fantasy, and you should know that because you've already dated her—girls like her, I mean—and you've seen, firsthand, how she acts when she's not working: just like everyone else. Actually, she's less sexual than most other women because she equates sexiness with her job. And, like most people, she likes to leave her work at the door.

Lesson Two: Stay Out of the Clubs

They're not meant for you. Not anymore. Sure, if you tip the bouncer $100, he's going to let you in. But nobody really wants to see you there.

Let's say you do go to a club and see a girl looking at you, and let's say you see her whisper something to her friends. I'll tell you this much: She ain't saying, "Who's the cute guy?" Those days are long gone. She's saying, "What's up with the old guy?"

If you don't notice that happening—the pointing and the whispering—it's only because you need a stronger prescription and a hearing aid.

(Obviously, Lesson Two doesn't apply if you've somehow become a celebrity. Also, if you're in a committed relationship and your suitably aged wife/girlfriend

comes to Vegas with you, then by all means do go to the club with her. Clubgoers love old couples. They're like love mascots.)

Lesson Three: You Can't Be a Professional Gambler
I don't care if you won three blackjack sessions in a row. I don't care if you won back-to-back poker tournaments.
A five-session losing streak is right around the corner. It always is.

Lesson Four: Get a Prenup
This lesson is actually a letter-within-a-letter, to my future fiancée:
Baby, I love you. I love you more than I ever imagined I could love anyone. I'm so excited to spend the rest of my life with you, and I never want us to be apart. I want us to move into a nursing home together and be the annoying lovey-dovey couple. And when one of us dies, I want the other one to die right after.
That said, I think we should get a prenup.
When you think about it, it's not me (the guy to whom you're engaged) asking for a prenup; it's Old Rick—a guy who didn't even know you. And if he did know you, there's no way he'd be pushing so hard for this prenup.
Please understand where Old Rick is coming from: Living in Vegas for three years, he witnessed an unending parade of young divorcées. All of them had one thing in common: They never imagined they'd one day get divorced.
So please sign here, here, and here.

Lovingly yours,
Rick

P.S., If we met before I wrote this letter, know that I never imagined our love would grow into something so beautiful. So please, no offense.

Lesson Five: Stop Comparing Yourself to Actors, Rock Stars and Reality-TV Stars.

They're always going to be having more fun than you are. At least, it's always going to seem that way, and that's because their business models depend on it. If you don't think they're attending cooler parties than you, with hipper friends and hotter women, then you're not going to buy their songs, see their movies, or watch their shows.

But many of them are miserable.

So, instead, compare yourself to the other 99.9 percent of the population—the ones who think you're having more fun. Maybe even tip them off as to how incorrect their perception is. Unless they're being jerks—then play up the act.

Lesson Six: Do What You Want in Life.

Most people do what they're told or what's expected of them. So then, when they visit Vegas and are encouraged to indulge, they run into trouble. But, if you marry the right girl, you won't have to worry about overdrawing your account for a night of "VIP" lap dances. And if you live an exciting life, you won't have to worry about losing everything at the blackjack tables—that only happens to people for whom gambling is the only excitement.

Live with passion and follow your gut. Because if you do that, you'll not only have a great time in Vegas, you'll have beaten the system.

Your Old Self,
Rick
March 24, 2011

The Perks and Perils of Professional Writing

They say, "Write what you know."
Terrible advice.

Writing what you know is a good idea only if you've got a challenging job, interesting hobbies, and eccentric friends. But if you had all that, you wouldn't have time to write; you'd be too busy working at your challenging job, dabbling in your interesting hobbies, and hanging out with your eccentric friends.

The only people with enough free time to write good stories are professional writers, and professional writers generally have boring lives. The only thing professional writers really know about is *writing*. So if writers were to follow the "Write what you know" maxim, we'd have a million stories about writing and no stories about anything else. Can you imagine anything more self-indulgent? The whole 'Writers on Writing' thing gets really boring, really fast.

Well, that being said, here are some things I wrote about writing:

Winning Immunity

Las Vegas Weekly was my first real writing job. Oh, I'd done some freelance gigs before, and I'd written a book, but my *Las Vegas Weekly* stories were read by people who weren't my parents.

Around the time I joined the *Weekly*, social media took over the world. The *Weekly* worked hard to capitalize on this. We shared our stories on every website that wasn't MySpace.[46] I'd write a story, post it, and then, the next day, I'd wake up to find dozens of comments about how right I was.

Well, I suppose that's not how it *always* went down …

Here's some actual reader feedback:

> —*"I wonder what Lax has in his résumé? Maybe he wants to be in politics where hatchet jobs are part of life."*
>
> —*"a tremendous amount of length and volume with no substance."*
>
> —*"BOTTOM LINE: The article is pure vicious trash."*
>
> —*"The article is tantamount to endorsing a departure from basic human decency. I take comfort in the knowledge that it will be ignored by well-thinking Las Vegans."*
>
> —*"Wow Ricky I sense some major anomosity [sic] from you. Why are you such a hater? … Is this article your claim to fame? A cover story in a free publication you pick up next to garage sale listings. Not exactly the Atlantic Monthly is it? Why don't you post your résumé so I can do some forensic investigating on you. I bet I could go back 15 years and find great stories on you (anything in your closet)???"[47]*
>
> —*"It is obvious, you need to write for the 'National Inquire' [sic] because you only have half of the 'Truth' and all of the BS. You didn't have any of the facts and it is obvious, you don't care to. Batman is not a jerk, YOU are. You're a lying, worthless 'Shock Jock,' living off the misery of others for pure amusement … Next time get the 'TRUE' facts or get out of your profession, because you really SUCK at it … Just a quick question???? Is your last name 'LAX' short for Laxative? Because, your last lying, misquoted, and BS article gave me the shits!"*

Comments like those upset a lot of writers. Generally speaking, we're a fragile people. But when it comes to criticism, I'm immune. And I'll tell you why:

---

[46] "If you post a story on MySpace" is the new, "If a tree falls in the middle of a forest and nobody is around to hear it."

[47] Yes, I did all sorts of evil things 15 years ago, when I was 13. Like skipping Brandon's Bar Mitzvah service.

A couple years before I started writing for *Las Vegas Weekly*, I made a stupid Internet video in which I sprung playing cards at my webcam for forty-four seconds. I called it "Card Spring." It took five hours to make. I cleared my afternoon schedule, cleared my living room, bought two decks of Bicycle cards, and then picked out a shirt and tie. I hit *record* and then sprung both decks at my MacBook's iSight camera. Then I got down on my hands and knees and picked up all the cards. I did that 37 times.

MySpace—remember this was back when people actually used MySpace—'featured' my video and it received over 100,000 hits and 1,600 comments in one day.

I read every single one of them.

MySpace users described my video as "awesome," "stupid," "neato," "freaky," "lame," and "creepy." But mostly, they described it as "gay."

Fifteen-year-old *Alan* from B-t*wn, Virginia called my video "pretty gay"; 17-year-old *QuEsO* from Mesa, Arizona called it "fucking gay"; 18-year-old *WOW* from "shh", Texas called it "really gay!!!!"; 17-year-old *M.O.B.* from Hazlet, New Jersey said that my video "could possibly be the gayest shit [he's] ever seen"; and 15-year-old *I NEED A GIRL* from YAY AREA, California confirmed that my video was "the gayest shit ever."

Fifteen-year-old *If Love Exists Then Where Is It?* from DAYTON, Ohio called my video "gayer than the power rangers," and 24-year-old *One PHAT Deigo* from DES PLAINES, Illinois said that it was "about as gay as bob sagat [sic]." Seventeen-year-old *Jake* from Wisconsin informed me that my video was "officially gay," but neglected to say which homosexual organization had bestowed the honor.

MySpace users didn't just comment on my video and its sexuality, they also commented on me.

Thirty-one-year-old *J* from PSL, Florida called me a "waste of sperm," 25-year-old *Doc* from Tulsa, Oklahoma called me a "piece of fucking shit ass hole"; 39-year-old *Magic-Man* from GOOSE CREEK, South Carolina called me a "moroon" [sic]; 15-year-old *THE CHOSEN 1* from Tokyo called me "a freakin jew bag"; 14-year-old *TOGA TOGA!!* From ALSIP, Illinois called me a "perverted gay freak"; and 15-year-old *YNOHTNA NEEDS NILDDIR* from Tiro, Ohio called me an "AIDS sucking cum sponge."

And then there was the mean stuff.

Twenty-eight-year-old *Dick* from Plano, Texas wrote, "I'm sure this dumbass thought he was being real cleaver [sic] and funny with this. Just so you know, jackass, this sucked and you are an idiot that sucks." Sixteen-year-old *Eric Bro* from BROWNSVILLE, Texas queried, "AM I GONNA HAVE CHOKE THIS DUDE GAY FAG QUEER?" Sixteen-year-old *Tony* from Stafford, Virginia speculated, "It

would be funnier if he had AIDS." Sixteen-year-old >G< from Your Mom's Bed, New York declared, "your a fuckin homo who lives with his mother and is probably a virgin asshole gay video you should kill ur self [sic]."

Did I mention that *the entire video consisted of nothing more than me springing two decks of cards at my webcam 37 times?*

Fourteen-year-old *Zeliox [6]SIC[6]* from Grand Island, Nebraska wrote, "you just wasted about three mins of my life ... I coulda used that three mins to shove my foot up your ass, shoot you, and laugh at your dead body ... faggot."

Three minutes? The video was just 44 seconds long. Did *Zeliox* watch it four times?

Of course, that was the least pressing question. And as for the more pressing ones, well, I decided to ask:

I wrote *Dick*, the guy who called me a dumbass, a jackass, and an idiot, to ask how I could have made my video less idiotic.

"If you could make it seem like you lose a finger or two due to those cards," Dick suggested, "that would be a little unexpected. Anyway take care and I hope I didn't offend, didn't realize anyone actually read those comments."

Next I wrote *Tony*, the guy who said my video would have been funnier if I had AIDS, to ask how, exactly, the tragic disease would have added humor.

"I just post that on every video I watch," Tony replied, "It's an old inside joke."

I wrote Tony back and asked him to tell me the inside joke.

"It's a long story. But all you have to know is me and my friend made a joke that involved AIDS and videos, so we post that on videos now."

I wrote Tony back again, claiming a particular fondness for AIDS humor and begging him to share the joke with me.

He refused again.

I'm starting to think there's no inside joke at all.

Next I wrote *Eric Bro*, the guy who wasn't sure whether he would have to choke "THIS DUDE GAY FAG QUEER," to see whether he'd reached a verdict.

He had: "naw men im not gonna choke u [sic]."

I wrote *Eric Bro* back, to express my relief and to ask how he'd come to his decision.

"i was yust bored and i comment it [sic]," he said.

Well that's a load off.

Lastly, I wrote *M.O.B.*, the guy who said that my video "could possibly be the gayest shit [he's] ever seen." I had to find out whether it was or wasn't.

M.O.B. determined that my video was *not* gayest shit he'd ever seen. Moreover, he now claimed that my video *wasn't even gay at all*: "nah i don [sic] see any gay shit there. and nah maybe it wasn [sic] the gayest shit ive [sic] ever seen ... .watched it again and it actually was pretty funny how ur [sic] face was serious the whole time kinda made me laugh."

A few hours later, *M.O.B.* wrote me a second time, unprompted, and he said this: "i looked at your myspace page and now that i have an idea of what you do im actually kinda embarassed ... once again im [sic] sorry."

I'm sorry, too—sorry that MySpace users are all talk and no walk.

Of course, that's not the point of this story. The point of the story is this: *If you didn't like this book, and if you want to make that clear to me in an insulting way, you're going to have to get really creative. Because I've heard it all.*

Solicitation Guilt

Even incredibly talented/incredibly famous/incredibly powerful/incredibly modest authors such as myself need help from time to time. For instance, when I wrote my last book, I needed other writers to blurb it, and I had to ask for those blurbs myself. [48] I felt guilty doing it—it's such a huge request. So I worked up this blurb-request letter introduction to acknowledge the magnitude of the request and soften the blow:

---

[48] Blurbs are those quotes of praise that go on the backs of books.

Dear _____,

Let's start here: You're welcome.

We'll figure out some way you can repay me—maybe a fancy lunch, maybe something as simple as a bottle of wine—but first, you probably want to know why you're so indebted to me.

Let me explain.

I'm offering you the opportunity to blurb a book that's pretty much certain to become a number-one bestseller and, by the year 2020, a "modern classic." Ten years from now, thousands of educated men and women will look back to this book's first edition to see which author had the brains and the courage to give his stamp of approval months before the literary lemmings jumped aboard the Rick Lax bandwagon, and when they do, they'll see your name starting right back at them, in big black letters. And then they'll rush out to buy all of your books, which, by the year 2020, will cost $600 a piece.

So you're welcome for your comfortable retirement and for your BMW hovercraft.

You might be interested to know that Dan Brown, J. K. Rowling, Malcolm Gladwell, and James Patterson have all committed to giving me blurbs. But then, when I told them I planned to solicit a blurb from you, Brown (speaking on behalf of Rowling, Gladwell, Patterson, and himself), said, "It's either _____ or us."

"Fine," I replied. "I pick _____."

Brown said, "Don't be silly, Rick. _____ hasn't even agreed to give you a blurb yet. Are you really going to turn down a sure thing—blurbs from four of the most famous authors of the new millennium—for the chance of getting a blurb from _____?"

"You're damn right I am. That's how much I respect _____'s work," I said.

So I'm not trying to guilt you into anything, but I am writing you today to ask for a book blurb …

Web Hits

I heard about a creative writing professor who asked her students to write the best Amazon.com reviews they could. The highest grade went to the student who tallied the most positive responses to the, "Was this review helpful to you?" question.

Best writing assignment I've ever heard of.

Today, most writing is done for the web.[49] And for my friends, most writing is done on Facebook.

A year ago, I gave myself the following writing assignment: Write a Facebook "Note" that gets as many comments and '*Likes*' as possible.

Two winners emerged.

Facebook Hit #1: Very Personal Ad

You don't want to date me. I'll break your heart. Or maybe you'll break mine. One way or another, this will end in heartbreak.

Or maybe it won't. Maybe this time it'll be different—I mean that. The truth is, I only started off with, "You don't want to date me," to make you want me more. Reverse psychology.

As you can see, I do play games. Because they work. Consistently. Don't try and tell me otherwise, because I've experimented. Don't tell me, "I like guys who don't play games," because it's not true. You do like them. You only dislike the guys who play games poorly.

I actually play fewer games than most guys.[50] Really—ask any of my ex-girlfriends. If you get in contact with them, they'll tell you the most wonderful things about me, and that's because I'm a nice guy.

I'm not "nice" in the platonic sense—I want to sleep with you, and I want it to happen sooner rather than later—I'm "nice" in the traditional sense. For example, if I like your black skirt and hate your beige one, I won't criticize the beige one when you put it on; I'll wait until you wear the black one and then say, "I love that black skirt so much. We should get you more just like it."

When I'm not being a romantic diplomat, I'm performing card tricks at the magic club, playing show tunes at Don't Tell Mama's on Fremont Street, and reading nonfiction books at Barnes & Noble. I also have some non-geeky hob-

---

[49] This is a total guess.

[50] You can believe this because, well, if I was going to lie about game playing (as most guys do), I'd tell you that I don't play games at all.

bies (e.g., working out at LVAC, playing poker at Mirage, clubbing at Wynn and Encore), but I lead with the geeky stuff because if any of it scares you off, then, well, off you go. If you think the geeky stuff is "weird" or "gay," then it's not going to work.

Did I mention I'm employed?

Also, I'm 29.

Now let's talk about you. Here's what I know about you already: you're still reading this. Like I said, I'm a big reader, too, so it appears we have at least one thing in common.

But aside from literacy, what do I look for in a girl?

Here goes:

1) Your Identity

You were gawky and unpopular in middle school and everybody made fun of you. But then, all of a sudden, you got really hot and everybody wanted to be your friend and kiss you. You resented them for only valuing you for your looks. So you left home, moved to Vegas, and are searching for a guy who not only appreciates the swan you've become but also identifies with and respects the ugly duckling you once were.[51]

2) Your Mind

On the one hand, your intelligence doesn't matter that much to me. On the other hand, I have a consistent track record of dating women who are smarter than me.

3) Your Looks

They're really important. Looks are really important to every guy. Including blind guys. If a guy tells you otherwise, he's lying. So please don't penalize me for saying that looks are "really important," because if you do penalize me for that, then I'll be afraid to be honest around you, and this will lead to conflict down the line.

4) Your Thoughts on Love

I can't decide if romance is the most important thing in the world or the

---

[51] If you were hot and popular in middle school, you won't 'get' me. You'll 'jokingly' call me "weird," but I won't find it funny. I'll find it dismissive and sad—sad for you, not me.

only important thing—I keep going back and forth on that one. If, for you, romance is just one of many important things (your job, your friends, your family, your religion) then you're going to think I'm needy and dramatic.

5) Everything Else

   I can deal with baggage and mental illness and addiction and lying and crazy Vegas work hours. The only deal-breaker is meanness.

   Talk to you soon, hopefully.
   —Ricky[52]

Facebook Hit #2: Re: "Grand Opening of Lexi Drew" Event Invitation
Hi C.,

   Just wanted to write and let you know that I can't make the "Grand Opening of Lexi Drew" party that you're hosting on Saturday.

   I must admit, I was surprised that you thought to invite me, seeing as though you didn't invite me to any parties when we went to high school together. But that was probably just because you didn't ever talk to me in high school, so no hard feelings.

   Anyway, the reason I can't make it to your party/promotional event is that I don't live in Michigan any more. Actually, I haven't lived in Michigan for about four years. I moved to Chicago in 2005 and then Las Vegas in 2008. But enough about me; what have you been up? You haven't told me a thing! We've got to catch up!

   Usually when I can't make it to a party to which I've been invited via Facebook, I simply click "Not Attending," but considering the number of times you graciously invited me to the promotional event that your employer, Six Degrees Magazine, is hosting, I felt obliged to write something more personal, hence this letter.

   By the way, I think you accidentally tagged me in a photo I'm not in. You can tell I'm not in the photo because the photo isn't actually a photo; it's an advertisement for your employer's promotional event, "The Grand Opening of Lexi Drew." (When I clicked on the Facebook message telling me I'd been

---

[52] Author's Note: I also posted this on Match.com. Got very few responses.

tagged in a photo, I was redirected to the advertisement.) I think I've figured out the source of the confusion: the advertisement contains a photograph of a five-woman music group called "The Paradiso Girls," and you probably mistook the brunette on the left for me because I have brown hair.

Sorry to digress, but I've got to admit, those Paradiso Girls are pretty cute! (Maybe that's why the Six Degrees Magazine design department put the **exact same photo** *of the Girls on the advertisement twice?) So I'm particularly sad that I can't fly back to Michigan, secure a "VIP TABLE RESERVATION," and listen to the Paradiso Girls sing their "hit single," "Patron Tequila."*

What a great song name!

Well, I've got to get going now, but before I do, I wanted to invite you to this event that my magazine, Las Vegas Weekly *("The Six Degrees Magazine of Las Vegas") is hosting this Thursday at Palms. PM me if you want the VIP table reservation number.*

Hope to see you there! It's been too long!

—Ricky[53]

---

[53] This was one of the meaner things I've ever written, but I hope it's apparent that the bulk of the joke is on me (and my inability to let parts of high school go), not on this poor C. girl.

Why You Should Believe
All the Crazy Stories
You Read in this Book

Writers lie. A lot. Every afternoon, I head to the bookstore and page through men's magazines that promise me six-pack abs in 30 days and mind-blowing sex with supermodels. Sometimes I browse bestsellers that purport to teach me how to cure cancer with milk, how to get rich by working four hours a week, and how to use the "Law of Attraction" to control the entire universe with my mind.

I find these books in the nonfiction section.

My bookstore carries all of the following "nonfiction" titles:

- *Awakening Your Psychic Powers*
- *Vibrational Medicine*
- *When Ghosts Speak: Understanding the World of Earthbound Spirits*
- *Book in a Month: The Fool-Proof System for Writing a Novel in 30 Days*
- *The Basics of Winning the Lotto*

Until recently, I didn't care that so many books were filled with lies. It didn't affect me. As a lifelong magician, I could identify and account for books' deceptions and misrepresentations up front. When I picked up *Get Anyone to Do Anything*, I hoped to find a few tips on persuasion; I didn't actually believe reading the book would give me absolute control over the entire human race. When I read, *Think and Grow Rich*, I knew that despite the book's title, there'd be more steps involved.

But James Frey's *A Million Little Pieces* was different.

I had no clue that the book was filled with fabrications, and no clue that the fabrications would have such a devastating impact on my life. To explain how, exactly, Frey's book devastated me, I have to tell you something that until recently I'd only revealed to my parents, my closest friends, my ex-girlfriends, and a handful of social workers. I wasn't planning on discussing it here, but my editor urged me, saying, "This is the exact kind of personal revelation that builds trust with readers."

So here goes:

I was addicted to alcohol from early 2003 to late 2005. Scotch, to be specific. My addiction wasn't nearly as bad as James Frey's, but it was bad. To make a long story short: my grades plummeted, my friendships suffered, and my relationships ended—including the one with my liver. The booze left me defeated, hopeless, and alone, and if that sounds cliché to you, go to a support group meeting and you'll see that no matter the age, no matter the sex, no matter the job, and no matter the drug, all addicts go through the same breakdown, the same steps to recovery, and the same bullshit.

I saw James Frey on "Oprah" in October of 2005. I read his book in November, and by December, things had taken a turn for the better. People say this all the time—particularly on "Oprah," come to think of it—so it too has become a cliché, but in my case, it was true: *The book changed my life*. Frey had been through what I'd been through—worse, even!—and had made it through in one piece.

So maybe I can too, I thought.

As I read the book a second and a third time—I carried it around with me like a Bible—I began to rekindle friendships and restore relationships. I even started jogging. Bought a tracksuit and everything. And apparently I wasn't alone; shortly after the "Oprah" appearance, Frey's book rose to the #1 slot on the *New York Times* Bestseller List. Within six months *A Million Little Pieces* had sold three million copies. That number alone comforted me; I felt like I was part of something bigger than myself.

In early 2006, I read TheSmokingGun.com's exposé of Frey's book, which revealed how the author had fabricated large parts of his memoir. Among other things, the website revealed that Frey had been in jail for only a few hours, not the 87 days he had claimed, and that Frey hadn't actually been involved with the train accident in which two girls died, as he'd claimed.

Shortly after this exposé, Frey admitted to Larry King that he had exaggerated some parts of his book. He also defended his decisions to do so: "A memoir is a subjective retelling of events. In every case, I did the best I could to recreate my life according to my memory of it." Oprah called in and defended Frey, but a few days later, she invited Frey back onto her show and told him that she felt "duped."

"Duped" isn't the right word to describe what I felt. "Duped" is how I felt when I learned that the mini-blender I ordered off the infomercial required considerably more cleaning than the TV pitchman had led me to believe. *Shattered* is how I felt when I learned that Frey was a sham. I didn't leave my parents' house for a week. When I finally did go out for the first time, I drove to Blockbuster and ran into my fifth grade teacher Mrs. Strauss. She asked whether everything was okay, and that was all it took; I burst into tears, and she hugged me for a couple minutes, right there in the New Releases section.

Random House promoted *A Million Little Pieces* as a "brutally honest" and "uncommonly genuine" memoir. In using the word "uncommon," it's unclear whether Random House meant that most memoirs aren't genuine or that the genuineness of Frey's memoir surpassed the genuineness of most others, but either way, Random House was wrong. That much was made clear to Random House when readers in

California, Illinois, Ohio, New York, and Washington banded together and filed class action lawsuits against the publishing giant, charging it with fraud, breach of contract, unjust enrichment, and violations of various state statutes based on unfair or deceptive acts and practices.

In June of 2006, the United States District Court of the Southern District of New York consolidated the lawsuits, and in September of 2006, the parties settled and Random House agreed to pay $2,350,000.00 in damages.

That's $2.35 per little piece.

✎ ✎ ✎

Frey isn't the only dishonest memoirist to get caught in recent memory. In 2006, mountaineer Greg Mortenson wrote a book, *Three Cups of Tea*, about how he got lost on a K2 descent. About how he found himself in the Pakistani town of Korphe. About how he fell in love with the village and its people, and about how he promised to return to the village to build them a proper school. The book stayed on the *New York Times* Bestseller list for three years. Over 300 cities selected it for their One City One Book programs. So Mortenson wrote a follow-up, *Stones into Schools*, which detailed his 1996 kidnapping by the Pakistani Taliban.

Another blockbuster bestseller.

After that came the "60 Minutes" investigation, which pointed out that Mortenson didn't actually get lost in Korphe on his way down from K2, that Mortenson didn't really promise the Korphe villagers he'd return to build them a school, and that Mortenson wasn't actually captured by the Pakistani Taliban.

But other than that his story checked out.

In 2008, Riverhead Books published *Love and Consequences*, the memoir of half-white, half-Native American author Margaret Jones, who grew up in South-Central Los Angeles and worked as a drug runner for a gang leader at the age of 13.

Turns out Margaret Jones was really Margaret Seltzer, who grew up in a rich neighborhood and is white.

Next came Holocaust survivor Misha Defonseca, whose book *Misha: A Memoire of the Holocaust Years* had been translated into 18 languages. Turns out she wasn't Jewish, wasn't trapped in the Warsaw ghetto, hadn't killed a Nazi soldier, and wasn't adopted by a pack of wolves, as she claimed. Apparently she spent the war years in Brussels.

Defonseca issued this press statement: "Ever since I can remember, I felt Jewish … There are times when I find it difficult to differentiate between reality and my inner world. The story in the book is mine. It is not the actual reality—it was my reality, my way of surviving."

Memoirists aren't the only writers prone to fabrication. Journalists do it, too. *New York Times* Staff Reporter Jayson Blair fabricated hundreds of facts for his articles on the Iraq war and the D.C. Sniper. *New Republic* Staff Reporter Stephen Glass made up lots of stories, including the one about the 15-year-old computer hacker who was hired as an information security analyst for a California software developer called Jukt Micronics. *New Republic* editor Charles Lane grew suspicious of the story because he couldn't find any proof of the existence of Jukt Micronics. As Lane's investigation progressed, Glass had his brother pose as a Jukt executive and confirm the story's details. Glass also set up a shell Jukt website and voicemail account, and fabricated Jukt memoranda and business cards.

When we hear about dishonest journalists like Blair and Glass and dishonest memoirists like Frey, Mortenson, Jones, and Defonseca, our instinct is to rope them off. "File Frey's book in fiction," we demand, forgetting that a made-up nonfiction book is different from a novel. "How could they do that?" we ask, as if we ourselves were immune to the pulls of money, success, sympathy, empathy, attention, and fame.

We mock and shun these discredited writers, and part of the reason we do it is so we can continue believing that *the rest* of writers we read are truthful. That *our* favorite writer would never lie to us.

Guess what. He would.

✒ ✒ ✒

A couple summers ago, I befriended a Holocaust survivor named Nathan Roth. We hung out at the same Barnes & Noble café and we chatted a couple times a week.

"I did an interview," Roth told me one afternoon, "at the University of Michigan. It was for the Holocaust Survivor Oral History organization—something like that; I forget the exact name. I told them about the war and the camp. This went on for a while; very long interview. And at the end they gave me a transcript. I read through it, and it's filled with 'um's and 'uh's and whatever else. To preserve accuracy. I know you're a writer, and I was hoping you might go through the transcript and clean it up for me. Don't change any of the details, just clean it up."

I cleaned it up and learned Roth's story in the process. Basically, the Nazis sent him to Ungvar, then to Jaworzno, which was part of Auschwitz. As the Jews evacuated Auschwitz, and the loudspeaker was blaring, and grenades were exploding in the distance, Nathan ripped off one of the latrine doors and pried from it one of the cast-iron hinges. He used the hinge to dig a hole through the mortar in the camp's wall. Then he ran through the forest, found shelter in a brothel, and eventually moved to America and started a big, successful family.

Best I can tell, Roth's story is 100 percent true. You can find the unedited interview on the Vision/Voice Holocaust Survival Oral History Archive. But let's be real: *You probably won't.*

It's a great story, and Roth loved sharing it, but as it is, it's not quite cinematic enough to take the world by storm. The narrative just can't compete with, say, that of retired television repairman Herman Rosenblat.

On two "Oprah Winfrey Show" appearances, Rosenblat told Oprah about the time he spent at the Schlieben concentration camp, about the nine-year-old girl who threw him apples over the camp fence, about his liberation, about his move to America, and about his Coney Island blind date … with, coincidentally, *the exact same girl who'd thrown him the apples 10 years earlier.* He called her the "Angel at the Fence," and Oprah called their reunion a miracle. Rosenblat married the Angel at the Fence and the two have lived together happily for over 50 years.

Oprah called the Rosenblats' story "the single greatest love story we've ever told on the air." Many agreed. The Rosenblats were featured on Lifetime, on the Hallmark Channel, and on "CBS News." Herman Rosenblat wrote a memoir, which Berkley Books, a Penguin imprint, promoted as "the true story of a Holocaust survivor whose prayers for hope and love were answered." It was all but certain to become a #1 *New York Times* bestseller.

Except one thing: Rosenblat made the story up.

Prof. Kenneth Waltzer, director of Jewish Studies at Michigan State University, was the first to speak up about how unlikely it was that a civilian on the outside could access the Schlieben fence without getting caught. Waltzer said the only place civilians could access the Schlieben fence was right next to the SS barracks.

In mid-2008, Rosenblat denied allegations of falsehood, but by December of 2008, he confessed and (kind of) apologized:

> To all who supported and believed in me and this story: I am sorry for all I have caused to you and everyone else in the world. Why did I do that and write the story with the girl and the apple, because I wanted to bring happiness to people, to remind them not to hate, but to love and tolerate all people. I brought good feelings to a lot of people and I brought hope to many. My motivation was to make good in this world.

Oprah called the Rosenblats' story "the single greatest love story we've ever told on the air." Many agreed. The Rosenblats were featured on Lifetime, on the Hallmark Channel, and on "CBS News."

Then, in February of 2009, Rosenbalt backed off from his quasipology. He went on "Good Morning America," and when reporter Dan Harris asked him whether his story was true, he replied, "It was my imagination. And in my imagination, in my mind, I believed it. Even now I believe it. That she was there, and she threw the apple to me."

"How can you say it wasn't a lie?" Harris asked. "You know it's not true."

"Yes, it's not true. But in my imagination, it was true."[54]

I asked Dr. Charles V. Ford, psychologist and author of the wonderful (though unfortunately-titled) book *Lies! Lies!! Lies!!!* whether he could make sense of Rosenblat's doublethink. Here's what Ford said: "Perhaps he's internalized the story. There's a possibility that he's made up a story surrounding something that *was* true, to a very a limited extent. In this case, Rosenblat's truth would be that not everybody outside of the camps wanted to kill *everybody* inside of them. We know that society as whole supported the Holocaust, but there were individuals who did things to help Jews in the camps, and maybe Rosenblat experienced that and then he made up the surrounding story. So in that sense, for him, the story might be true to a very limited extent."

"And what about Frey?" I asked.

"I haven't examined Frey," Dr. Ford told me, "and I'm not a mind reader, but I can make suppositions using general theoretical principles. That said, two factors might be in play here. The first is simple artistic license. I doubt the events in Hemmingway's life occurred exactly the way he recounted them in *A Movable Feast*. We all use artistic license when, let's say, we're sitting around dinner table, enjoying some wine, and recalling our collegiate exploits."

"And the second possible factor?"

---

[54] Maybe that statement isn't as crazy as it sounds. According to *Lying* author Sissela Bok, the idea of memory as truth was once common:

> One pre-Socratic Greek tradition saw truth—aletheia—as encompassing all that we remember … The oral tradition required that information be memorized and repeated, often in song, so as not to be forgotten. Everything thus memorized—stories about the creation of the world, genealogies of gods and heroes, advice about health—all partook of truth, even if in another sense completely fabricated or erroneous.

"Pathological narcissism. Some men subconsciously feel like they're not 'manly enough.' They want to present themselves to world as highly masculine, as one tough hombre, so they exaggerate accounts of their military exploits, of their athletic competitions, and of their suffering, as in the case of Frey. And when the public believes these stories, it helps the men who tell them believe the stories too. It goes back to internalization."

🖋 🖋 🖋

Sometimes I use artistic license. Sometimes I'm guilty of internalization. I'm certainly not immune to the pulls of money, success, sympathy, empathy, attention, and fame. Nobody is.

Many of the stories in this book—I'll flatter myself for a second here—are good ones. So I wouldn't be offended if you'd questioned whether I made some of them up.

I didn't. I didn't have to. I live in Las Vegas.

Yes, I probably made some small factual mistakes—all writers do—and, yes, in several stories, I changed names, rearranged timelines, and altered specific details of certain events. But in most cases, I told it just like it is.

One big exception: This story.

I was never actually addicted to alcohol. I can't stand the taste of scotch. I have no idea whether "all addicts go through the same breakdown and the same steps to recovery." Part of the reason I don't know is that I never read *A Million Little Pieces*. For all I know, addictions are like snowflakes, each one unique. My editor never said, "personal revelations build trust with readers." I never bought a Nike tracksuit and don't have a fifth-grade teacher named Mrs. Strauss.

I said all that because I wanted to *show* you how easy it is for authors to lie in print, and how easy it is for you to believe them. I couldn't have just *told* you—the message wouldn't have hit home. I'm not making a moral judgment here; I'm just letting you know how often it happens.

Now, you've got to figure, if I'm honest enough to admit this, and if I'm honest enough to admit to making factual mistakes, and honest enough to admit internalization, and honest enough to admit that I'm not above the pulls of money, success, sympathy, empathy, attention, and fame, I'm probably one of the most honest writers out there.

So I do hope you'll believe me when I say, *the stories in this book were true.*

contacting the author

If you made it through the whole book, you might as well take a couple seconds and let me know what you thought of it: LawyerBoyChicago@gmail.com.

acknowledgments

Thanks to Heidi Barwell. She pushed for this book and edited it. Thanks to Deke Castleman for bringing the book to Huntington Press' attention, to Laurie Cabot for laying it out—no small task!—and thanks to Anthony Curtis for welcoming me into the family.

Thanks to Bruce Spotleson at Greenspun Media Group for going out of his way to help me secure permission to reprint these stories. He didn't have to do it, and he didn't really get anything out of it. It was big favor, and I do appreciate it. Thanks also to Bryan Allison, Kelli Maruca, Paula Pettit, Michael Uriarte, Janice Van Gorder, my new *Las Vegas Weekly* publisher Travis Keys, and everyone else on the Westside.

Thanks to my former *Las Vegas Weekly* editor Scott Dickensheets for all the great notes. If you enjoy the big stories in the middle of this book (the Town Square story, the skeptic convention story), Scott deserves credit. Thanks also to my awesome current *Las Vegas Weekly* editor, Sarah Feldberg. If you like the muscle-suit story or the "Vegas Escape," piece, credit goes to Sarah.

Thanks to my other *LVW* editors, past and present, too: Ken Miller, Spencer Patterson, Xania Woodman, Joe Brown, Deanna Rilling, and April Corbin. Thanks to Erin, to Abby G, to Abby T, to Ryan, Wes, Allison, Mark, Emma, Rebecca, Nadine, Justin, Leila, and everyone else on the Eastside.

Thanks to all my temporary coworkers in Chapter One. Thanks to Jungle Josh and Alesha and everyone else on the street; thanks to Keith Ragano and "Brian" at Crazy Horse III; thanks to Chris at Studio Lites; thanks to Michelle and Daniel and the entire staff at P.J. Clarke's; thanks to Jenn and Scott for helping set up my day at Mirage; and thanks to Felix and the Mirage team for having me.

Thanks to Brandon at Flex Design Costumes for letting me use one of his beautiful muscle suits. If your want one for yourself—and I know you do—visit Brandon at FlexDesignCostumes.com.

Big thanks to Bryan Adams for the fantastic photos. It would be great if more books had photos, and it would be really great if the photos in those books were as half as good as the ones Bryan took for this one. To see more of Bryan's work, visit him at http://www.facebook.com/flashadamsphotography.

Thanks to Maggie Feldman for letting us shoot at Palazzo's LAVO, for letting us use photos from my birthday party at Marquee's Library Room, and for letting us use many more TAO Group photos. Thanks also to Lisa Long Adler for letting us shoot at now-closed-but-not-forgotten Blush at Wynn.

Thanks to my parents for editing many of these stories before my various editors got to them. Check's in the mail.

The past year has been a good one, and I've been lucky enough to make some great Vegas friends since my last book came out. So, along with all the friends thanked in *Fool Me Once*, thanks to Angie, to Justin and Jocelynn, to Chris, Katie, Calen, Andrei, Blake, Jonathan, and David, and everyone else in the DC/Theory11 crew; to Richard, Vic, Mark, Megan, Lindsay, Amber, Ellen, and everybody else in the Las Vegas Writers Group/SNLAC crew; and thanks to all my new friends at Gary Darwin's Magic Club.

legal notices

Many of preceding stories were originally published in *Las Vegas Weekly*. They appear in this book with prior, written permission of Greenspun Media Group.

The first chapter is new, with the exception of the footnote dealing with the Festival Fountain Show, which ran in *Las Vegas Weekly* in June of 2009. Most of the seventh chapter is new, too. All of the chapter introductions are new. The Wyrick postscript is new. Many of the story titles have been changed since their original appearance in *Las Vegas Weekly*.

The essay "It's Not Us; It's Them: The Moral History of America, Starring Sin City" originally appeared as part of the 2011 Vegas Valley Book Festival's *Fade Sag Crumble: Ten Las Vegas Writers Confront Decay*.

The stories in this book are true, though certain names, dates, and details of specific events have been changed.

about huntington press

Huntington Press is a specialty publisher of gambling- and Las Vegas-related books and periodicals, including the award-winning consumer newsletter, *Anthony Curtis' Las Vegas Advisor*. To receive a copy of the Huntington Press catalog, call **1-800-244-2224** or write to the address below.

Huntington Press
3665 Procyon Street
Las Vegas, Nevada 89103